MODERN THOUGHT

The Age of Analysis, which has been edited by the eminent teacher and author, Morton White, covers the *thoughts, writings, times* and *personalities* of *twentieth century philosophers.*

Professor White illuminates modern philosophy by clear and brilliant commentaries on the writings of leading philosophers in the fields of logic, philosophical and linguistic analysis, existentialism and phenomenology and deals with the concepts of time, instinct and organism. Here are well-chosen selections from G. E. Moore and Bertrand Russell, deans of contemporary British philosophy; Benedetto Croce, foremost Italian philosopher of this century; Sartre, existentialist; William James, John Dewey and Charles Peirce, leaders in the American movement of pragmatism, and from the works of George Santayana, Alfred North Whitehead, Ludwig Wittgenstein and others whose philosophies are of importance to 20th century thinking.

MORTON WHITE, Professor of Philosophy Harvard, has taught at Columbia University and at the University of Pennsylvania. He held a Guggenheim Fellowship, and has been a visiting member of The Institute for Advanced Study in Princeton, New Jersey, as well as Tokyo University. The author of numerous articles and reviews, he has written such books as *The Origin of Dewey's Instrumentalism, Social Thought in America,* and *Toward Reunion in Philosophy.* He is also the author of a forthcoming book of essays entitled *Religion, Politics and the Higher Learning.*

This is what the *New York Times* has said about the Mentor Philosophers Series—"Paper-backed books have clearly come of age in this country . . . Mentor Books is to be congratulated on this ambitious bit of editing."

MENTOR Books of Interest

The Mentor Philosophers

THE AGE OF ANALYSIS

20th Century Philosophers

SELECTED, WITH INTRODUCTION AND INTERPRETIVE COMMENTARY

by

MORTON WHITE

A MENTOR BOOK

Published by The New American Library

FIRST PRINTING, SEPTEMBER, 1955
SECOND PRINTING, MARCH, 1956
(With Minor Corrections)
THIRD PRINTING, JUNE, 1957
FOURTH PRINTING, OCTOBER, 1958

A cloth-bound edition of *The Age of Analysis*
is published by Houghton Mifflin Co.

MENTOR BOOKS are published by
The New American Library of World Literature, Inc.
501 Madison Avenue, New York 22, New York

TO

G. E. MOORE

Preface

THE EDITOR OF A VOLUME ON TWENTIETH-CENTURY PHILOSO-
phy must make more than the usual explanations of the
anthologist. The recency of the period makes for uncharted
terrain, for embarrassing riches, and for strong partisan feeling
about the figures to be selected. The historian of earlier centuries need only retouch the portraits bequeathed to him by
tradition, but the historian of contemporary philosophy must
paint under the watchful eyes of living subjects or their admirers. The choice of the subjects in this volume will provoke
little dispute, for even their philosophical opponents will acknowledge their influence. But the influence of a philosopher
must be distinguished from the philosophical value of what
he says—from his originality and his insight—and I have tried
to think of originality, insight, and influence in making my
selections and my comments.

Because of the present importance of the pragmatic, the
logical, the analytic, and the linguistic strains in contemporary
philosophy, the writings of Charles Peirce, Bertrand Russell,
G. E. Moore, and Ludwig Wittgenstein will appear in greater
quantity than is usual in volumes offered to the general reader,
who is too frequently treated as a kind of sponge, able to soak
up only a more fluid philosophical prose. Most popular an-
thologies of the twentieth century concentrate on Santayana
because of his style, or on James because of his charm, or on
Whitehead because of an unusual combination of intellectual
grandeur and generosity; and for a closely related reason,
Russell the moralist or journalist is more honored by editors
than Russell the great logical analyst. It is with this in mind
that I have tried to present a more catholic selection than
usual, confident that there is an audience willing to hear what
the other half of philosophy says. And so, along with Bergson's
poetry of time and instinct, existentialist speculations, and
phenomenological reflections, the reader will find passages
in the workmanlike literature of logical analysis, the philosophy of science, and linguistic philosophy. The more sprawling
figures of the twentieth century will continue to live in these
pages, only in smaller apartments.

Because the volume is edited for the general reader among

others, I have designed it, in part, to show that philosophy in the twentieth century has not been wholly remote from the concerns of the ordinary man or from the problems of culture in the widest sense. For this reason I have chosen some of the readings with an eye to the institution, discipline, concept, or aspect of the universe which holds peculiar interest for the philosopher from whose writing they have been selected. Therefore I have selected passages from Whitehead that bring out his special interest in the concept of *life,* from Croce one that illustrates his concern with *history,* from Charles Peirce a piece that shows his pragmatic interest in *natural science,* one from Bertrand Russell that reveals the extent to which *logic* plays a role in his philosophy, from G. E. Moore a statement on the relation between philosophy and *common sense,* and so on. And since these focal interests emerge as parts of the development of philosophy as a discipline and as elements in the culture of the twentieth century, I have tried to describe some of the intellectual currents and philosophical movements that are significantly related to the ideas expressed in the selections themselves. Taken as a whole, therefore, this volume is not the story of Western philosophy in the twentieth century so much as a selective survey of some of its leading doctrines as expounded by its leading philosophers. Hegel once observed that the owl of Minerva awakens only after the shades of night have fallen, and so with twentieth century philosophy at high noon we may not expect wise hooting or bedtime tales about its ultimate significance.

The philosophers presented here are not drawn up historically in a rigid line of march, or as a series of ideological dominoes who push each other into action or out of dogmatic slumbers, or as roughnecks who turn each other inside out or upside down. Nevertheless there are certain clearly observable historical trends and movements which are worth setting down in historical order, like the early decline of hegelian idealism, which is treated in the opening chapters, and the latterly active existentialism, pragmatism, and logical positivism, which are presented and discussed toward the end of the volume. Because they are the views of *groups* of philosophers, movements like these may sometimes receive more extensive discussion than the views of a single philosopher, but I think this is understandable. Some single philosophers may receive more extensive discussion than others because they require more elucidation or because I think they are more important or more interesting. This is unavoidable. It should go without saying that the relative lengths of the excerpts are not intended as measures of their authors' importance.

One word in explanation of the purpose and title of the volume. I have tried to present a fair but selective survey of twentieth-century philosophy in the West. In conformity with the pattern observed by other volumes in this series, this one has been entitled "The Age of Analysis," but that should not lead the reader to expect a volume which is limited to philosophers of the so-called analytic school, like Carnap, Moore, Russell, and Wittgenstein. It is intended to record succinctly, and in full recognition of the dangers in any title, the fact that the twentieth century has witnessed a great preoccupation with analysis as opposed to the large, synthetic, system-building of some other periods in the history of philosophy. I have found it useful to label the century by seizing one of its more powerful tendencies and not by trying to capture its essence.

My greatest debt, of course, is to those distinguished thinkers of the twentieth century who have made this book possible, and to their co-operative publishers. My own writing, selections, and arrangements have been immeasurably improved by the counsel and the delightfully unsparing criticism of my wife, Lucia Perry White. She has toiled over and helped me eliminate many unreadable comments, and has overseen the volume with the eye of a literate, unprofessional reader of philosophy. She has tried the selections for size and meaning, and I can thank her for any success I may have in communicating to the general reader. I also wish to thank my friend Isaiah Berlin of Oxford for reading the manuscript and for making many useful suggestions. I can only regret that the Atlantic Ocean prevented me from making greater use of his learning and his genius for seeing important things in the development of philosophical ideas.

For an over-all view of the subject the reader may wish to study my comments consecutively before turning to the selections, while the student who is using this volume as a text may prefer to read it straight through.

Cambridge, Massachusetts
August 12, 1954

Contents

CHAPTER I

The Decline and Fall

of the Absolute

IT IS A REMARKABLE TRIBUTE TO AN ENORMOUSLY muddled but brilliant German professor of the nineteenth century that almost every important philosophical movement of the twentieth century begins with an attack on his views. I have in mind Hegel, whose philosophy is more fully presented in another volume of this series, but without whom we cannot begin a discussion of the twentieth century. Not only did he influence the originators of marxism, existentialism, and instrumentalism—now three of the most popular philosophies in the world—but at one time or another he dominated the founders of the more technical movements, logical positivism, realism, and analytic philosophy. The point is that Karl Marx, Kierkegaard the existentialist, John Dewey, Bertrand Russell, and G. E. Moore were at one time or another close students of Hegel's thought and some of their most distinctive doctrines reveal the imprint or the scars of previous contact or struggle with that strange genius. Therefore, it will be necessary to say something about Hegel's views, if only to make clear the historical background of some of the readings in this volume.

Hegel held that the universe reveals the workings, the development, the realization, the unfolding of a World Spirit or Absolute Idea (sometimes called the Absolute for short). On his view the universe is not unlike an animate being that has a soul, desires, aims, intentions, and goals. The universe is spiritual; it has direction; and the explanation of ordinary facts, human actions, historical changes, and institutions may be grasped once we recognize how they are imbedded in this cosmic organism, how they are directed by the cunning of the Absolute, how they play their part in the Universe's progressive realization of the World Spirit.

Because the idea of change and development was so central to his thought, Hegel was forced to conclude that the traditional, formal, and (as he called it in derogation) static logic of Aristotle was hopelessly inadequate, and that it had to be replaced by what he called a dialectical logic more adequate to deal with the fluid workings of the Absolute. Aristotle had said that a thing must either have an attribute or its opposite at a given time but Hegel disagreed, usually by calling attention to intermediate or twilight zones when, he said, a thing appears to possess neither. We need not review this cloudy chapter in the history of logical theory. It is sufficient to say that hegelians abandoned or professed to abandon traditional logic, and replaced it by their own dialectical formula, which they applied to all aspects of the universe but which received its most active illustration in social history, usually by marxists. Hegel's philosophy may well be called dialectical idealism since according to it the World Spirit unfolds itself in a dialectical pattern, a pattern in which one step, usually called thesis, is followed by its opposite, antithesis, and in which this conflict is partially resolved by a synthesis of both contending elements. The outstanding application of the purely dialectical aspect of Hegel's thought is that of Marx in his philosophy of history, where the capitalist class is viewed as a thesis that gives rise to the working class as antithesis, and where the struggle between them is supposed to result in a synthesis. But the method has been forcibly extended to other fields, notably to physics, biology, and mathematics, where it has frequently resulted in sheer nonsense.

Even apart from its influence on marxism, we cannot fail to see the attraction that Hegel's general view must have had for a century that was reeling under the blows of Hume, the Enlightenment, and Kant. For Hegel did two things of immense historical importance. He provided a defense of religious belief for those who could not accept atheism or Kant's practical theology, and he encouraged philosophers and historians in the feeling that there are modes of explanation other than those available in Newtonian mechanics. This second aspect of his thinking fitted in with the growth of history as a discipline and with the influence of darwinian biology in the nineteenth century. Therefore hegelianism became the gathering place of some who sought a peaceable resolution of the warfare between science and theology and of others committed to the historical, evolutionary emphasis of the time. The Absolute or World Spirit was easily identified with the God of Christianity, and Hegel's emphasis on historical, contextual explanation became the ally of genetic method. Instead of a bleak, evolutionary positivism of the kind that many Englishmen and Americans found congenial in the work of Herbert Spencer, who was also trying to reconcile science and religion, young men all over the Western world were provided with a rich, highly complex philosophical system that covered every corner of the universe in deep rich velvet, soft to the touch and warming.

At a price, of course. A good part of this price Marx was willing to pay, if he could just turn the system upside down. That is to say, if he could take the dialectic off its idealistic head where he found it, and put it on its materialistic feet. This was the marxian shift from dialectical idealism to dialectical materialism. Kierkegaard, on the other hand, was no mere revisionist and he shivered at being, as he said, "a paragraph in a system." His response was an emotional outburst that has continued to echo through philosophy and theology.

Marx and Kierkegaard had gone through their hegelian phases before Hegel was taken up at the end of the nineteenth century in England and America by the teachers of many who have become important professional philosophers of the twentieth century. Therefore, there were two distinct waves of disenchantment with Hegel—an early one on the continent in the middle of the nineteenth century and another at the beginning of the twentieth century in England and America. But the second wave was different from the first, because this time the disenchanted had been enchanted with another Hegel. The siren had sung in many different keys. Marx and Kierkegaard had begun with Hegel the theological, historical, political, ethical, esthetic thinker—the greater Hegel, I think. But Dewey, Russell, and Moore—the most notable ex-hegelians of the twentieth century—came in contact with Hegel through the writings of British neo-hegelians as they were called, who were far more interested in the logical, metaphysical, epistemological aspect of idealism.

The British philosophers F. H. Bradley and J. E. McTaggart were acute thinkers who concentrated on the less humanistic, more technical aspects of the hegelian system. It was Bradley and McTaggart who gripped the young Russell and the young Moore, and it was the logically minded American idealist Josiah Royce who exercised a similar influence on young Americans. All these neo-idealists exerted their influence in spite of the influence of William James who had cried out early against the block universe of Hegel, and who was poking fun at his system for reasons very like Kierkegaard's—for personal, psychological, and emotional reasons. Indeed it was precisely because James seemed like a mere literary rebel against idealism and not like a tough, technical opponent that he had little immediate effect on the younger men. It was only after they had seen through the bluff of idealistic logic that the spirit of James was vindicated. James had said "Damn the Absolute!" to his colleague Royce, but that no more convinced the young professional philosophers than Kierkegaard's passionate outburst against the "system." What came to worry them was not so much the hegelian air that stifled Kierkegaard, nor the apotheosis of the Prussian state that Marx hated. They were far more aggravated by the idealistic theory of knowledge, by the view of Hegel that linked him with the Irish idealist, Bishop Berkeley, who had said: "To be is to be perceived," and upon this they concentrated their attack.

As a result of this division within the anti-hegelian camp we may say that the process which I shall call "dehegelization" took two forms. Some of the twentieth-century admirers of Hegel, like Dewey and Santayana, rejected hegelianism with a certain amount of sadness. They could not take the dialectic, the sophistry, or the myth, but they continued to think of philosophy as a grand, monumental enterprise that demanded sensibility, historical learning, and wisdom as well as technical skill, so that even while rejecting the Absolute, they remained, like Croce, sympathetic to Hegel's view of philosophy as synoptic, as a total view of the universe and man. Indeed, even those who followed Kierkegaard in emphasizing the importance of the *existent* individual as against the abstract system and the Absolute—existentialists like Heidegger, Jaspers, Marcel, and Sartre—continued to do philosophy in a sprawling and turgid manner that reminds one of Hegel even when it is directed against him. It is only when we come to the tradition of Russell and Moore, to Wittgenstein, to logical positivists like Carnap and his followers, to some of the American realists, that we find a complete and total rejection of hegelian doctrine *and* hegelian style. Philosophers in these traditions deny that philosophy must construct a world-view that will encompass and illuminate science, art, morals, religion, and politics. They do so not only because some of them reject metaphysics as meaningless, but also because none of them thinks of philosophy as a super-discipline, as an instrument of cultural criticism, or as a substitute for religion. With the exception of their acknowledged leader, Russell, who is a complicated and large figure in twentieth-century philosophy, most philosophers in the logico-analytic tradition shy away from the issues of public and personal life, from the problems of culture and practice, as though they are of no concern to philosophers.

In illustration of these two forms of dehegelization I begin with a selection from the writings of G. E. Moore who, along with Russell, is a dean of contemporary British philosophy, and then follow it with one from Croce, the foremost Italian philosopher of the twentieth century. Though never a full-fledged hegelian, Croce has been indelibly influenced by Hegel's method. Moore is the very antithesis. I deliberately juxtapose them at the beginning of the volume in order to dramatize one of the great contrasts in twentieth-century philosophy.

In the light of this contrast one is tempted to say (after

the Greek poet Archilochus and Isaiah Berlin in his brilliant study of Tolstoi, *The Hedgehog and The Fox*) that the history of philosophy in the twentieth century is a history of hedgehogs and foxes, a history of philosophers who strive to know one big thing and those who are content to know many little things, or indeed *one* little thing. With something like this in mind I have divided the volume into three major parts which follow the paradigmatically contrasting selections from Croce and Moore. In the first of these parts (through Chapter VIII) I present the views of philosophers who try to see the world in terms of a central concept which is to organize all their attitudes and beliefs. Here I have in mind Henri Bergson and Alfred North Whitehead, who share so much with Croce in this respect, not only in their search for a guiding concept but also in the concepts upon which they fix, concepts as romantic as history and art (Croce), time and instinct (Bergson), life, process, and organism (Whitehead). I also have in mind the work of Husserl and the existentialists who, though preoccupied with immediate experience and human decision, think of their philosophies as maps of the universe or as total insights into man's desperate, anxious, forlorn existence.

It is easy to understand why this way of doing philosophy—and I recognize, of course, that there are vast differences among these philosophers—has attracted the attention of religious thinkers and political movements seeking foundations and scaffolds for their moral philosophies and their programs. Bergson's philosophy was seized upon by syndicalists; Croce's became the philosophy of Italian liberalism; Heidegger the existentialist lent his voice to the Nazis, Sartre was a figure in the French underground, and other existentialists have their connections with theology and literature. All of these thinkers commit themselves in ways which bring them into friendly or unfriendly contact with the dogma of organized religions like Catholicism; they compete with marxism for the minds and hearts of intellectuals throughout the world; they appeal to feelings and impulses which are deeper and more strongly felt than those that underlie the more surgical attitudes of logic, of epistemology, of the philosophy of science. While lecturing in Japan a few years ago I was struck by the extent to which young Japanese philosophers were excited by these more cosmic varieties of Western philosophy, how they sought some kind of large, comfortable and protective system which would unify their values and attitudes after they had abandoned traditional religious beliefs or the systems of Kant and Hegel. This is one reason for the hold of Communist ideology on intellectuals throughout Europe and Asia, and it also explains the power of existentialism, for both of them are street-corner philosophies, café philosophies, philosophies which claim to have and which, unfortunately, often do have an influence on life.

With very few exceptions, like that of Whitehead and Santayana, this large conception of philosophy is concentrated on the continent of Europe which remains the home of philosophy conceived in a hegeloid, that is a Hegel-like though not a hegelian, way. In some degree of contrast to this I have devoted the section following the philosophical hedgehogs to a characteristically American movement in philosophy—pragmatism, and have illustrated it by selections from Charles Peirce, William James, and John Dewey, who make their main contributions to different aspects of the doctrine. It is a mediating movement in philosophy, as James said, because it aspires to a total, metaphysical, systematic view of reality without losing sight of scientific and logical detail or of human problems. It is concerned with the methods of science as in Peirce and Dewey, in the psychology and justification of religious belief as in James, and in the significance of science for ethics as in Dewey. Therefore pragmatism stands between the more traditional view of philosophy as world-view and the more recent analytic tendencies which are to be represented in the last part of the volume. Dewey has influenced educational practice in America, his political philosophy has been attacked by the extreme right and by the Communists; James saw deeply into human psychology; a great liberal tradition in history, law, economics, and social science was allied with pragmatism. But we must also remember the important logical contribution of Peirce and his contributions to semantics and the philosophy of language, for these bring pragmatism into close contact with the philosophers represented in the last part of the volume.

They are in the tradition of Moore's attack on Hegel; indeed some of them even outdo Moore by calling Hegel's doctrine meaningless rather than merely false. Some of them are not only connected with the tradition of British empiricism, particularly with David Hume, but also with an international movement in philosophy that sprang from important logical, mathematical, and scientific developments in the nineteenth and twentieth centuries: logical positivism. Some of its leaders, like Wittgenstein and Carnap have been uncompromisingly anti-metaphysical and opposed to all manifestations of what one of its devotees calls "school philosophy," but at the present time variants of it dominate English philosophy and it is quite strong in many American universities and colleges. It too has its focal concepts, language and meaning, but it aims to treat them as objects of intensive logical study and as instruments of analysis rather than as the central notions of an expansive, metaphysical examination of reality or as a guide to life. Hegel would have called it the antithesis of the kind of philosophy represented by himself and by Croce, Bergson, and Whitehead in this volume, and the pragmatists often think of themselves as making up the higher synthesis of both.

This third mode of philosophizing is the victim of an understandable paradox so far as the common man is concerned. For while it is officially dedicated in one of its manifestations to great respect for ordinary language (Moore and Wittgenstein) and in another to preferring the purified language of logic, science, and mathematics (Russell and Carnap), it often frightens readers who understand ordinary language and admire the language of science. The great contemporary devotees of clarity who seem to demand no more than the good sense which Descartes thought so well distributed, find fewer sympathetic readers among the laity than those philosophers who keep the reader in tow by touching his deepest anxieties, hopes, and fears. Partly with this in mind, and partly because I think it represents the most lively and important tendency in phi-

avidity, and admired him more than any other recent philosopher." It was a passage from Bradley's *Principles of Logic* that set Moore to thinking in 1897-98 that "the meaning of an idea" was "something wholly independent of mind," and this was the beginning, Moore says, "of certain tendencies in me which have led some people to call me a 'Realist,' and was also the beginning of a break-away from belief in Bradley's philosophy." Russell describes the results of this break-away more dramatically. He reports that Moore "took the lead in rebellion, and I followed, with a sense of emancipation. Bradley argued that everything common sense believes in is mere appearance; we reverted to the opposite extreme, and thought that *everything* is real that common sense, uninfluenced by philosophy or theology, supposes real. With a sense of escaping from prison, we allowed ourselves to think that grass is green, that the sun and stars would exist if no one was aware of them, and also that there is a pluralistic timeless world of Platonic ideas. The world, which had been thin and logical, suddenly became rich and varied and solid. Mathematics could be *quite* true, and not merely a stage in dialectic."

Russell's statement reminds us of two distinct elements within twentieth-century realism. One is represented by its common-sense belief that physical objects like the sun and stars exist independently of the mind, and the other by its highly uncommonsensical belief that there are such things as platonic ideas or universals that also exist independently. The first belief was directed against the idealists in a way that could easily command the assent and produce the applause of solid and sober citizens. The realists' arguments were supposed to make mad the guilty idealists, who, as Moore once said, thought that trains had wheels only when they were in stations. But the second step, that of asserting the existence of a static, timeless, and spaceless *wheelhood* in addition to palpable, rolling wheels appalled a later generation of philosophers who had learned from Russell himself the principle called Occam's Razor, according to which entities are not to be multiplied beyond necessity. The point is that some of the realists were not only anti-hegelians but also platonists, and it was the latter tendency that led them to be inflationary as well as deflationary philosophers. In alliance with a group of continental thinkers of whom Franz Brentano, Alexius Meinong, and Gottlob Frege were the most influential, some of the realists held that when we understand a word like "wheel," we mentally grasp an attribute or characteristic—*wheelness* or *wheelhood*—which is the meaning of the word "wheel."

In a similar vein they held that when we see a physical object, we are directly aware of what they called a *sensedatum,* which is an *appearance* of that object and quite distinct from the solid, three-dimensional object itself. The sense-datum is a glimpse of the physical object that we get and a glimpse is something different from those who do the glimpsing and from the object of which they get a glimpse. This passion for interposing queer entities between the human being and words or physical objects was characteristic of many philosophers who had been emboldened by their success in rescuing the external world from its idealist fate. Some of them, like Meinong, were even driven to supposing that there must be some unusual entity whose existence is implied when we say (truly) that the golden mountain does not exist. It cannot be the golden mountain, of course, for *it* is said not to exist, and so it must be something whose exact nature is quite puzzling. It is to Russell's great and everlasting credit that he devised a very ingenious and plausible solution to Meinong's puzzle called the Theory of Descriptions which we shall meet later, but it is important to point out that at the very moment when he was devising it, he also accepted many other peculiar entities of realistic invention.

Although they concentrated their attention on problems of knowledge, the realists were also interested in ontology, or a theory of being, which they constructed on the basis of their epistemological conclusions. Their attempts at analyzing the meaning of a statement like "I see the wheel" or "I understand the word 'wheel,'" were modeled on the philosophically innocuous analysis of "John D. Rockefeller I is the grandfather of John D. Rockefeller III," according to which there is an intervening individual of whom John D. I was the parent and John D. III a child. But John D. II, the intermediary in this case, is a human being, an entity of the same general kind as his father and his son, whereas the sense-data and the universals pressed into service by the realists were very different from the extremes between which they were sandwiched. In asserting the existence of these different kinds of things—physical objects, sense-data, meanings, and others too technical to consider here—the realists were pluralists and philosophical foxes. They began by rejecting Hegel's one big, queer thing—the Absolute—but concluded by putting many little queer things in its place.

The selection from Moore is indicative of this pluralistic tendency in the realism of the period, this interest in showing that there are many different categories of things in heaven and earth. But insofar as Moore in this selection thinks of philosophy as a description of "the whole universe" his departure from traditional philosophy was less decisive than that of a number of younger philosophers whom he taught and influenced. In 1910–11 when Moore gave the lectures from which I have made this selection he was actively interested in metaphysics and to that extent connected with the philosophical tradition, but even then he did not adopt a theory which would show all the things in the universe to be stages in the development of the Absolute or manifestations of some one stuff or substance. In 1910 he and his friend Russell were metaphysical pluralists in their description of the whole universe but they were already laying the groundwork for a radical rejection of all metaphysics by philosophers who think that the only task of philosophy is to analyze the meanings of statements and not to speculate about the whole universe. We shall consider *their* views later.

The following selection shows what the late J. M. Keynes meant when he spoke of the "beauty of the literalness of Moore's mind, the pure and passionate intensity of his vision, *un*fanciful and *un*dressed up. Moore had a nightmare once in which he could not distinguish propositions from tables. But even when he was awake, he could

26 THE AGE OF ANALYSIS

not distinguish love and beauty and truth from the furniture. They took on the same definition of outline, the same stable, solid, objective qualities and common sense reality."[3] And the mention of Keynes brings to mind a point about Moore's influence that is worth stressing after we have contrasted philosophies that deal directly with human problems in a large and emotional way, and those that don't. Keynes has reported the great influence Moore had had in the early years of the century on a number of young men who were to become distinguished writers and social thinkers: among them himself, Lytton Strachey, Leonard Woolf, Desmond MacCarthy. And what this shows is that philosophers may have an impact on the humanistic, historical, literary, and political tradition without discoursing directly on those matters, though it is true that it was Moore's great ethical work *Principia Ethica* that had been the vehicle of his influence on so many future members of the Bloomsbury circle. Even so, that is a highly technical, analytical work. Its influence on sensitive and learned men suggests the purity and power of Moore's thinking and shows it to be closer to the humanistic tradition than some of his detractors make out. There is a Socratic simplicity about Moore's writing, an honesty, and even a sweetness about its air, as Keynes has said. It may be that his appeal to literate intellectuals is a typically English phenomenon, but one hopes that it is not, and that serious, technical philosophy can play its role in the cultural life of any civilized people, even when it is not explicitly devoted to politics, history, art, or matters of science.

The following is a selection from Chapter I of Moore's *Some Main Problems of Philosophy* (1953) entitled "What is Philosophy?"[4]

[3] J. M. Keynes, *Two Memoirs* (Hart-Davis, 1949), p. 94.

[4] For permission to reprint pp. 1-2, pp. 15-27, of *Some Main Problems of Philosophy* by G. E. Moore, grateful acknowledgment is made to George Allen and Unwin, Ltd., London, and The Macmillan Company, New York.

⟨ I want, as a start, to try to give you a general idea of what philosophy *is*: or, in other words, what sort of questions it is that philosophers are constantly engaged in discussing and trying to answer. I want to begin in this way for two reasons. In the first place, by doing this, I shall be giving you some idea of what the problems are which I myself mean to discuss in the rest of this course. And, in the second place, I think it is the best way of beginning any discussion of the main problems of philosophy. By attempting to give, first of all, a general sketch or outline of the whole subject, you point out how the different separate problems are connected with one another and can give a better idea of their relative importance.

I am going, then, first of all to try to give a description of the *whole* range of philosophy. But this is not at all an easy thing to do. It is not easy, because, when you come to look into the matter, you find that philosophers have in fact discussed an immense variety of different sorts of questions; and it is very difficult to give any general description, which will embrace *all* of these questions, and also very difficult to arrange them properly in relation to one another. I cannot hope really to do more than to indicate roughly the main sorts of questions with which philosophers are concerned, and to point out some of the most important connections between these questions. I will try to begin by describing those questions which seem to me to be the *most* important and the most generally interesting, and will then go on to those which are subordinate.

To begin with, then, it seems to me that the most important and interesting thing which philosophers have tried to do is no less than this; namely: To give a general description of the *whole* of the Universe, mentioning all the most important kinds of things which we *know* to be in it, considering how far it is likely that there are in it important kinds of things which we do not absolutely *know* to be in it, and also considering the most important ways in which these various kinds of things are related to one another. I will call all this, for short, 'Giving a general description of the *whole* Universe,' and hence will say that the first and most important problem of philosophy is: To give a general description of the *whole* Universe. Many philosophers (though by no means all) have, I think, certainly tried to give such a description: and the very different descriptions which different philosophers have given are, I think, among the most important differences between them. And the problem is, it seems to me, plainly one which is peculiar to philosophy. There is no other science which tries to say: Such and such kinds of things are the *only* kinds of things that there are in the Universe, or which we know to be in it. And I will now try to explain more clearly, by means of examples, exactly what I mean by this first problem—exactly what I mean by a general description of the *whole* Universe. I will try, that is, to mention the most important differences between the descriptions given by different philosophers. And I wish, for a particular reason, to begin in a particular way. There are, it seems to me, certain views about the nature of the Universe, which are held, now-a-days, by almost everybody. They are so universally held that they may, I think, fairly be called the views of Common Sense. I do not know that Common Sense can be said to have any views about the *whole* Universe: none of its views, perhaps, amount to this. But it has, I think, very definite views to the effect that certain kinds of things certainly are in the Universe, and as to some of the ways in which these kinds of things are related to one another. And I wish to begin by describing these views, because it seems to me that what is most amazing and most interesting about the views of many philosophers, is the way in which they go beyond or positively contradict the views of Common Sense: they profess to know that there are in the Universe most important kinds of things, which Common Sense does not profess to know of, and also they profess to know that there are *not* in the Universe (or, at least, that, if there are, we do not know it), things of the existence of which Common Sense is most sure. I think, therefore, you will best realise what these philosophical descriptions of the Universe really mean, by realising how very different they are from the views of Common Sense—how far, in some points, they go beyond Common Sense, and how absolutely, in others, they contradict it. I wish, therefore, to begin by describing what I take to be the most important views of Common Sense: things which we all commonly assume to be true about the Universe, and which we are sure that we know to be true about it. . . .

Starting, therefore, from the view of Common Sense that there certainly are in the Universe (1) material objects in space and (2) the acts of consciousness of men and animals upon the earth, we might most simply get a general description of the Universe in one or other of two ways: Either by saying, these two kinds of things *are* the only kinds in the Universe; or by saying: they are the only kinds we *know* to be in it, *but* there may possibly also be others. And as regards the first of these two views, I doubt whether any one, on reflection, would be willing to accept it quite as it stands. The most obvious objection to it is that by asserting that there are no acts of consciousness in the Universe, except those of men and animals on the earth, it denies the possibility that there *may* be or have been on other planets living beings endowed with consciousness. And this is a possibility which almost everybody would think it rash to deny. But still, by slightly modifying it to allow of this possibility, we get a view which might, I think, seem very plausible to many people. We might, for instance, say: There really is not, and never has been anything in the Universe, except material objects in space, on the one hand, and acts of consciousness, more or less similar to those of men and animals, attached to living bodies more or less similar to theirs, on the other hand. This is, I think, really a plausible view of the Universe; at least as plausible as many that have been proposed by philosophers. But, no doubt, the second view is more plausible still: it does seem more plausible to add the proviso: These are the only things we *know* to be in it; *but* there *may* be other kinds of things unknown to us. And this, I think, is a view which really has been held by many people, philosophers and others. They have held, that is, that the only kinds of things which we *know* to be in the Universe are material objects in space, and the acts of consciousness of men and animals on the earth; while adding also that there *may* be other kinds of things unknown to us.

No doubt, philosophers who have said this or something like it have not meant by it quite what they said. Those who hold that there are and *have been* in the Universe material objects in space, and that there are and have been acts of consciousness, can hardly deny that there certainly are in the Universe *also* at least two other things beside these—things which are neither material objects nor acts of consciousness—namely, Space and Time themselves. It must be admitted on this view that Space and Time themselves really *are*—that they are *something*; and it is obvious that they are *neither* material objects *nor* acts of consciousness. And similarly there may be in the Universe other kinds of things known to us, besides Space and Time, which are neither material objects nor yet acts of consciousness. For my part, I think, there certainly are several other kinds of things, and that it is one of the objects of philosophy to point them out. But those philosophers who have spoken as if material objects and acts of consciousness were the *only* kinds of things known by us to be in the Universe, have, I think, not really meant to deny this. They have meant, rather, that material objects and acts of consciousness are the only kinds of things known to us, which are in a certain sense *substantial*: substantial in a sense in which Space and Time themselves do not seem to be substantial. And I may say, at once, that, for my part, if we make suitable modifications of this sort, this view does seem to me to be a correct view. I hold, that is to say, that material objects in space, and the acts of consciousness of men and animals on the earth, really are the only *substantial* kinds of things *known* to us; though I should admit that there may possibly be others unknown to us; and though I think that there are certainly several *unsubstantial* kinds of things, which it is very important to mention, if we are to give a really complete general description of the *whole* Universe—Time and Space for instance.

One way, therefore, in which we might get a general

description of the whole Universe, is by making additions to the views of Common Sense of the comparatively simple sort which I have just indicated. But many philosophers have held that any such view as this is very incorrect indeed. And different philosophers have held it to be incorrect in three different ways. They have either held that there certainly are in the Universe some most important kinds of things—*substantial* kinds of things—*in addition* to those which Common Sense asserts to be in it. Or else they have positively contradicted Common Sense: have asserted that some of the things which Common Sense supposes to be in it, are *not* in it, or else, that, if they are, we do not know it. Or else they have done *both*; both added and contradicted.

I wish now to give some examples of all three kinds of views. Both of those which *add* something very important to the views of Common Sense; and of those which *contradict* some of the views of Common Sense; and of those which do both.

To begin then with those which *add* something to the views of Common Sense.

There is, first of all, one view of this type which everybody has heard of. You all know, that enormous numbers of people, and not philosophers only, believe that there certainly is a God in the Universe: that, besides material objects and our acts of consciousness, there is also a Divine Mind, and the acts of consciousness of this mind; and that, if you are to give any complete description of the sum of things, of everything that is, you must certainly mention God. It might even be claimed that this view—the view that there is a God, is itself a view of Common Sense. So many people have believed and still do believe that there certainly is a God, that it might be claimed that this is a Common Sense belief. But, on the other hand, so many people now believe that, even if there is a God, we certainly do not *know* that there is one; that this also might be claimed as a view of Common Sense. On the whole, I think it is fairest to say, that Common Sense has *no* view on the question whether we do know that there is a God or not: that it neither asserts that we do know this, nor yet that we do not; and that, therefore, Common Sense has *no* view as to the Universe as a *whole*. We may, therefore, say that those philosophers who assert that there certainly *is* a God in the Universe do go *beyond* the views of Common Sense. They make a most important addition to what Common Sense believes about the Universe. For by a God is meant something so different both from material objects and from our minds, that to add that, besides these, there is also a God, is certainly to make an important addition to our view of the Universe.

And there is another view of this type, which also everybody has heard of. Everybody knows that enormous numbers of men have believed and still do believe that there *is* a future life. That is to say, that, besides the acts of consciousness attached to our bodies, while they are alive upon the earth, our minds go on performing acts of consciousness after the death of our bodies—go on performing acts of consciousness *not* attached to any living body on the surface of the earth. Many people believe that we *know* this: so many people believe it that, here again, as in the case of God, it might be claimed that this is a belief of Common Sense. But, on the other hand, so many people believe that, even if we have a future life, we certainly do not *know* that we have one; that here again it is perhaps fairest to say that Common Sense has no view on the point: that it asserts neither that we *do* know of a future life nor that we do *not*. This, therefore, also may be called an *addition* to the views of Common Sense; and certainly it is a most important addition. If there really are going on in the Universe at this moment, not only the acts of consciousness attached to the living bodies of men and animals on the surface of this earth, but also acts of consciousness performed by the minds of millions of men, whose bodies have long been dead—then certainly the Universe is a very different place from what it would be, if this were not the case.

Here, then, are two different views of the type which I describe as making important *additions* to the views of Common Sense, while not contradicting it. And there is only one other view of this type which I wish to mention.

Some philosophers have held, namely, that there certainly is in the Universe, *something* else, beside material objects and our acts of consciousness, and something substantial too—but that we do not know what the nature of this something is—that it is something Unknown or Unknowable. This view, you see, must be carefully distinguished from that which I mentioned above as *not* going much beyond Common Sense: namely the view that there *may* be in the Universe, things which are neither material objects nor the acts of consciousness of men and animals, but that we do not know whether there are or not. There is a great difference between saying: There *may* be in the Universe some other kind of thing, but we do not know whether there is or not; and saying: There certainly *is* in the Universe some other important kind of thing, though we do not know *what* it is. This latter view may, I think, fairly be said to go a great way beyond the views of Common Sense. It asserts that in addition to the things which Common Sense asserts to be *certainly* in the Universe—namely, material objects in Space and the Acts of consciousness attached to living bodies—there *certainly* is something else besides, though we do not know what this something is. This view is a view which has, I think, been held by people who call themselves Agnostics; but I think it hardly deserves the name. To know, not only that there may be, but that there *certainly* is in the Universe something substantial besides material objects and our acts of consciousness is certainly to know a good deal. But I think it is a view that is not uncommonly held.

I have given, then, three examples of views which add to Common Sense without contradicting it and I now pass to the second type of views: those which contradict Common Sense, without *adding* to it; those which deny something which Common Sense professes to know, without professing to *know* anything, which Common Sense does *not* profess to know. I will call these, for the sake of a name, *sceptical views*.

Of this second type, there are, I think, two main varieties, both of which consist in saying that we do *not* know, certain things which Common Sense says we *do* know. No views of this type, I think, positively deny that there are in the Universe those things which Common Sense says certainly are in it: they only say that we simply do not know at all whether these things are in it or not; whereas Common Sense asserts quite positively that we *do* know that they are.

The first variety of this type is that which asserts that we simply do not know at all whether there are any material objects in the Universe at all. It admits that there *may* be such objects; but it says that none of us knows that there are any. It denies, that is to say, that we can know of the existence of any objects, which continue to exist when we are not conscious of them, except other minds and their acts of consciousness.

And the second view goes even further than this. It denies also that we can know of the existence of any minds or acts of consciousness except our own. It holds, in fact, that the only substantial kind of thing which any man can know to be in the Universe is simply his owns acts of consciousness. It does not deny that there *may* be in the Universe other minds and even material objects too; but it asserts that, if there are, we cannot know it. This is, of course, an illogical position; since the philosopher who holds it, while asserting positively that no man can know of the existence of any other mind, also positively asserts that there are other men beside himself, who are all as incapable as he is of knowing the existence of any one else. But though it is illogical, it has been held. And it would cease to be illogical, if, instead of asserting that *no* man knows of the existence of any other mind, the philosopher were to confine himself to the assertion that *he* personally does not.

But now I come to the third type of views—views which depart *much* further from Common Sense than any that I have mentioned yet; since they *both* positively deny that there are in the Universe certain things which Common Sense asserts certainly *are* in it, and *also* positively assert that there are in it certain kinds of things, which Common Sense does not profess to know of. Views of this type are, I may say, very much in favour among philosophers.

The chief views of this type may, I think, be divided into two classes: first, those whose contradiction of Common Sense merely consists in the fact that they positively deny the existence of space and material objects; and secondly, those which positively deny many other things as well. Both kinds, I must insist, do positively deny the existence of material objects; they say that there certainly *are* no such things in the Universe; not merely, like the sceptical views, that we do not *know* whether there are or not.

First, then, for those views which merely contradict Common Sense by denying the existence of Space and material objects.

These views all, I think, start by considering certain things, which I will call the Appearances of material objects. And I think I can easily explain what I mean by this. You all know that, if you look at a church steeple from the distance of a mile, it has a different appearance from that which it has, when you look at it from the distance of a hundred yards; it looks smaller and you do not see in it many details which you see when you are nearer. These different appearances which the same material objects may present from different distances and different points of view are very familiar to all of us: there certainly are such things in the Universe, as these things which I call Appearances of material objects. And there are two views about them, both of which might be held quite consistently with Common Sense, and between which, I think, Common Sense does not pronounce. It might be held that some, at least, among them really are parts of the objects,* of which they are appearances: really are situated in space, and really continue to exist, even when we are not conscious of them. But it might also be held, quite consistently with Common Sense, that *none* of these appearances are in space, and that they all exist only so long as they appear *to* some one: that, for instance, the appearance which the church tower presents to me on a particular occasion, exists only so long as I see it, and cannot be said to be in the same space with any material object or to be at any

* I should now say 'parts of the *surfaces* of the objects' (1952). AUTHOR'S NOTE.

distance from any material object. Common Sense, I think, does not contradict either of those views. All that it does insist on, I think, is that these appearances are appearances of material objects—of objects which do exist, when we are not conscious of them, and which *are* in space. Now the philosophers whose views I am now considering have, I think, all accepted the second of the two views about appearances, which I said were consistent with Common Sense—namely the view that these appearances only exist, so long as the person to whom they appear is seeing them, and that they are *not* in space. And they have then gone on to contradict Common Sense, by adding that these appearances are *not* appearances of material objects—that there are no material objects, for them to be appearances *of*.

And there are two different views of this kind, which have been held.

The first is the view of one of the most famous of English philosophers, Bishop Berkeley. Berkeley's view may, I think, be said to have been that these Appearances are in fact not Appearances *of* anything at all. He himself says, indeed, that these Appearances are themselves material objects—that they are what we mean by material objects. He says that he is not denying the existence of matter, but only explaining what matter is. But he has been commonly held to have denied the existence of matter, and, I think, quite rightly. For he held that these Appearances do not exist except at the moment when we see them; and anything of which this is true can certainly not properly be said to be a material object: what we mean to assert, when we assert the existence of material objects, is certainly the existence of something which continues to exist even when we are *not* conscious of it. Moreover he certainly held, I think, that these appearances were not *all* of them in the same space: he held, for instance, that an appearance, which appears to me, was not at any distance or in any direction from an appearance which appears to you: whereas, as I have said, we should, I think, refuse to call anything a material object, which was not at some distance, in space, in some direction from all *other* material objects. I think, then, it may fairly be said that Berkeley denies the existence of any material objects, in the sense in which Common Sense asserts their existence. This is the way in which he contradicts Common Sense. And the way in which he *adds* to it, is by asserting the existence of a God, to whom, he thinks, there appear a set of appearances exactly like all of those which appear to us.

But Berkeley's view has not, I think, been shared by many other philosophers. A much commoner view is that these things which I have called the appearances of material objects, are in fact the appearances of *something,* but not, as Common Sense asserts, of material objects, but of minds or conscious beings. This view, therefore, both contradicts Common Sense, by denying the existence of material objects, and also goes beyond it by asserting the existence of immense numbers of minds, in addition to those of men and of animals. And it insists, too, that these minds are not *in space*: it is, it says, not true that they are at any distance in any direction from one another; they are, in fact, all simply *nowhere,* not in any place at all.

These views are, I think, startling enough. But there are other philosophers who have held views more startling still —who have held not only that space and material objects do not really exist, but also that time and our own conscious acts do not really exist either: that there are not really any such things in the Universe. At least, this is, I think, what many philosophers have meant. What they *say* is that all these four kinds of things, material objects, space, our acts of consciousness and time, are Appearances; that they are all of them Appearances *of* something else—either of some one thing, or else some collection of things, which is *not* a material object, not an act of consciousness of ours, and which also is not in space nor yet in time. And, as you see, this proposition is ambiguous: whether it contradicts Common Sense or not depends on the question what these philosophers mean by calling these things Appearances. They might conceivably mean that these Appearances were just as real, as the things of which they are appearances; by asserting that they are Appearances of something else, they might only mean to assert that there is in the Universe something else *besides*—something to which these things are related in the same sort of way in which the appearance of a church-tower, which I see when I look at it from a distance, is related to the real church-tower. And, if they did only mean this, their views would merely be of the type of those that *add* to Common Sense: they would merely be asserting that, in addition to the things which Common Sense believes to be in the Universe, there is *also* something else *beside* or *behind* these things. But it seems to me quite plain that they do not really mean this. They do mean to maintain that matter and space and our acts of consciousness and time are *not* real in the sense in which Common Sense believes them to be real, and in which they themselves believe that the *something* else behind Appearances is real. And holding this, it seems to me that what they really mean is that these things are not real at all: that there are not really any such things in the Universe. What, I think, they really mean (though they would not all admit that they mean it) is something like this. There is a sense in which the pole-star, when we look at it, *appears* to be much smaller than the moon. We may say, then, that *what* appears—the *appearance,* in this case—is simply this: *that the pole-star is smaller than the moon.* But there simply *is* no such thing in the Universe as this which appears: the pole-star is *not* smaller than the moon: and, therefore, what appears to be in the Universe—namely, *that* it is smaller than the moon —is a simple nonentity—there is no such thing. It is in this sense, I think, that many philosophers have believed and still believe that not only matter and space but also our acts of consciousness and time simply do not exist: that there are no such things. They have believed that they are something which appears; but that what appears simply is *not* anything—that there is no such thing in the Universe. This, I think, is what they really mean, though they would not all admit that they mean it. And as to what they hold to be in the Universe, *instead* of the things which Common Sense holds to be in it, they have held different views. Some have held that it is a collection of different minds; others that it is one mind; others that it is something which is in some sense mental or spiritual, but which cannot be properly said either to be one mind or many.

These, then, are some of the views which have been held as to the nature of the Universe as a *whole*. And I hope these examples have made clear the sort of thing I mean by the first problem of philosophy—a *general* description of the whole Universe. Any answer to the problem must consist in saying one or other of three things: it must say *either* that certain large classes of things are the *only* kinds of things in the Universe, *i.e.*, that everything in it belongs to one or other of them; or else it must say that everything in the Universe is of one kind; or else it must say that everything which we *know* to be in the Universe belongs to some one of several classes or to some one class. And it must also, if it holds that there are several different classes of things, say something about the relation of these classes to one another.

This, then, is the first and most interesting problem of philosophy. And it seems to me that a great many others can be defined as problems bearing upon this one.

For philosophers have not been content simply to express their opinions as to what there is or is not in the Universe, or as to what we know to be in it or do not know to be in it. They have also tried to prove their opinions to be true. And with this, you see, a great many subordinate problems are opened up.

In order to prove, for instance, that any one of these views I have mentioned is true, you must both prove *it* and *also* refute all the others. You must prove either that there is a God, or that there is not, or that we do not know whether there is one or not. Either that there is a future life, or that there is not, or that we do not know whether there is one or not. And so on with all the other kinds of things I have mentioned: matter and space and time; and the minds of other men; and other minds, *not* the minds of men or animals. In order to prove that any particular view of the Universe is correct, you must prove, in the case of each of these things, either that they do exist, or that they do not, or that we do not know whether they do or not. And all these questions, you see, may be treated separately for their own sakes. Many philosophers, indeed, have not tried to give any general description of the *whole* Universe. They have merely tried to answer some one or more of these subordinate questions.

And there is another sort of subordinate questions, which ought, I think, to be specially mentioned. Many philosophers have spent a great deal of their time in trying to define more clearly what is the difference between these various sorts of things: for instance, what is the difference between a material object and an act of consciousness, between matter and mind, between God and man, etc. And these questions of definition are by no means so easy to answer as you might think. Nor must it be thought that they are mere questions of words. A good definition of the sorts of things you hold to be in the Universe, obviously adds to the clearness of your view. And it is not only a question of clearness either. When, for instance, you try to define what you mean by a material object, you find that there are several different properties which a material object might have, of which you had never thought before; and your effort to define may thus lead you to conclude that whole classes of things have certain properties, or have *not* certain others, of which you would never have thought, if you had merely contented yourself with asserting that there are material objects in the Universe, without enquiring what you meant by this assertion.

We may, then, say that a great class of subordinate philosophical problems consist in discussing whether the great classes of things I have mentioned do exist or do not, or whether we are simply ignorant as to whether they do or not; and also in trying to define these classes and considering how they are related to one another. A great deal of philosophy has consisted in discussing these questions with regard to God, a future life, matter, minds, Space and Time. And all these problems could be said to belong to that department of philosophy which is called Metaphysics.

But now we come to a class of questions which may be said to belong to other departments of philosophy, but which also have an evident bearing on the first main problem as to the general description of the Universe. One of

the most natural questions to ask, when anybody asserts
some fact, which you are inclined to doubt, is the question:
How do you know that? And if the person answers the
question in such a way as to show that he has not learnt the
fact in any one of the ways in which it is possible to acquire
real knowledge, as opposed to mere belief, about facts of
the sort, you will conclude that he does *not* really know
it. In other words, we constantly assume in ordinary life
that there are only a limited number of ways in which it is
possible to acquire real *knowledge* of certain kinds of facts;
and that if a person asserts a fact, which he has not learnt
in any of these ways, then, in fact, he does not *know* it.
Now philosophers also have used this sort of argument very
largely. They have tried to classify exhaustively all the
different kinds of ways in which we can know things; and
have then concluded that, since certain things, which other
philosophers have asserted or which they themselves
formerly believed, are *not* known in any of these ways,
therefore these things are not known at all.

Hence a large part of philosophy has, in fact, consisted
in trying to classify completely all the different ways in
which we can *know* things; or in trying to describe exactly
particular ways of knowing them.

And this question—the question: How do we *know*
anything at all? involves three different kinds of questions.

The first is of this sort. When you are asked: How do
you know that? it may be meant to ask: What sort of a
thing *is* your knowledge of it? What sort of a process goes
on in your mind, when you *know* it? In what does this
event, which you call a *knowing,* consist? This first question
as to what sort of a thing knowledge is—as to what happens when we *know* anything—is a question which
philosophy shares with psychology; but which many
philosophers have tried to answer. They have tried to
distinguish the different kinds of things, which happen in
our minds, when we know different things; and to point
out, what, if anything, is common to them all.

But there is, secondly, something else which may be
meant; when it is asked what knowledge *is*. For we do not
say that we *know* any proposition, for instance the proposi-

tion that matter exists, unless we mean to assert that this proposition is *true*: that it is *true* that matter exists. And hence there is included in the question what knowledge *is,* the question what is meant by saying that any proposition is *true*. This is a different question from the psychological question as to what happens in your mind, when you know anything; and this question as to what *truth* is has generally been said to be a question for *Logic,* in the widest sense of the term. And Logic, or at least parts of it, is reckoned as a department of philosophy.

And, finally, there is still another thing which may be meant, when it is asked: How do you know that? It may be meant, namely, what reason have you for believing it? or in other words, what *other* thing do you know, which *proves* this thing to be *true?* And philosophers have, in fact, been much occupied with this question also: the question what are the different ways in which a proposition can be proved to be true; what are all the different sorts of reasons which are good reasons for believing anything. This also is a question which is reckoned as belonging to the department of Logic.

There is, therefore, a huge branch of philosophy which is concerned with the different ways in which we know things; and many philosophers have devoted themselves almost exclusively to questions which fall under this head.

But finally, if we are to give a complete account of philosophy, we must mention one other class of questions. There is a department of philosophy which is called Ethics or ethical philosophy; and this department deals with a class of questions quite different from any which I have mentioned yet. We are all constantly in ordinary life asking such questions as: Would such and such a result be a good thing to bring about? or would it be a bad thing? Would such and such an action be a right action to perform or would it be a wrong one? And what ethical philosophy tries to do is to classify all the different sorts of things which *would* be good or bad, right or wrong, in such a way as to be able to say: Nothing would be good, unless it had certain characteristics, or one or other of certain characteristics; and similarly nothing would be bad, unless it had certain properties or one or other of certain properties: and similarly with the question, what sort of actions would be right, and what would be wrong.

And these ethical questions have a most important bearing upon our general description of the Universe in two ways.

In the first place, it is certainly one of the most important facts about the Universe that there are in it these distinctions of good and bad, right and wrong. And many people have thought that, from the fact that there are these distinctions, other inferences as to what is in the Universe can be drawn.

And in the second place, by combining the results of Ethics as to what *would* be good or bad, with the conclusions of Metaphysics as to what kinds of things there are in the Universe, we get a means of answering the question whether the Universe is, on the whole, good or bad, and how good or bad, compared with what it might be: a sort of question, which has in fact been much discussed by many philosophers.

To conclude, then, I think the above is a fair description of the sort of questions with which philosophers deal.]

CHAPTER III

Philosophy and History:

Benedetto Croce (1866–1952)

IN SHARP CONTRAST TO MOORE AND RUSSELL, AND IN SPITE of his own criticisms of Hegel's philosophy, Croce remained closer to the spirit of Hegel's thought than any other distinguished thinker of the twentieth century. Croce was an idealist; he was more closely in touch with history and literature than any of his famous contemporaries in philosophy; he holds the strange-sounding view that philosophy and history are identical. For more than a generation he dominated Italian culture: as Minister of Education in the Giolitti government of 1920, as the opponent whom Mussolini dared not destroy during the fascist regime, and finally as the spiritual voice of Italy just after her collapse in the second world war. More than any philosopher of the twentieth century he has united scholarship with active wisdom, while living a long and productive life outside of the university.

Croce was born in 1866 and spent his early childhood in Naples. His parents were landowners who died in an earthquake in 1883, leaving him a wealthy orphan and ultimately, one gathers, a man of independent means. In addition to Hegel the most powerful intellectual forces in his life were his countrymen Giambattista Vico and Francesco de Sanctis. Vico's *The New Science,* published in 1725, celebrates the importance of history; de Sanctis, a nineteenth-century figure, wrote one of the important histories of Italian literature. Along with Hegel they represent Croce's three great interests: philosophy, history, and literature, which he encouraged so brilliantly during his long editorship of the magazine *La Critica.*

Like so many philosophers who have been influenced by or sympathetic to Hegel, Croce has a tendency to blur lines, to challenge sharp and rigid distinctions, and this is most strikingly illustrated in his thesis that history and philosophy are identical. This identification of subjects which have been so sharply separated by philosophical tradition is a product of Croce's passionate interest in both of them and his obvious desire to combine his study of them in an unmechanical way. His intellectual development has been almost dialectical in the hegelian sense. After abandoning an attempt to study law in Rome, Croce threw himself into antiquarian studies of Neapolitan folklore and history. But throughout this period he was moved by deep inner promptings, by exciting memories of conversations with the philosopher Antonio Labriola, whom he had met in Rome and whose lectures on ethics he had attended, by ruminations on the ideas of de Sanctis, Vico, and German

MORTON WHITE   45

estheticians. In 1893 this all burst out in a swiftly composed essay called *History Subsumed under the General
Concept of Art,* his first philosophical venture after achieving a substantial reputation as an antiquarian and a philologist. But the philosophical fires were quickly extinguished
and Croce turned back to his philology once again, though
not for long. By now the hegelian antithesis to antiquarian
studies had become philosophy as he saw it practiced by
others, for example by Labriola in his studies of marxism.
Croce read them with great interest and in reaction produced a series of essays in the late nineties which were
later published under the title *Historical Materialism and
Marxian Economics.*

From that time on Croce was a philosopher in his own
right, who came to argue that the antiquarian studies of his
youth were only the bare bones of history and that the
work of his predecessors was not true philosophy. The
truth presumably lay in his own synthesis, his own philosophical history or historical philosophy, and this he expounded in a series of four volumes that appeared before
the first world war had ended. They are all parts of a general work called *Philosophy of Spirit* and they deal in order
with esthetics, logic, economics and ethics, history. We get
an indication of one kind of mind to whom Croce appealed
from a letter of William Butler Yeats's: "I am now deep
in Croce. I have finished his *Philosophy of the Practical,* all
of his *Aesthetics* except the historical chapters, which I
shall return to, and am half through the *Logic.* I find this
kind of study helps my poetry which has I believe been at
its best these last few months."[1] Yeats's appreciation of
Croce (and Whitehead and Bergson) contrasts dramatically with his hostility toward Russell and his misunderstandings of Moore, the "very British brother" of Yeats's cor-
respondent, T. Sturge Moore.

The title of Croce's major work and its four divisions
are a clue to the fundamentals of his philosophy. I have already said that Croce is an idealist who believes that reality
or the subject matter of our thinking is mind, life, or spirit.

[1] Ursula Bridge (ed.), *W. B. Yeats and T. Sturge Moore: Their
Correspondence 1901-1937* (Routledge and Kegan Paul, 1953),
p. 113.

It is difficult for one who cannot accept this view to know even what is meant by it. One is likely to reply (in the manner of G. E. Moore) "What about tables and chairs? Surely they are not spirits." Such a reply would undoubtedly be rejected as irrelevant by a follower of Croce and it is only by trying to understand why that we can penetrate the elements of his philosophy. I think that Croce is trying to say that we can only be sure of the existence of mental or spiritual *activity* and that any postulation of what he calls a "transcendent" entity is unjustified. If I judge that this page is white and analyze my judgment, I find two active elements in it. First, the esthetic element, the direct awareness, or immediate experience, or intuition that prompts my judgment; second, my linking of this experience with others and my abstraction of a common concept that applies to all of them. If I remove these two elements, if I try to think of anything beyond these activities of intuition and abstraction I find nothing. (Some may ask about the experiences intuited and the concepts abstracted, but I do not know Croce's answer.) Those philosophers who are prepared to assert the existence of something else commit themselves, as Kant did, to the existence of transcendent beings, to things-in-themselves which are supposed to lie behind the appearances, and on Croce's view even Hegel's Absolute Idea was such a transcendent entity and therefore inadmissible.

After identifying spiritual activity as the subject-matter of philosophy Croce distinguishes between intellectual activity, whose two forms are intuition and abstraction, and practical activity, whose two forms are economic and ethical activity. Corresponding to intuition, abstraction, economic activity, and ethical activity respectively are the concepts of beauty, truth, utility, and goodness, and the disciplines that study them: esthetics, logic, economics, and ethics.

This accounts for the first three volumes of the *Philosophy of Spirit,* but how does the fourth on history fit into the picture? History is the concrete study of the spirit, of life, of human activity, and it employs all of the four concepts to which we have just referred. It is therefore the

grandest and deepest discipline of all and identical with
philosophy itself. The true historian must understand and
evaluate the events he studies and in doing so he becomes
a philosopher. In understanding and evaluating them he
must re-enact them, relive them, in a way that leads Croce
to say that all history is contemporary history (in what is
obviously a Pickwickian sense, though not so recognized).
It is not surprising, therefore, that Croce should have been
one of the most learned and active of philosophers. In one
respect, however, he abandoned the encyclopedic ideal:
he was not interested in mathematics or the natural
sciences. He did not deny their importance, but he often
said that they dealt with reality in an abstract way while
philosophy and history as he conceived them sought greater
and greater concreteness, closer connection with the active,
living spirit of man. This led him to an attack on the pretensions of scientific method.

Much of this attack was stimulated by certain tendencies in the nineteenth century against which Croce argued.
Like the British idealists, Croce was in reaction against
the empiricism of Auguste Comte and John Stuart Mill
and the evolutionary agnosticism of Herbert Spencer. As a
literary historian he had read the work of their continental counterparts in the nineteenth century, Hippolyte Taine
and Ernest Renan, whose admiration for science and interest in applying it to historical studies Croce continued
to oppose for the rest of his life. In protecting history from
the encroachments of science he was, of course, also protecting its identical twin philosophy.

I have selected a passage from Croce in which his views
on history are set forth. Since the task of the historian is
to relate individual events, he is not only obliged to use his
intuition in order to identify the subject of his study and
his individual judgments, say Italy at a given period, but
he must also use his powers of abstraction in characterizing Italy at that period, in concluding that it was a fascist
state. And in saying that Italy was fascist at a certain time
the historian is applying a concept or a predicate which
requires analysis of the kind usually associated with philosophy. As the selection will indicate, this relatively in-

nocuous doctrine is overlaid with other views of Croce that are not as straightforward. But *it* is there and *it* is undeniable. Its effect is to make the historian more conscious of the need for theoretical analysis and the philosopher more conscious of the need to analyze his concepts in a given context, to treat them not as inhabitants of a transcendent, platonic heaven but as predicates of a specific statement or as components of a specific judgment. By one of those meetings of extremes that frequently occur in the history of philosophy Croce's view seems as though it might be congenial to those latter-day philosophers who have surrendered the platonism of the early Moore and Russell, who stress the importance of discussing the behavior of words and sentences in their living context, and who view the context itself as an indefinitely long story or passage in which they appear. Where Croce differs from them is in his concentration on stories of general human interest, stories told by historians of human culture rather than nurses at bedtime. Were his powers of logical analysis as acute and subtle as his subject matter is profound, Croce might have anticipated a good deal of philosophy that is not usually identified with his own tradition.

The selection that follows is a chapter drawn from Croce's *History as the Story of Liberty* (1941), "Historical Knowledge Considered as Complete Knowledge."[2]

It is not enough to say that history is historical judgment, it is necessary to add that every judgment is an historical judgment or, quite simply, history. If judgment is a relation between a subject and a predicate, then the subject or the event, whatever it is that is being judged, is always an historical fact, a becoming, a process under way, for there are no immobile facts nor can such things be envisaged in the world of reality. Historical judgment is embodied even in the merest perception of the judging mind (if it did not judge there would not even be perception but merely blind and dumb sensation): for example the perception

[2] I wish to thank George Allen and Unwin, Ltd., London, for permission to reprint pp. 32-36 of *History as the Story of Liberty* by Benedetto Croce, translated from the Italian by Sylvia Sprigge. The original appeared under the title *La storia come pensiero e come azione* in 1938.

that the object in front of me is a stone, and that it will not fly away of its own accord like a bird at the sound of my approach, makes it expedient that I should dislodge it with my stick or with my foot. The stone is really a process under way, struggling against the forces of disintegration and yielding only bit by bit, and my judgment refers to one aspect of its history.

But we may not rest here either, nor renounce further consequences: historical judgment is not a variety of knowledge, but it is knowledge itself; it is the form which completely fills and exhausts the field of knowing, leaving no room for anything else.

In point of fact all concrete knowledge whatever is on a par with historical judgment, bound to life, that is to action, of which it marks a pause or an anticipation having for its function to break down (as we have said) any obstacles barring a clear view of the situation from which it must specifically and with determination emerge. Knowledge for the sake of knowledge, so far from having anything aristocratic or sublime about it (as some believe), would be an idiotic pastime for idiots, or for the idiotic moments which we all have in us; in reality there is no such thing, it is intrinsically impossible and the stimulus ceases with the failure of the material itself and of the end of knowledge. Those intellectuals who see salvation in the withdrawal of the artist or the thinker from the world around him, in his deliberate non-participation in vulgar practical contests—vulgar in so far as they are practical— do without knowing it compass the death of the intellect. In a paradisal state without work or struggle in which there were no obstacles to overcome, there could be no thought, because every motive for thought would have disappeared; neither any real contemplation, because active and poetic contemplation contains in itself a world of practical struggles and of affections.

Nor are great efforts necessary to demonstrate that natural science with its complement and instrument, mathematics, is also based upon the practical requirements of life, and is out to satisfy them; Francis Bacon, its great initiator in modern times, taught this convincingly enough.

The question is, however, at what stage in its development does natural science exercise this useful office and become true and proper knowledge? Certainly not when it makes abstractions, builds classes, stabilizes relations between classes and calls them laws, gives mathematical formulae to these laws, and so on. All these are accessory labours useful for storing up knowledge already acquired or to be acquired, but they are not the act of knowing. A man may possess in books or by rote all medical knowledge, all the kinds and sub-kinds of illnesses with their characteristics, and so possess "bien Galien, mais nullement le malade," as Montaigne would have said, and he will know as little (or nothing) as another man knows of history, who owns one of these many universal history books which have been compiled, and has furnished his memory out of it. The latter will not truly know anything until under the stimulus of events that knowledge loses its deadly rigidity, and his thought studies some political or other situation: and the same is true of the medical expert up to the moment when he has a patient to deal with and must by intuition and understanding diagnose the sickness of that patient, and that patient alone, in that way and under those conditions, and he grapples not with the formula of the illness but with its concrete and individual reality. The natural sciences have their beginning in individual cases, which the mind does not yet or not fully understand, and they execute a lengthy and complicated series of efforts in order finally to bring the mind, which has been thus prepared, up against these same cases, setting it in direct communication with them so that it may form a proper judgment.

Natural science, therefore, is not seriously at variance or in opposition to the theory that all genuine knowledge is historical knowledge; like history it deals with the actual and humble world. It is not so with philosophy, or, if you like, with the traditional idea of a philosophy which has its eyes fixed on heaven, and expects supreme truth from that quarter. This division of heaven and earth, this dualist conception of a reality which transcends reality, of metaphysics over physics, this contemplation of the concept without or outside judgment, for ever imprints the same character, whatever denomination the transcendental reality may bear: God or Matter, Idea or Will; it makes no difference, while beneath or against each of them there is presumed to subsist some inferior or merely phenomenal reality.

But historical thought has played a nasty trick on this respectable transcendental philosophy, as upon its twin, transcendental religion, of which the former is the reasoned or theological form; the trick of turning it into history, by interpreting all its concepts, doctrines, disputes, and even its disconsolate sceptical renunciations, as historical facts and affirmations, which arose out of certain requirements, that were thus partly satisfied and partly unsatisfied. In this way historical thought did due justice to the age-long domination of transcendental philosophy (a domination which was also a service to human society) and marked its end with a decent obituary. It can be said that once transcendental philosophy was subjected to historical criticism, philosophy itself ceased to enjoy an autonomous existence because its claim to autonomy was founded upon its metaphysical character. That which has taken its place is no longer philosophy, but history, or, which amounts to the same thing, philosophy in so far as it is history and history in so far as it is philosophy: "History-Philosophy," of which the principle is the identity of the universal and the individual, of the intellect and the intuition, and which regards as arbitrary and illegitimate any separation of those two elements, they being in reality a single element. It is a curious fate that history should for a long time have been considered and treated as the most humble form of knowledge, while philosophy was considered as the highest, and that now it not only is superior to philosophy but annihilates it. This so-called history which had been relegated to a back seat was not in truth history, but chronicles and research, superficially considered and based on hearsay: the other kind of history which has now asserted itself is historical thought, sole and integral form of knowledge. When the old metaphysical philosophy tried to lend a helping hand to history in order to draw it out of the depths, it was not to history but to the chronicle that the hand was given, and as this could not be raised to the rank of history by reason of its metaphysical character, a "philosophy of history" was superimposed upon it, a process of excogitation and guess-work, to which we have referred above, a sort of divine programme which history carries out like someone who tries to make a more or less careful copy of a model. The "philosophy of history" was a consequence of mental impotence, or, as Vico said of myths, of bankruptcy of the mind.

Among the various didactic forms of literature there certainly are works which may be classed as philosophy and not as history because they seem to treat of abstract concepts, purged of any intuitive elements. But if these treatises are not mere circlings in the void, if they contain full and concrete judgments, then the intuitive element is always there, even if it is latent to the vulgar eye, which is only on the lookout for it when it appears as an incrustation of chronicle writing or of erudition. The intuitive element is there, in the very fact that the philosophical arguments formulated in it answer the need for light on particular historical conditions: the knowledge of these conditions explains the argument just as these conditions are themselves explained by the arguments. I was going to say, to take a living example, that even the methodological elucidations which I am giving here are not really intelligible unless with an explicit mental reference (normally made by me simply in an implicit way) to the political, moral and intellectual conditions of our times, which they help to describe and judge.

Then there are the specialists, or professors of philosophy whose occupation appears to be to act as a counterweight to the philologists, that is to the erudites who profess to be historians. The latter collect bare facts and produce them as history, while the former marshal the abstract ideas, thus complementing one form of ignorance with another form of ignorance, by which means there is not much progress to be made. These are the natural preservers of transcendental philosophy who even when in words they assert the unity of philosophy and history, deny it in fact, or at the most they descend from time to time out of their super-world in order to pronounce some musty generalization or some historical falsehood. As the historic sense grows more refined and an historical way of thinking becomes more general, the historical-philologists will be sent back to the realm of pure and simple and useful philology and the professional philosophers can be thanked and gracefully dismissed, because philosophy will have found in the true writings of history a scope for its labours which they lacked. They philosophized coldly, shunned the excitement of passions and interests, wrote "without reference to any occasion." But every serious history, and every serious philosophy, ought to be a history and a philosophy "for the occasion," as Goethe said of genuine poetry, though the occasion of poetry is in the passions, that of history in the conduct of life and in morality.]

CHAPTER IV

Myth, Morals, and Religion:

George Santayana (1863–1952)

WHILE MOORE PUSHED ENGLISH PHILOSOPHY IN THE direction of analysis and really had no principled objection to metaphysics done respectably, and while Croce went to the other extreme of identifying philosophy with history, Santayana's *Life of Reason,* which appeared in 1905-06, gave moral philosophy a central position in reaction to the cult of history in the nineteenth century and in marked contrast to the logical tendencies of the twentieth. Santayana tells us of his early absorption in "the historical spirit of the nineteenth century, and in that splendid panorama of nations and religions, literatures and arts, which it unrolled before the imagination. These picturesque vistas into the past came to fill in circumstantially that geographical and moral vastness to which my imagination was already accustomed."[1] But elsewhere he tells us of his reservations about Hegel's *Phenomenology of Mind*: "It had seemed to me that myth and sophistry there spoiled a very fine subject. The subject was the history of human ideas: the sophistry was imposed on Hegel by his ambition to show that the episodes he happened to review formed a dialectical chain, and the myth sprang from the constant suggestion that this history of human ideas made up the whole of cosmic evolution, and that those episodes were the scattered syllables of a single eternal oracle."[2] That very fine subject became Santayana's own in his *Life of Reason,* which was subtitled "The Phases of Human Progress" in a way that illuminates Santayana's relation to the good, the past, and Hegel. Unlike Hegel he did not try to describe the dialectical development of human ideas, but rather engaged in a moral review of Western civilization.

History, therefore, is not the essence of philosophy for Santayana as it is for Croce. On Santayana's view history is a "servile science," dedicated to a superhuman and an infrahuman ideal: superhuman because it aims to describe *all* past existence, infrahuman because, like Aristotle, Santayana thought there were many things beneath human interest. But he did think the philosopher might *use* the results of historians, that he might select from them whatever illustrated his own ideals, as he might pick out his friends in a crowd. *The Life of Reason* is a critical survey of the chief goods that have been achieved by man in his efforts to harmonize and satisfy his various impulses—to *live* the life of reason. Its five volumes on common sense, society, religion, art, and science are connected essays on the transformation of man's natural impulses into high ideals. Santayana's treatment of love is usually regarded as a paradigm of his philosophizing in *The Life of Reason.* It is a sensible and sensitive recognition of the fact that love is animal in its basis and ideal in its aspiration. In the same

[1] "A Brief History of my Opinions," *Contemporary American Philosophy,* ed. Adams and Montague (Macmillan, 1930), Vol. II, pp. 244-45.

[2] *The Life of Reason,* Preface to the second edition (1924), pp. x-xi.

way, the family, government, and industry are moments in man's march toward his ideal; they are instruments in the life of reason, which reaches its highest expression in religion, art, and science. These are the chief constituents of an ideal society.

In the selection to follow, Santayana expresses some of his views on religion, which are made somewhat intriguing by the fact that he regards himself as an atheist and a Catholic. He rejects the theology of Catholicism but rejoices in the poetry and the ritual of its religious ceremony. For him religion is not a literal account of anything but an allegorical and metaphorical rendering of moral truth. It becomes almost a species of poetry and is therefore to be measured by esthetic and moral standards rather than by scientific methods. His treatment of theology is part of a general movement in the twentieth century in which one field of traditional knowledge after another has come to be viewed as a body of myth. Santayana does it for theology, and the logical positivists do something similar for metaphysics and ethics, as we shall see.

All along the line there is a progressive retreat from the view that theological, metaphysical, and ethical statements are about their ostensible subject matters—gods, transcendent entities, and moral qualities—and in this way they are contrasted with science. The contrast is that of useful, pleasing, or moving myth-making, and true, literal transcription of reality. But because of its conviction that tables and chairs are just as much constructs as gods are, pragmatism applies a similar analysis to science itself, treating it as a myth that is useful in a sense which varies with the kind of pragmatism one has in mind. For James, as we shall see, it is useful in a relatively subjective sense; for John Dewey it is useful as an instrument in the solution of a public, objective problem. Naturally, when everything becomes mythical it becomes hard to see the value of any distinction between the mythical and the non-mythical. Literal truth must be assigned to something and very often the direct reports of sensation or satisfaction are elected to this role. On the rock bottom, then, we have the literal truth about "the given," the data of experience or satisfaction, and then, towering above it, the constructed symbols of art, religion, and science which achieve their value either by causing certain experiences or by helping us predict them. Santayana's view is not always as extreme as this, but his treatment of religion was a kind of harbinger of things to come, a preface to the interest in myth which dominates not only twentieth-century philosophy but also its literature and its religious thinking. Extreme mythicalism was naturally in conflict with the outlook of 'realism in epistemology and it explains a good deal of the controversy between pragmatism and realism in the twentieth century. Moreover, it is related to the influence of marxism and freudianism in the twentieth century, for they construe seemingly objective truths as mere ideological devices or as reflections of psychosexual demands. Instead of asking whether a statement is true they tend to ask for the background and consequences of its affirmation.

Santayana was for a number of years a professor of philosophy at Harvard but then left this country to become one of America's distinguished expatriates along with Henry James and T. S. Eliot. He had been born a Spaniard and his return to Europe meant going home to a culture which he admired more and which he may have understood better. After *The Life of Reason* he continued to write prolifically and is thought by some to be one of the great stylists in the English language. He has written poetry, criticism, a novel, and an autobiography in addition to numerous philosophical works. His main influence on American thought has been in the direction of the kind of naturalism which is illustrated by the relatively early *Life of Reason,* but close students of his thinking often debate whether there might not be one, two, or *n* Santayanas who exhibit varying degrees of fidelity to the earlier doctrine.

The following is Chapter I of Santayana's *Reason in Religion,* "How Religion May Be An Embodiment of Reason." This is the third volume of *The Life of Reason* (1905-06).[3]

[3] Reprinted from *The Life of Reason: Reason in Religion* by George Santayana. Copyright, 1905, by Charles Scribner's Sons; 1933, by George Santayana. Used by permission of Charles Scribner's Sons, New York, and Constable and Company, Ltd., London.

[*Religion certainly significant.*

Experience has repeatedly confirmed that well-known maxim of Bacon's that "a little philosophy inclineth man's mind to atheism, but depth in philosophy bringeth men's minds about to religion." In every age the most comprehensive thinkers have found in the religion of their time and country something they could accept, interpreting and illustrating that religion so as to give it depth and universal application. Even the heretics and atheists, if they have had profundity, turn out after a while to be forerunners of some new orthodoxy. What they rebel against is a religion alien to their nature; they are atheists only by accident, and relatively to a convention which inwardly offends them, but they yearn mightily in their own souls after the religious acceptance of a world interpreted in their own fashion. So it appears in the end that their atheism and loud protestation were in fact the hastier part of their thought, since what emboldened them to deny the poor world's faith was that they were too impatient to understand it. Indeed, the enlightenment common to young wits and worm-eaten old satirists, who plume themselves on detecting the scientific ineptitude of religion—something which the blindest half see—is not nearly enlightened enough: it points to notorious facts incompatible with religious tenets literally taken, but it leaves unexplored the habits of thought from which those tenets sprang, their original meaning, and their true function. Such studies would bring the sceptic face to face with the mystery and pathos of mortal existence. They would make him understand why religion is so profoundly moving and in a sense so profoundly just. There must needs be something humane and necessary in an influence that has become the most general sanction of virtue, the chief occasion for art and philosophy, and the source, perhaps, of the best human happiness. If nothing, as Hooker said, is "so malapert as a splenetic religion," a sour irreligion is almost as perverse.

But not literally true.

At the same time, when Bacon penned the sage epigram we have quoted he forgot to add that the God to whom depth in philosophy brings back men's minds is far from being the same from whom a little philosophy estranges them. It would be pitiful indeed if mature reflection bred no better conceptions than those which have drifted down the muddy stream of time, where tradition and passion have jumbled everything together. Traditional conceptions, when they are felicitous, may be adopted by the poet, but they must be purified by the moralist and disintegrated by the philosopher. Each religion, so dear to those whose life it sanctifies, and fulfilling so necessary a function in the society that has adopted it, necessarily contradicts every other religion, and probably contradicts itself. What religion a man shall have is a historical accident, quite as much as what language he shall speak. In the rare circumstances where a choice is possible, he may, with some difficulty, make an exchange; but even then he is only adopting a new convention which may be more agreeable to his personal temper but which is essentially as arbitrary as the old.

All religion is positive and particular.

The attempt to speak without speaking any particular language is not more hopeless than the attempt to have a religion that shall be no religion in particular. A courier's or a dragoman's speech may indeed be often unusual and drawn from disparate sources, not without some mixture of personal originality; but that private jargon will have a meaning only because of its analogy to one or more conventional languages and its obvious derivation from them. So travellers from one religion to another, people who have lost their spiritual nationality, may often retain a neutral and confused residuum of belief, which they may egregiously regard as the essence of all religion, so little may they remember the graciousness and naturalness of that ancestral accent, which a perfect religion should have. Yet a moment's probing of the conceptions surviving in such minds will show them to be nothing but vestiges of old beliefs, creases which thought, even if emptied of all dogmatic tenets, has not been able to smooth away at its first unfolding. Later generations, if they have any religion at all, will be found either to revert to ancient authority, or to attach themselves spontaneously to something wholly novel and immensely positive, to some faith promulgated by a fresh genius and passionately embraced by a converted people. Thus every living and healthy religion has a marked idiosyncrasy. Its power consists in its special and surprising message and in the bias which that revelation gives to life. The vistas it opens and the mysteries it propounds are another world to live in; and another world to live in—whether we expect ever to pass wholly into it or no—is what we mean by having a religion.

It aims at the Life of Reason.

What relation, then, does this great business of the soul, which we call religion, bear to the Life of Reason? That the relation between the two is close seems clear from several circumstances. The Life of Reason is the seat of all ultimate values. Now the history of mankind will show us that whenever spirits at once lofty and intense have seemed to attain the highest joys, they have envisaged and attained them in religion. Religion would therefore seem to be a vehicle or a factor in rational life, since the ends of rational life are attained by it. Moreover, the Life of Reason is an ideal to which everything in the world should be subordinated; it establishes lines of moral cleavage everywhere and makes right eternally different from wrong. Religion does the same thing. It makes absolute moral decisions. It sanctions, unifies, and transforms ethics. Religion thus exercises a function of the Life of Reason. And a further function which is common to both is that of emancipating man from his personal limitations. In different ways religions promise to transfer the soul to better conditions. A supernaturally favoured kingdom is to be established for posterity upon earth, or for all the faithful in heaven, or the soul is to be freed by repeated purgations from all taint and sorrow, or it is to be lost in the absolute, or it is to become an influence and an object of adoration in the places it once haunted or wherever the activities it once loved may be carried on by future generations of its kindred. Now reason in its way lays before us all these possibilities: it points to common objects, political and intellectual, in which an individual may lose what is mortal and accidental in himself and immortalise what is rational and human; it teaches us how sweet and fortunate death may be to those whose spirit can still live in their country and in their ideas; it reveals the radiating effects of action and the eternal objects of thought.

Yet the difference in tone and language must strike us, so soon as it is philosophy that speaks. That change should remind us that even if the function of religion and that of reason coincide, this function is performed in the two cases by very different organs. Religions are many, reason one. Religion consists of conscious ideas, hopes, enthusiasms, and objects of worship; it operates by grace and flourishes by prayer. Reason, on the other hand, is a mere principle or potential order, on which, indeed, we may come to reflect, but which exists in us ideally only, without variation or stress of any kind. We conform or do not conform to it; it does not urge or chide us, nor call for any emotions on our part other than those naturally aroused by the various objects which it unfolds in their true nature and proportion. Religion brings some order into life by weighting it with new materials. Reason adds to the natural materials only the perfect order which it introduces into them. Rationality is nothing but a form, an ideal constitution which experience may more or less embody. Religion is a part of experience itself, a mass of sentiments and ideas. The one is an inviolate principle, the other a changing and struggling force. And yet this struggling and changing force of religion seems to direct man toward something eternal. It seems to make for an ultimate harmony within the soul and for an ultimate harmony between the soul and all the soul depends upon. So that religion, in its intent, is a more conscious and direct pursuit of the Life of Reason than is society, science, or art. For these approach and fill out the ideal life tentatively and piecemeal, hardly regarding the goal or caring for the ultimate justification of their instinctive aims. Religion also has an instinctive and blind side, and bubbles up in all manner of chance practices and intuitions; soon, however, it feels its way toward the heart of things, and, from whatever quarter it may come, veers in the direction of the ultimate.

But largely fails to attain it.

Nevertheless, we must confess that this religious pursuit of the Life of Reason has been singularly abortive. Those within the pale of each religion may prevail upon themselves to express satisfaction with its results, thanks to a fond partiality in reading the past and generous draughts of hope for the future; but anyone regarding the various religions at once and comparing their achievements with what reason requires, must feel how terrible is the disappointment which they have one and all prepared for mankind. Their chief anxiety has been to offer imaginary remedies for mortal ills, some of which are incurable essentially, while others might have been really cured by well-directed effort. The Greek oracles, for instance, pretended to heal our natural ignorance, which has its appropriate though difficult cure, while the Christian vision of heaven pretended to be an antidote to our natural death, the inevitable correlate of birth and of a changing and conditioned existence. By methods of this sort little can be done for the real betterment of life. To confuse intelligence and dislocate sentiment by gratuitous fictions is a short-sighted way of pursuing happiness. Nature is soon avenged. An unhealthy exaltation and a one-sided morality have to be followed by regrettable reactions. When these come, the real rewards of life may seem vain to a relaxed vitality, and the very name of virtue may irritate young spirits untrained in any natural excellence. Thus religion too often debauches the morality it comes to sanction, and impedes the science it ought to fulfil.

Its approach imaginative.

What is the secret of this ineptitude? Why does religion, so near to rationality in its purpose, fall so far short of it in its texture and in its results? The answer is easy: Religion pursues rationality through the imagination. When it explains events or assigns causes, it is an imaginative substitute for science. When it gives precepts, insinuates ideals, or remoulds aspiration, it is an imaginative substitute for wisdom—I mean for the deliberate and impartial pursuit of all good. The conditions and the aims of life are both represented in religion poetically, but this poetry tends to arrogate to itself literal truth and moral authority, neither of which it possesses. Hence the depth and importance of religion becomes intelligible no less than its contradictions and practical disasters. Its object is the same as that of reason, but its method is to proceed by intuition and by unchecked poetical conceits. These are repeated and vulgarised in proportion to their original fineness and significance, till they pass for reports of objective truth and come to constitute a world of faith, superposed upon the world of experience and regarded as materially enveloping it, if not in space at least in time and in existence. The only truth of religion comes from its interpretation of life, from its symbolic rendering of that moral experience which it springs out of and which it seeks to elucidate. Its falsehood comes from the insidious misunderstanding which clings to it, to the effect that these poetic conceptions are not merely representations of experience as it is or should be, but are rather information about experience or reality elsewhere—an experience and reality which, strangely enough, supply just the defects betrayed by reality and experience here.

When its poetic method is denied its value is jeopardised.

Thus religion has the same original relation to life that poetry has; only poetry, which never pretends to literal validity, adds a pure value to existence, the value of a liberal imaginative exercise. The poetic value of religion would initially be greater than that of poetry itself, because religion deals with higher and more practical themes, with sides of life which are in greater need of some imaginative touch and ideal interpretation than are those pleasant or pompous things which ordinary poetry dwells upon. But this initial advantage is neutralised in part by the abuse to which religion is subject, whenever its symbolic rightness is taken for scientific truth. Like poetry, it improves the world only by imagining it improved, but not content with making this addition to the mind's furniture—an addition which might be useful and ennobling—it thinks to confer a more radical benefit by persuading mankind that, in spite of appearances, the world is really such as that rather arbitrary idealisation has painted it. This spurious satisfaction is naturally the prelude to many a disappointment, and the soul has infinite trouble to emerge again from the artificial problems and sentiments into which it is thus plunged. The value of religion becomes equivocal. Religion remains an imaginative achievement, a symbolic representation of moral reality which may have a most important function in vitalising the mind and in transmitting, by way of parables, the lessons of experience. But it becomes at the same time a continuous incidental deception; and this deception, in proportion as it is strenuously denied to be such, can work indefinite harm in the world and in the conscience.

It precedes science rather than hinders it.

On the whole, however, religion should not be conceived as having taken the place of anything better, but rather as having come to relieve situations which, but for its presence, would have been infinitely worse. In the thick of active life, or in the monotony of practical slavery, there is more need to stimulate fancy than to control it. Natural instinct is not much disturbed in the human brain by what may happen in that thin superstratum of ideas which commonly overlays it. We must not blame religion for preventing the development of a moral and natural science which at any rate would seldom have appeared; we must rather thank it for the sensibility, the reverence, the speculative insight which it has introduced into the world.

It is merely symbolic and thoroughly human.

We may therefore proceed to analyse the significance and the function which religion has had at its different stages, and, without disguising or in the least condoning its confusion with literal truth, we may allow ourselves to enter as sympathetically as possible into its various conceptions and emotions. They have made up the inner life of many sages, and of all those who without great genius or learning have lived steadfastly in the spirit. The feeling of reverence should itself be treated with reverence, although not at a sacrifice of truth, with which alone, in the end, reverence is compatible. Nor have we any reason to be intolerant of the partialities and contradictions which religions display. Were we dealing with a science, such contradictions would have to be instantly solved and removed; but when we are concerned with the poetic interpretation of experience, contradiction means only variety, and variety means spontaneity, wealth of resource, and a nearer approach to total adequacy.

If we hope to gain any understanding of these matters we must begin by taking them out of that heated and fanatical atmosphere in which the Hebrew tradition has enveloped them. The Jews had no philosophy, and when their national traditions came to be theoretically explicated and justified, they were made to issue in a puerile scholasticism and a rabid intolerance. The question of monotheism, for instance, was a terrible question to the Jews. Idolatry did not consist in worshipping a god who, not being ideal, might be unworthy of worship, but rather in recognising other gods than the one worshipped in Jerusalem. To the Greeks, on the contrary, whose philosophy was enlightened and ingenuous, monotheism and polytheism seemed perfectly innocent and compatible. To say God or the gods was only to use different expressions for the same influence, now viewed in its abstract unity and correlation with all existence, now viewed in its various manifestations in moral life, in nature, or in history. So that what in Plato, Aristotle, and the Stoics meets us at every step—the combination of monotheism with polytheism—is no contradiction, but merely an intelligent variation of phrase to indicate various aspects or functions in physical and moral things. When religion appears to us in this light its contradictions and controversies lose all their bitterness. Each doctrine will simply represent the moral plane on which they live who have devised or adopted it. Religions will thus be better or worse, never true or false. We shall be able to lend ourselves to each in turn, and seek to draw from it the secret of its inspiration.]

CHAPTER V

Time, Instinct, and Freedom:

Henri Bergson (1859–1941)

FOR ALL OF THEIR SHARP DIFFERENCES, CROCE, MOORE, and Santayana represent relatively moderate positions in the previous selections. Croce recognises the philosophical importance of something like the logical analysis of concepts that became so fundamental in the philosophy of Moore and Russell; Moore is much more metaphysical than the wild men of the analytic party; and Santayana is a naturalist. But in this chapter and the next we shall consider the philosophies of Bergson and the later Whitehead, who represent something far more extreme, and in Whitehead's own account of the genealogy of his viewpoint, something far more romantic, far more opposed to the logical and scientific tradition in philosophy.

Bergson was born in 1859, the year in which Darwin's *Origin of Species* appeared, and also the year in which John Dewey and Edmund Husserl were born. The philosophical background of his thinking was a good deal like that of Croce insofar as Bergson was repelled by the positivism and evolutionism of the second half of the nineteenth century. He had been far more Spencerian than Croce in his youth, however, and this may explain the greater extremes to which he went in his attack on what has been called "scientism." Like Croce, Bergson rejected the excessive claims of science in the interest of doing justice to the concrete, the immediate, the vital, but unlike Croce he thought of intuition as vastly superior to the scientific intellect in its power to see all these things and to describe them accurately. It is very difficult to classify Bergson under the conventional philosophical labels, to catch him in the nets of materialism, idealism, or empiricism; some of his antagonisms are easy to formulate in this way but not his positive doctrines.

Bergson's philosophy was the most influential French reaction in the twentieth century to the iron grip of mechanics, intellect, rationalism, determinism, and science. The positivism of Comte, the evolutionary philosophy of Spencer, and the utilitarianism of John Stuart Mill and his followers had formed the intellectual opposition of Croce and the British idealists. It was a similar constellation of opinions and attitudes that Bergson rejected, along with the platonic respect for abstract, eternal ideas and the cartesian respect for rational thought. Not without support or traditional backing in France, however, for Bergson was the culmination of a line of nineteenth-century French voluntarists who emphasized the importance of will as against intellect and who also influenced the thinking of William James. One of the first in this line, Maine de Biran, had replaced Descartes' "I think" by "I will" as the basic philosophical premise. Bergson emphasized the primacy of intuition and instinct over intellect, made time and change the central categories of his philosophy, and urged direct contact with life and the surging aspects of experience as the alternative to the dry, geometrizing, discursive techniques of science.

Bergson was an outspoken irrationalist, a spokesman for the anti-intellectual tendencies that had been accumulating in the writings of the romantics, in Nietzsche, and in Dostoevski. But while Nietzsche and Dostoevski spoke for an agonized Underground Man, Bergson was the polished and urbane representative of a more dandified opposition to science and logic. His writings were attacked, devoured, and regurgitated by an endless number of critics, admirers, and disciples, and he became the most popular and most widely translated philosopher of his day. His style moves in a way that resembles his own picture of consciousness—not as a series of sentences that can be understood separately, but rather like a series of "interpenetrating" experiences that lack definiteness, independence, and clarity.

Their effect is like that of poetry rather than philosophical prose and they communicate moods that periodically explode into insights rather than propositions that hang together logically and imply a conclusion. "You must take things by storm; you must thrust intelligence outside itself by an act of will," Bergson said in a passage that describes his philosophy and his prose.

While it is extremely difficult to present a logically consecutive account of his thinking, it is possible to make up a pattern into which the conventional Bergsonian phrases fit: "vital impetus," "duration," and "creative evolution." First of all, the vital impulse or *élan vital*. For Bergson living is a far more basic process than knowing. Life is an unceasing, continuous, undivided process, a sort of cosmic movement of which we are expressions rather than parts. As such we are all motivated by this *élan vital*. It, rather than mind or matter, is the fundamental reality, and we become aware of it in ourselves through direct, immediate experience, and in others through sympathy or "intuition." Intuition, or the immediate awareness of life itself, is sharply distinguished from the activity of the intellect, which is an artificial process of symbolically representing things beyond itself. As such, intellect is further removed from fundamental reality and is at best conversant with the solids which it cuts out (another frequent Bergsonian phrase) from the continuous stream of experience and impulse. Intellect is essentially geometrical in character and is therefore incapable of dealing with the really and truly living, the preanalytic data of sympathy and intuition. At best intellect can *surround* a prefabricated house of science whereas intuition has the noble privilege of entering the mansion of life and feeling and experience.

When we study vital phenomena under the influence of a scientific point of view we miss what is unique and original, what is unforeseeable and irreversible. "To get a notion of this irreducibility and irreversibility," Bergson says, "we must do violence to the mind, go counter to the natural bent of the intellect. But that is just the function of philosophy." This is an epitome of his attitude toward philosophy conceived as science or logical analysis, but

what is the alternative? What is the Bergsonian way of
reaching true reality, of getting beneath the artificial concepts and categories constructed by the intellect? In answering this question we shall discover the significance of
what Bergson calls experienced, lived, or real time—duration, as he also calls it.

Bergson says that our own awareness of what goes on
in ourselves is the most illuminating of all our experiences.
While we sometimes think of ourselves as passing from
state to state, from a feeling of warmth to a feeling of cold,
from a thought of the sun to a thought of the moon, in
which each feeling or thought is a separate, unchanging
thing that succeeds one and precedes another, a little attention will show us that this is a misleading picture created by a mechanically oriented psychology. It neglects
the fact that these states are themselves changing and that
each is related to its predecessor and its successor not as
externally related things but as interpenetrating, organi-
cally linked experiences. Instead of regarding our inner
life as a flux of fleeting shades merging into each other, we
treat it as an array of solid colors set side by side like the
beads of a necklace. In doing so we neglect the most important feature of our lives, the fact that we *endure*. This
qualitative process of enduring is what identifies real or
lived time and must be carefully distinguished from the
artificial, quantitative time of the mathematician and the
physicist; indeed real time or duration is the stuff, says
Bergson, of which our psychical life is made. What the
physicist does is to geometrize real time, to identify it with
a line, with the time-axis of physical graphs, and in this
way he illustrates the spatial orientation of the intellect.
This, Bergson says, is not to be deplored because physics
and mathematics are indispensable human activities. But,
he says, in a passage that endeared him to a pragmatist
like William James, physics and mathematics and all the
devices of the intellect are practical devices, constructed
in order to facilitate action, and do not, therefore, penetrate to the instinctual stream of consciousness that rushes
underneath (or through) them. To reach it is the aim of

philosophy, which proceeds by less practical methods and which is bound to use intuition as the only way to the truth about ultimate, *real* reality.

One of the chief results of Bergson's philosophy was his doctrine of creative evolution and his defense of freedom. He offers the theory of creative evolution as the only defensible alternative to mechanism—the idea that we can characterize and explain evolution by reference to purely physical and chemical transformations—and also to teleology—the view that everything proceeds by prearranged plan. Both of them suffer the same defects that scientific psychology does by comparison to Bergsonian methods, since they concentrate on physical time, neglect duration and therefore they fail to see that real time *bites into* things in a way that allows for real change. Once we recognize the shortcomings of mechanism and teleology as the inherent shortcomings of a scientific, static, mechanical, geometrical, logical approach, we see that there is room for real change and real freedom, unhampered by causality and determinism.

It is easy to see why this point of view proved so exciting and liberating to a generation brought up on the formulae of nineteenth-century positivism and materialism, why it appealed to artists and writers, to religious thinkers and to fashionable ladies who came to Bergson's crowded lectures at the Collège de France to understand the mysteries of evolution, mind, matter, time, and free will, "part of it with the mind and to divine the rest with the heart." For Bergson had gone much further than Hegel in attacking the rationalism and intellectualism of the platonic and cartesian traditions, *so far* that William James greeted the appearance of *Creative Evolution* with ecstasy while the logical Bertrand Russell said that if one were to ask whether there are any reasons for accepting such a restless view of the world, "he will find, if I am not mistaken, that there is no reason whatever for accepting this view, either in the universe or in the writings of M. Bergson."

The following passage is selected from Chapter III of Bergson's *Creative Evolution* (1911), "On the Meaning of Life—the Order of Nature and the Form of Intelligence."[1]

[In the course of our first chapter we traced a line of demarcation between the inorganic and the organized, but we pointed out that the division of unorganized matter into separate bodies is relative to our senses and to our intellect, and that matter, looked at as an undivided whole, must be a flux rather than a thing. In this we were preparing the way for a reconciliation between the inert and the living.

On the other side, we have shown in our second chapter that the same opposition is found again between instinct and intelligence, the one turned to certain determinations of life, the other molded on the configuration of matter. But instinct and intelligence, we have also said, stand out from the same background, which, for want of a better name, we may call consciousness in general, and which must be coextensive with universal life. In this way, we have disclosed the possibility of showing the genesis of intelligence in setting out from general consciousness, which embraces it.

We are now, then, to attempt a genesis of intellect at the same time as a genesis of material bodies—two enterprises that are evidently correlative, if it be true that the main lines of our intellect mark out the general form of our action on matter, and that the detail of matter is ruled by the requirements of our action. Intellectuality and materiality have been constituted, in detail, by reciprocal adaptation. Both are derived from a wider and higher form of existence. It is there that we must replace them, in order to see them issue forth.

Such an attempt may appear, at first, more daring than the boldest speculations of metaphysicians. It claims to go further than psychology, further than cosmology, further

[1] I wish to thank Henry Holt and Co., New York, Macmillan and Co., Ltd., London, and Mlle. J. A. Bergson for their kind permission to reprint pp. 186-99 of *Creative Evolution* by Henri Bergson, translated from the French by Arthur Mitchell. Copyright, 1911, by Henry Holt and Company, Inc.; 1938, by Arthur Mitchell. The original appeared under the title *L'Evolution Créatrice* in 1907.

than traditional metaphysics; for psychology, cosmology and metaphysics take intelligence, in all that is essential to it, as given, instead of, as we now propose, engendering it in its form and in its matter. The enterprise is in reality much more modest, as we are going to show. But let us first say how it differs from others.

To begin with psychology, we are not to believe that it *engenders* intelligence when it follows the progressive development of it through the animal series. Comparative psychology teaches us that the more an animal is intelligent, the more it tends to reflect on the actions by which it makes use of things, and thus to approximate to man. But its actions have already by themselves adopted the principal lines of human action; they have made out the same general directions in the material world as we have; they depend upon the same objects bound together by the same relations; so that animal intelligence, although it does not form concepts properly so called, already moves in a conceptual atmosphere. Absorbed at every instant by the actions it performs and the attitudes it must adopt, drawn outward by them and so externalized in relation to itself, it no doubt plays rather than thinks its ideas; this play none the less already corresponds, in the main, to the general plan of human intelligence.* To explain the intelligence of man by that of the animal consists then simply in following the development of an embryo of humanity into complete humanity. We show how a certain direction has been followed further and further by beings more and more intelligent. But the moment we admit the direction, intelligence is given.

In a cosmogony like that of Spencer, intelligence is taken for granted, as matter also at the same time. We are shown matter obeying laws, objects connected with objects and facts with facts by constant relations, consciousness receiving the imprint of these relations and laws, and thus adopting the general configuration of nature and shaping itself into intellect. But how can we fail to see that intelligence is supposed when we admit objects and facts? *A*

* We have developed this point in *Matière et mémoire,* chaps. ii. and iii., notably pp. 78-80 and 169-86. AUTHOR'S NOTE.

priori and apart from any hypothesis on the nature of the matter, it is evident that the materiality of a body does not stop at the point at which we touch it: a body is present wherever its influence is felt; its attractive force, to speak only of that, is exerted on the sun, on the planets, perhaps on the entire universe. The more physics advances, the more it effaces the individuality of bodies and even of the particles into which the scientific imagination began by decomposing them: bodies and corpuscles tend to dissolve into a universal interaction. Our perceptions give us the plan of our eventual action on things much more than that of things themselves. The outlines we find in objects simply mark what we can attain and modify in them. The lines we see traced through matter are just the paths on which we are called to move. Outlines and paths have declared themselves in the measure and proportion that consciousness has prepared for action on unorganized matter—that is to say, in the measure and proportion that intelligence has been formed. It is doubtful whether animals built on a different plan—a mollusc or an insect, for instance—cut matter up along the same articulations. It is not indeed necessary that they should separate it into bodies at all. In order to follow the indications of instinct, there is no need to perceive *objects,* it is enough to distinguish *properties.* Intelligence, on the contrary, even in its humblest form, already aims at getting matter to act on matter. If on one side matter lends itself to a division into active and passive bodies, or more simply into coexistent and distinct fragments, it is from this side that intelligence will regard it; and the more it busies itself with dividing, the more it will spread out in space, in the form of extension adjoining extension, a matter that undoubtedly itself has a tendency to spatiality, but whose parts are yet in a state of reciprocal implication and interpenetration. Thus the same movement by which the mind is brought to form itself into intellect, that is to say, into distinct concepts, brings matter to break itself up into objects excluding one another. *The more consciousness is intellectualized, the more is matter spatialized.* So that the evolutionist philosophy, when it imagines in space a matter cut up on the very lines that our action will follow, has given itself in advance, ready-made, the intelligence of which it claims to show the genesis.

Metaphysics applies itself to a work of the same kind, though subtler and more self-conscious, when it deduces *a priori* the categories of thought. It compresses intellect, reduces it to its quintessence, holds it tight in a principle so simple that it can be thought empty: from this principle we then draw out what we have virtually put into it. In this way we may no doubt show the coherence of intelligence, define intellect, give its formula, but we do not trace its genesis. An enterprise like that of Fichte, although more philosophical than that of Spencer, in that it pays more respect to the true order of things, hardly leads us any further. Fichte takes thought in a concentrated state, and expands it into reality; Spencer starts from external reality, and condenses it into intellect. But, in the one case as in the other, the intellect must be taken at the beginning as given—either condensed or expanded, grasped in itself by a direct vision or perceived by reflection in nature, as in a mirror.

The agreement of most philosophers on this point comes from the fact that they are at one in affirming the unity of nature, and in representing this unity under an abstract and geometrical form. Between the organized and unorganized they do not see and they will not see the cleft. Some start from the inorganic, and, by compounding it with itself, claim to form the living; others place life first, and proceed towards matter by a skillfully managed *decrescendo;* but, for both, there are only differences of *degree* in nature—degrees of complexity in the first hypothesis, of intensity in the second. Once this principle is admitted, intelligence becomes as vast as reality; for it is unquestionable that whatever is geometrical in things is entirely accessible to human intelligence, and if the continuity between geometry and the rest is perfect, all the rest must indeed be equally intelligible, equally intelligent. Such is the postulate of most systems. Anyone can easily be convinced of this by comparing doctrines that seem to have no common point, no common measure, those of

Fichte and Spencer for instance, two names that we happen to have just brought together.

At the root of these speculations, then, there are the two convictions, correlative and complementary, that nature is one and that the function of intellect is to embrace it in its entirety. The faculty of knowing being supposed coextensive with the whole of experience, there can no longer be any question of engendering it. It is already given, and we merely have to use it, as we use our sight to take in the horizon. It is true that opinions differ as to the value of the result. For some, it is reality itself that the intellect embraces; for others, it is only a phantom. But, phantom or reality, what intelligence grasps is thought to be all that can be attained.

Hence the exaggerated confidence of philosophy in the powers of the individual mind. Whether it is dogmatic or critical, whether it admits the relativity of our knowledge or claims to be established within the absolute, a philosophy is generally the work of a philosopher, a single and unitary vision of the whole. It is to be taken or left.

More modest, and also alone capable of being completed and perfected, is the philosophy we advocate. Human intelligence, as we represent it, is not at all what Plato taught in the allegory of the cave. Its function is not to look at passing shadows nor yet to turn itself round and contemplate the glaring sun. It has something else to do. Harnessed, like yoked oxen, to a heavy task, we feel the play of our muscles and joints, the weight of the plow and the resistance of the soil. To act and to know that we are acting, to come into touch with reality and even to live it, but only in the measure in which it concerns the work that is being accomplished and the furrow that is being plowed, such is the function of human intelligence. Yet a beneficent fluid bathes us, whence we draw the very force to labor and to live. From this ocean of life, in which we are immersed, we are continually drawing something, and we feel that our being, or at least the intellect that guides it, has been formed therein by a kind of local concentration. Philosophy can only be an effort to dissolve again into the

Whole. Intelligence, reabsorbed into its principle, may thus live back again its own genesis. But the enterprise cannot be achieved in one stroke; it is necessarily collective and progressive. It consists in an interchange of impressions which, correcting and adding to each other, will end by expanding the humanity in us and making us even transcend it.

But this method has against it the most inveterate habits of the mind. It at once suggests the idea of a vicious circle. In vain, we shall be told, you claim to go beyond intelligence: how can you do that except by intelligence? All that is clear in your consciousness is intelligence. You are inside your own thought; you cannot get out of it. Say, if you like, that the intellect is capable of progress, that it will see more and more clearly into a greater and greater number of things; but do not speak of engendering it, for it is with your intellect itself that you would have to do the work.

The objection presents itself naturally to the mind. But the same reasoning would prove also the impossibility of acquiring any new habit. It is of the essence of reasoning to shut us up in the circle of the given. But action breaks the circle. If we had never seen a man swim, we might say that swimming is an impossible thing, inasmuch as, to learn to swim, we must begin by holding ourselves up in the water and, consequently, already know how to swim. Reasoning, in fact, always nails us down to the solid ground. But if, quite simply, I throw myself into the water without fear, I may keep myself up well enough at first by merely struggling, and gradually adapt myself to the new environment: I shall thus have learnt to swim. So, in theory, there is a kind of absurdity in trying to know otherwise than by intelligence; but if the risk be frankly accepted, action will perhaps cut the knot that reasoning has tied and will not unloose.

Besides, the risk will appear to grow less, the more our point of view is adopted. We have shown that intellect has detached itself from a vastly wider reality, but that there has never been a clean cut between the two; all around conceptual thought there remains an indistinct fringe which recalls its origin. And further we compared the intellect to a solid nucleus formed by means of condensation. This nucleus does not differ radically from the fluid surrounding it. It can only be reabsorbed in it because it is made of the same substance. He who throws himself into the water, having known only the resistance of the solid earth, will immediately be drowned if he does not struggle against the fluidity of the new environment: he must perforce still cling to that solidity, so to speak, which even water presents. Only on this condition can he get used to the fluid's fluidity. So of our thought, when it has decided to make the leap.

But leap it must, that is, leave its own environment. Reason, reasoning on its powers, will never succeed in extending them, though the extension would not appear at all unreasonable once it were accomplished. Thousands and thousands of variations on the theme of walking will never yield a rule for swimming: come, enter the water, and when you know how to swim, you will understand how the mechanism of swimming is connected with that of walking. Swimming is an extension of walking, but walking would never have pushed you on to swimming. So you may speculate as intelligently as you will on the mechanism of intelligence; you will never, by this method, succeed in going beyond it. You may get something more complex, but not something higher nor even something different. You must take things by storm: you must thrust intelligence outside itself by an act of will.

So the vicious circle is only apparent. It is, on the contrary, real, we think, in every other method of philosophy. This we must try to show in a few words, if only to prove that philosophy cannot and must not accept the relation established by pure intellectualism between the theory of knowledge and the theory of the known, between metaphysics and science.

At first sight, it may seem prudent to leave the consideration of facts to positive science, to let physics and chemistry busy themselves with matter, the biological and psychological sciences with life. The task of the philosopher is then clearly defined. He takes facts and laws from the scientist's hand; and whether he tries to go beyond them in order to reach their deeper causes, or whether he thinks it impossible to go further and even proves it by the analysis of scientific knowledge, in both cases he has for the facts and relations, handed over by science, the sort of respect that is due to a final verdict. To this knowledge he adds a critique of the faculty of knowing, and also, if he thinks proper, a metaphysic; but the *matter* of knowledge he regards as the affair of science and not of philosophy.

But how does he fail to see that the real result of this so-called division of labor is to mix up everything and confuse everything? The metaphysic or the critique that the philosopher has reserved for himself he has to receive, ready-made, from positive science, it being already contained in the descriptions and analyses, the whole care of which he left to the scientists. For not having wished to intervene, at the beginning, in questions of fact, he finds himself reduced, in questions of principle, to formulating purely and simply in more precise terms the unconscious and consequently inconsistent metaphysic and critique which the very attitude of science to reality marks out. Let us not be deceived by an apparent analogy between natural things and human things. Here we are not in the judiciary domain, where the description of fact and the judgment on the fact are two distinct things, distinct for the very simple reason that above the fact, and independent of it, there is a law promulgated by a legislator. Here the laws are internal to the facts and relative to the lines that have been followed in cutting the real into distinct facts. We cannot describe the outward appearance of the object without prejudging its inner nature and its organization. Form is no longer entirely isolable from matter, and he who has begun by reserving to philosophy questions of principle, and who has thereby tried to put philosophy above the sciences, as a "court of cassation" is above the courts of assizes and of appeal, will gradually come to make no more of philosophy than a registration court, charged at most with wording more precisely the sentences that are brought to it, pronounced and irrevocable.

Positive science is, in fact, a work of pure intellect. Now, whether our conception of the intellect be accepted or rejected, there is one point on which everybody will agree with us, and that is that the intellect is at home in the presence of unorganized matter. This matter it makes use of more and more by mechanical inventions, and mechanical inventions become the easier to it the more it thinks of matter as mechanism. The intellect bears within itself, in the form of natural logic, a latent geometrism that is set free in the measure and proportion that the intellect penetrates into the inner nature of inert matter. Intelligence is in tune with this matter, and that is why the physics and metaphysics of inert matter are so near each other. Now, when the intellect undertakes the study of life, it necessarily treats the living like the inert, applying the same forms to this new object, carrying over into this new field the same habits that have succeeded so well in the old; and it is right to do so, for only on such terms does the living offer to our action the same hold as inert matter. But the truth we thus arrive at becomes altogether relative to our faculty of action. It is no more than a *symbolic* verity. It cannot have the same value as the physical verity, being only an extension of physics to an object which we are *a priori* agreed to look at only in its external aspect. The duty of philosophy should be to intervene here actively, to examine the living without any reservation as to practical utility, by freeing itself from forms and habits that are strictly intellectual. Its own special object is to speculate, that is to say, to see; its attitude toward the living should not be that of science, which aims only at action, and which, being able to act only by means of inert matter, presents to itself the rest of reality in this single respect. What must the result be, if it leave biological and psychological facts to positive science alone, as it has left, and rightly left, physical facts? It will accept *a priori* a mechanistic conception of all nature, a conception unreflected and even unconscious, the outcome of the material need. It will *a priori* accept the doctrine of the simple unity of knowledge and of the abstract unity of nature.

The moment it does so, its fate is sealed. The philosopher has no longer any choice save between a metaphysical dogmatism and a metaphysical skepticism, both of which rest, at bottom, on the same postulate, and neither of which adds anything to positive science. He may hypostasize the unity of nature, or, what comes to the same thing, the unity of science, in a being who is nothing since he does nothing, an ineffectual God who simply sums up in himself all the given; or in an eternal Matter from whose womb have been poured out the properties of things and the laws of nature; or, again, in a pure Form which endeavors to seize an unseizable multiplicity, and which is, as we will, the form of nature or the form of thought. All these philosophies tell us, in their different languages, that science is right to treat the living as the inert, and that there is no difference of value, no distinction to be made between the results which intellect arrives at in applying its categories, whether it rests on inert matter or attacks life.

In many cases, however, we feel the frame cracking. But as we did not begin by distinguishing between the inert and the living, the one adapted in advance to the frame in which we insert it, the other incapable of being held in the frame otherwise than by a convention which eliminates from it all that is essential, we find ourselves, in the end, reduced to regarding everything the frame contains with equal suspicion. To a metaphysical dogmatism, which has erected into an absolute the factitious unity of science, there succeeds a skepticism or a relativism that universalizes and extends to all the results of science the artificial character of some among them. So philosophy swings to and fro between the doctrine that regards absolute reality as unknowable and that which, in the idea it gives us of this reality, says nothing more than science has said. For having wished to prevent all conflict between science and philosophy, we have sacrificed philosophy without any appreciable gain to science. And for having tried to avoid the seeming vicious circle which consists in using the intellect to transcend the intellect, we find ourselves turning in a real circle, that which consists in laboriously rediscovering by metaphysics a unity that we began by positing *a priori,* a unity that we admitted blindly and unconsciously by the very act of abandoning the whole of experience to science and the whole of reality to the pure understanding.

Let us begin, on the contrary, by tracing a line of demarcation between the inert and the living. We shall find that the inert enters naturally into the frames of the intellect, but that the living is adapted to these frames only artificially, so that we must adopt a special attitude towards it and examine it with other eyes than those of positive science. Philosophy, then, invades the domain of experience. She busies herself with many things which hitherto have not concerned her. Science, theory of knowledge, and metaphysics find themselves on the same ground. At first there may be a certain confusion. All three may think they have lost something. But all three will profit from the meeting.

Positive science, indeed, may pride itself on the uniform value attributed to its affirmations in the whole field of experience. But, if they are all placed on the same footing, they are all tainted with the same relativity. It is not so if we begin by making the distinction which, in our view, is forced upon us. The understanding is at home in the domain of unorganized matter. On this matter human action is naturally exercised; and action, as we said above, cannot be set in motion in the unreal. Thus, of physics—so long as we are considering only its general form and not the particular cutting out of matter in which it is manifested— we may say that it touches the absolute. On the contrary, it is by accident—chance or convention, as you please— that science obtains a hold on the living analogous to the hold it has on matter. Here the use of conceptual frames is no longer natural. I do not wish to say that it is not legitimate, in the scientific meaning of the term. If science is to extend our action on things, and if we can act only with inert matter for instrument, science can and must continue to treat the living as it has treated the inert. But, in doing so, it must be understood that the further it penetrates the depths of *life,* the more symbolic, the more relative to the contingencies of action, the knowledge it supplies to us becomes. On this new ground philosophy ought then to follow science, in order to superpose on scientific truth a knowledge of another kind, which may be called metaphysical. Thus combined, all our knowledge, both scientific and metaphysical, is heightened. In the absolute we live and move and have our being. The knowledge we possess of it is incomplete, no doubt, but not external or relative. It is reality itself, in the profoundest meaning of the word, that we reach by the combined and progressive development of science and of philosophy.

Thus, in renouncing the factitious unity which the understanding imposes on nature from outside, we shall perhaps find its true, inward and living unity. For the effort we make to transcend the pure understanding introduces us into that more vast something out of which our understanding is cut, and from which it has detached itself. And, as matter is determined by intelligence, as there is between them an evident agreement, we cannot make the genesis of the one without making the genesis of the other. An identical process must have cut out matter and the intellect, at the same time, from a stuff that contained both. Into this reality we shall get back more and more completely, in proportion as we compel ourselves to transcend pure intelligence.]

CHAPTER VI

Nature and Life:

Alfred North Whitehead (1861–1947)

HAD THIS VOLUME BEEN PREPARED THIRTY YEARS AGO THE selection from Whitehead's writings certainly would not have followed those from Croce and Bergson, nor would it have preceded that from Husserl. Whitehead would not have been a central figure among the metaphysicians and the humanists, classified with the proponents of insight and intuition, with the prophets of life, time, history, and instinct. If he had been linked with any group in the twentieth century, it would have been with the logicians because of his great collaboration with Russell that resulted in their *Principia Mathematica* (1910-13), a systematic derivation of mathematics from logic. Or he might have been linked with Moore and the realists because of his brilliant studies in the philosophy of science: *Enquiry Concerning the Principles of Natural Knowledge* (1919), *The Concept of Nature* (1920), and *The Principle of Relativity* (1922). His logical and mathematical phase is usually identified with his teaching at Cambridge, England, and his work on the foundations of physics dates from his shift to London, but his metaphysical period is identified with Cambridge, Massachusetts, where at sixty-three he became professor of philosophy at Harvard and began what is thought to be the most important phase of his career. It was there that he wrote his *Science and the Modern World* (1925), his *Process and Reality* (1929), and his *Adventures of Ideas* (1933)—all of them devoted to the exposition and application of his philosophy of organism.

By putting Whitehead in the company of Croce and Bergson I do not intend to suggest that they constitute a school. I mean only to call attention to their preoccupation with notions as dark and difficult as intuition and organism, their interest in seeing things whole, and their opposition to the traditions of rationalism, empiricism, and the more analytical tendencies of this century. The matter may be put somewhat differently and perhaps more clearly. Every philosopher is limited and even somewhat sectarian in what he reads and takes seriously; he uses a circumscribed library of works by his contemporaries. Croce, Bergson, Whitehead, Husserl, and the existentialists are likely to appear simultaneously in the working libraries of many philosophers who pay little or no attention to the works of Moore, Russell, Wittgenstein, and Carnap. And vice versa, of course. This split is based on profound affinities and contrasts of attitude, style, interest, and doctrine which we cannot blink even though they may be difficult to formulate with exactness.

Because of his peculiar intellectual development Whitehead is the only distinguished philosopher of the twentieth century who crosses these lines. Even Russell, who is notorious for shifting his point of view, commands no such wide audience, for one thing because of a persistent respect for logic, science, clarity, and analysis throughout all his changes. But Whitehead is three things to all men—logician, philosopher of science, and metaphysician—and therefore even the most narrowly conceived libraries contain at least some of his works.

While close students may see unity and continuity in Whitehead's development from a universal algebra to a sort of universal biology, his third period is generally regarded as radically different from the others. His emergence into it has been hailed by some as a major conversion, much as if a logical and scientific sinner had come back to the metaphysical fold. During this third period Whitehead won an audience that resembles Bergson's in its composition (though not in size, I suspect) precisely because of Whitehead's serene dealings with adventure and life, his serious dealings with religion and education, his scoffing at the ideals of clarity and precision. Coming from someone who had been through mathematics and logic and physics, this bucked up a number of people who had no taste or competence for such matters. But because of the difficulty of his later terminology and his radical redefinition of so many terms of ordinary language, many of Whitehead's readers find his more technical and positive systematic work extremely difficult to understand—even when they make concerted efforts to talk his language, to abandon the language of the streets and the schools while living in *Process and Reality* (or in the less charming and darker parts of *Science and the Modern World*). I am sure, therefore, that an excerpt from the *magnum opus, Process and Reality,* would be unintelligible out of context. In fact, I suspect that the great numbers of people who read the historical and less technical sections of *Science and the Mod-*

ern World with admiration may have their fingers on the greater Whitehead, and so for various reasons I have selected something from one of the less jargonized works, first published as two lectures entitled *Nature and Life* (1934) and later incorporated as the last two chapters of *Modes of Thought* (1938).

One of Whitehead's basic points is that nature is alive, a conclusion that is not unrelated to the emphasis on life in Bergson and Croce. But what distinguishes Whitehead from Bergson, who relies mainly on biology, and Croce, who is a historian, is the fact that Whitehead tries to support his philosophy of process and activity by referring to the results of modern physics and mathematics. He is a heroic thinker who tries to beard the lions of intellectualism, materialism, and positivism in their own bristling den. His early training and distinction in these subjects give him courage, but he is not alone; the twentieth century has an established tradition of philosophically minded scientists like Jeans and Eddington who have enlisted in a closely related crusade.

Whitehead protests against the view that parts of nature are dead, a point of view which he identifies with a scientifically discredited common-sense outlook that is made to sound very much like the outlook Moore defended against the idealists. But while Whitehead pays homage to Bradley, his position is presumably different; he is not interested in reviving older idealistic or spiritualistic doctrines but in advancing a new view of the universe.

Before presenting the selection in which Whitehead outlines his own point of view it is desirable to summarize the philosophy he rejects and his reasons for rejecting it. Basically it is the view that nature is composed of permanent things, bits of matter moving about, as he says, in a space otherwise empty, each one having its shape, its mass, its motion, its color, its smell. It is the view of the great thinkers of the sixteenth and seventeenth centuries, the view of the ordinary man today, and according to Whitehead it has never been successfully extruded from the minds of scientists even though science has thoroughly discredited it. The result is a modern muddle, a series of inconsistencies that must be clarified and resolved.

According to Whitehead the first great scientific attack on the common-sense point of view arose when the transmission theories of light and sound showed that color and sound are *secondary* qualities which are not really *in* the objects but are subjective reactions to bodily motions, much as pain is in us and not in the knife with which we cut ourselves. Color and sound were thereby removed from nature, the superficiality of sense perception as a source of insight into the nature of things was demonstrated, and the modern epistemologists' belief that sense perception provides data for the interpretation of nature was shown to be misguided. It was left to Hume, Whitehead says, to see the "hybrid character" of this view of our perceptions, a view which implies that we come to know the redness of the rose in the garden in one way and its position in another, that is to say as a blend of secondary qualities "in here" and primary qualities "out there."

This is Whitehead's first bit of adverse testimony against common sense. It is supplemented by a second expert opinion that comes from Newton. Newton was forced to accept the universal law of gravitation, according to which all bodies attract each other, as an ultimate principle, derivable from nothing more fundamental. He could not say *why* all bodies attract each other, and so he was forced to say (in Latin) "I do not use hypotheses," meaning by that that he refused to go beyond the available evidence in order to provide an explanation for gravitation. In remaining so agnostic, says Whitehead, Newton "illustrated a great philosophic truth, that a dead nature can give no reasons," much as dead men tell no tales, I suppose. Moreover, Whitehead adds homiletically, "All ultimate reasons are in terms of aim at value. A dead nature aims at nothing." With this he concludes his reflections on what might be called the Hume-Newton syndrome, pointing out that in 1933 the President of the United States was inaugurating a new chapter in the history of mankind which we need to understand intuitively, but all the Hume-Newton point of view can see in it is "a complex transition of sensa, and an entangled motion of molecules."

This familiar testimony is finally buttressed by the statement of a much more powerful and respected figure—the twentieth-century scientist—who not only drives the last nail into the coffin of common sense but also launches Whitehead into his activistic philosophy of process. The doctrine of empty space has been eliminated by modern physics, Whitehead says, and replaced by the idea of a field of force, a field of incessant activity. Moreover, "Matter has been identified with energy, and energy is sheer activity." Since any local agitation shakes the whole universe there is no point in treating anything as a local, detached existence. The environment enters into the very nature of each thing. The common-sense and older scientific view of self-contained particles of matter is an abstraction, and a useless one when we are plumbing the depths of the universe. It may suffice for lawyers and ignorant philosophers, Whitehead says, but it prevents us from seeing that the basic fact of modern physics is activity. However, this figure of activity that the modern physicist places at the center of his picture of the universe is what Whitehead calls "bare activity," and it remains for the philosopher to veil it decently with the answers to the very large questions: "Activity for what, producing what, Activity involving what?" To this exacting task Whitehead turns his attention in the selection that follows. It is an abridgment, with omissions indicated, of Lecture Eight, "Nature Alive," of Whitehead's *Modes of Thought* (1938).[1]

[The status of life in nature . . . is the modern problem of philosophy and of science. Indeed it is the central meeting point of all the strains of systematic thought, humanistic, naturalistic, philosophic. The very meaning of life is in doubt. When we understand it, we shall also understand its status in the world. But its essence and its status are alike baffling. . . .

[1] The present abridgment is printed with the permission of The Macmillan Co., New York, publishers of *Modes of Thought*. The lecture previously appeared in *Nature and Life* (University of Chicago Press, 1934).

The doctrine that I am maintaining is that neither physical nature nor life can be understood unless we fuse them together as essential factors in the composition of "really real" things whose interconnections and individual characters constitute the universe.

The first step in the argument must be to form some concept of what life can mean. Also we require that the deficiencies in our concept of physical nature should be supplied by its fusion with life. And we require that, on the other hand, the notion of life should involve the notion of physical nature.

Now as a first approximation the notion of life implies a certain absoluteness of self-enjoyment. This must mean a certain immediate individuality, which is a complex process of appropriating into a unity of existence the many data presented as relevant by the physical processes of nature. Life implies the absolute, individual self-enjoyment arising out of this process of appropriation. I have, in my recent writings, used the word "prehension" to express this process of appropriation. Also I have termed each individual act of immediate self-enjoyment an "occasion of experience." I hold that these unities of existence, these occasions of experience, are the really real things which in their collective unity compose the evolving universe, ever plunging into the creative advance. . . .

This concept of self-enjoyment does not exhaust that aspect of process here termed "life." Process for its intelligibility involves the notion of a creative activity belonging to the very essence of each occasion. It is the process of eliciting into actual being factors in the universe which antecedently to that process exist only in the mode of unrealized potentialities. The process of self-creation is the transformation of the potential into the actual, and the fact of such transformation includes the immediacy of self-enjoyment.

Thus in conceiving the function of life in an occasion of experience, we must discriminate the actualized data presented by the antecedent world, the non-actualized potentialities which lie ready to promote their fusion into a new unity of experience, and the immediacy of self-enjoyment which belongs to the creative fusion of those data with those potentialities. This is the doctrine of the creative advance whereby it belongs to the essence of the universe, that it passes into a future. It is nonsense to conceive of nature as a static fact, even for an instant devoid of duration. There is no nature apart from transition, and there is no transition apart from temporal duration. This is the reason why the notion of an instant of time, conceived as a primary simple fact, is nonsense.

But even yet we have not exhausted the notion of creation which is essential to the understanding of nature. We must add yet another character to our description of life. This missing characteristic is "aim." By this term "aim" is meant the exclusion of the boundless wealth of alternative potentiality, and the inclusion of that definite factor of novelty which constitutes the selected way of entertaining those data in that process of unification. The aim is at that complex of feeling which is the enjoyment of those data in that way. "That way of enjoyment" is selected from the boundless wealth of alternatives. It has been aimed at for actualization in that process. . . .

The question at once arises as to whether this factor of life in nature, as thus interpreted, corresponds to anything that we observe in nature. All philosophy is an endeavor to obtain a self-consistent understanding of things observed. Thus its development is guided in two ways, one is the demand for a coherent self-consistency, and the other is the elucidation of things observed. It is therefore our first task to compare the above doctrine of life in nature with our direct observations.

Without doubt the sort of observations most prominent in our conscious experience are the sense-perceptions. Sight, hearing, taste, smell, touch, constitute a rough list of our major modes of perception through the senses. . . . The truth is that our sense-perceptions are extraordinarily vague and confused modes of experience. Also there is every evidence that their prominent side of external reference is very superficial in its disclosure of the universe.

. . . For example, pragmatically a paving-stone is a hard, solid, static, irremovable fact. This is what sense-perception, on its sharp-cut side, discloses. But if physical science be correct, this is a very superficial account of that portion of the universe which we call the paving-stone. Modern physical science is the issue of a co-ordinated effort, sustained for more than three centuries, to understand those activities of Nature by reason of which the transitions of sense-perception occur.

Two conclusions are now abundantly clear. One is that sense-perception omits any discrimination of the fundamental activities within nature. For example, consider the difference between the paving-stone as perceived visually, or by falling upon it, and the molecular activities of the paving-stone as described by the physicist. The second conclusion is the failure of science to endow its formulae for activity with any meaning. The divergence of the formulae about nature from the appearance of nature has robbed the formulae of any explanatory character. It has even robbed us of reason for believing that the past gives any ground for expectation of the future. In fact, science conceived as resting on mere sense-perception, with no other source of observation, is bankrupt, so far as concerns its claim to self-sufficiency. . . .

Yet it is untrue to state that the general observation of mankind, in which sense-perception is only one factor, discloses no aim. The exact contrary is the case. All explanations of the sociological functionings of mankind include "aim" as an essential factor in explanation. For example, in a criminal trial where the evidence is circumstantial the demonstration of motive is one chief reliance of the prosecution. In such a trial would the defence plead the doctrine that purpose could not direct the motions of the body, and that to indict the thief for stealing was analogous to indicting the sun for rising? . . . In fact we are *directly* conscious of our purposes as *directive* of our actions. Apart from such direction no doctrine could in any sense be acted upon. The notions entertained mentally would have no effect upon bodily actions. Thus what happens would happen in complete indifference to the entertainment of such notions.

Scientific reasoning is completely dominated by the presupposition that mental functionings are not properly part of nature. Accordingly it disregards all those mental antecedents which mankind habitually presuppose as effective in guiding cosmological functionings. As a method this procedure is entirely justifiable, provided that we recognize the limitations involved. These limitations are both obvious and undefined. The gradual eliciting of their definition is the hope of philosophy. . . .

A rough division can be made of six types of occurrences in nature. The first type is human existence, body and mind. The second type includes all sorts of animal life, insects, the vertebrates, and other genera. In fact all the various types of animal life other than human. The third type includes all vegetable life. The fourth type consists of the single living cells. The fifth type consists of all large-scale inorganic aggregates, on a scale comparable to the size of animal bodies, or larger. The sixth type is composed of the happenings on an infinitesimal scale, disclosed by the minute analysis of modern physics.

Now all these functionings of Nature influence each other, require each other, and lead on to each other. The list has purposely been made roughly, without any scientific pretension. The sharp-cut scientific classifications are essential for scientific method. But they are dangerous for philosophy. Such classification hides the truth that the different modes of natural existence shade off into each other. There is the animal life with its central direction of a society of cells, there is the vegetable life with its organized republic of cells, there is the cell life with its organized republic of molecules, there is the large-scale inorganic society of molecules with its passive acceptance of necessities derived from spatial relations, there is the infra-molecular activity which has lost all trace of the passivity of inorganic nature on a larger scale. . . .

Again, another consideration arises. How do we observe nature? Also, what is the proper analysis of an observation? The conventional answer to this question is that we perceive nature through our senses. Also in the analysis of sense-perception we are apt to concentrate upon its most clear-cut instance, namely sight. Now visual perception is the final product of evolution. It belongs to high grade animals—to vertebrates and to the more advanced type of insects. There are numberless living things which afford no evidence of possessing sight. Yet they show every sign of taking account of their environment in the way proper to living things. Also human beings shut off sight with peculiar ease, by closing our eyes or by the calamity of blindness. The information provided by mere sight is peculiarly barren—namely external regions disclosed as coloured. There is no necessary transition of colours, and no necessary selection of regions, and no necessary mutual adaptation of the display of colours. Sight at any instant merely provides the passive fact of regions variously coloured. If we have memories, we observe the transition of colours. But there is nothing intrinsic to the mere coloured regions which provides any hint of internal activity whereby change can be understood. It is from this experience that our conception of a spatial distribution of passive material substances arises. Nature is thus described as made up of vacuous bits of matter with no internal values, and merely hurrying through space.

But there are two accompaniments of this experience which should make us suspicious of accepting it at its face value as any direct disclosure of the metaphysical nature of things. In the first place, even in visual experience we are also aware of the intervention of the body. We know directly that we see *with our eyes*. That is a vague feeling, but extremely important. Secondly, every type of crucial experiment proves that what we see, and where we see it, depend entirely upon the physiological functioning of our body. Any method of making our body function internally in a given way, will provide us with an assigned visual sensation. The body is supremely indifferent to the happenings of nature a short way off, where it places its visual sensa.

Now the same is true of all other modes of sensation, only to a greater extent. All sense-perception is merely one outcome of the dependence of our experience upon bodily functionings. Thus if we wish to understand the relation of our personal experience to the activities of nature, the proper procedure is to examine the dependence of our personal experiences upon our personal bodies.

Let us ask about our overwhelming persuasions as to our own personal body-mind relation. In the first place, there is the claim to unity. The human individual is one fact, body and mind. This claim to unity is the fundamental fact, always presupposed, rarely explicitly formulated. I am experiencing and my body is mine. In the second place, the functioning of our body has a much wider influence than the mere production of sense-experience. We find ourselves in a healthy enjoyment of life by reason of the healthy functionings of our internal organs—heart, lungs, bowels, kidneys, etc. The emotional state arises just because they are not providing any sensa directly associated with themselves. Even in sight, we enjoy our vision because there is no eyestrain. Also we enjoy our general state of life, because we have no stomach-ache. I am insisting that the enjoyment of health, good or bad, is a positive feeling only casually associated with particular sensa. For example, you can enjoy the ease with which your eyes are functioning even when you are looking at a bad picture or a vulgar building. This direct feeling of the derivation of emotion from the body is among our fundamental experiences. There are emotions of various types—but every type of emotion is at least modified by derivation from the body. It is for physiologists to analyze in detail the modes of bodily functioning. For philosophy, the one fundamental fact is that the whole complexity of mental experience is either derived or modified by such functioning. Also our basic feeling is this sense of derivation, which leads to our claim for unity, body and mind.

But our immediate experience also claims derivation from another source, and equally claims a unity founded upon this alternative source of derivation. This second source is our own state of mind directly preceding the immediate present of our conscious experience. A quarter of a second ago, we were entertaining such and such ideas, we were enjoying such and such emotions, and we were making such and such observations of external fact. In our present state of mind, we are continuing that previous state.

The word "continuing" states only half the truth. In one sense it is too weak, and in another sense it overstates. It is too weak, because we not only continue, but we claim absolute identity with our previous state. It was our very identical self in that state of mind, which is of course the basis of our present experience a quarter of a second later. In another sense the word "continuing" overstates. For we do not quite continue in our preceding state of experience. New elements have intervened. All of these new elements are provided by our bodily functionings. We fuse these new elements with the basic stuff of experience provided by our state of mind a quarter of a second ago. Also, as we have already agreed, we claim an identification with our body. Thus our experience in the present discloses its own nature as with two sources of derivation, namely, the body and the antecedent experiential functionings. Also there is a claim for identification with each of these sources. The body is mine, and the antecedent experience is mine. Still more, there is only one ego, to claim the body and to claim the stream of experience. I submit that we have here the fundamental basic persuasion on which we found the whole practice of our existence. While we exist, body and soul are inescapable elements in our being, each with the full reality of our own immediate self. But neither body nor soul possesses the sharp observational definition which at first sight we attribute to them. Our knowledge of the body places it as a complex unity of happenings within the larger field of nature. But its demarcation from the rest of nature is vague in the extreme. The body consists of the co-ordinated functionings of billions of molecules. It belongs to the structural essence of the body that, in an indefinite number of ways, it is always losing molecules and gaining molecules. When we consider the question with microscopic accuracy, there is no definite boundary to determine where the body begins and external nature ends. Again the body can lose whole limbs, and yet we claim identity with the same body. Also the vital functions of the cells in the amputated limb ebb slowly. Indeed the limb survives in separation from the body for an immense time compared to the internal vibratory periods of its molecules. Also apart from such catastrophes, the body requires the environment in order to exist. Thus there is a unity of the body with the environment, as well as a unity of body and soul into one person.

But in conceiving our personal identity we are apt to emphasize rather the soul than the body. The one individual is that co-ordinated stream of personal experiences, which is my thread of life or your thread of life. It is that succession of self-realization, each occasion with its direct memory of its past and with its anticipation of the future. . . .

Yet when we examine this notion of the soul, it discloses itself as even vaguer than our definition of the body. First, the continuity of the soul—so far as concerns consciousness —has to leap gaps in time. We sleep or we are stunned. And yet it is the same person who recovers consciousness. We trust to memory, and we ground our trust on the continuity of the functionings of nature, more especially on the continuity of our body. Thus nature in general and the body in particular provide the stuff for the personal endurance of the soul. Again there is a curious variation in the vividness of the successive occasions of the soul's existence. We are living at full stretch with a keen observation of external occurrence; then external attention dies away and we are lost in meditation; the meditation gradually weakens in vivid presentation: we doze; we dream; we sleep with a total lapse of the stream of consciousness. These functionings of the soul are diverse, variable, and discontinuous. The claim to the unity of the soul is analogous to the claim to the unity of the body, and is analogous to the claim to the unity of body and soul, and is analogous to the claim to the community of the body with an external nature. It is the task of philosophic speculation to conceive the happenings of the universe so as to render understandable the outlook of physical science and to combine this outlook with these direct persuasions representing the basic facts upon which epistemology must build. The weakness of the epistemology of the eighteenth and nineteenth centuries was that it based itself purely upon a narrow formulation of sense-perception. Also among the various modes of sensation, visual experience was picked out as the typical example. The result was to exclude all the really fundamental factors constituting our experience.

In such an epistemology we are far from the complex data which philosophic speculation has to account for in a system rendering the whole understandable. Consider the types of community of body and soul, of body and nature, of soul and nature, or successive occasions of bodily existence, or the soul's existence. These fundamental interconnections have one very remarkable characteristic. Let us ask what is the function of the external world for the stream of experience which constitutes the soul. This world, thus experienced, is the basic fact within those experiences. All the emotions, and purposes, and enjoyments, proper to the individual existence of the soul are nothing other than the soul's reactions to this experienced world which lies at the base of the soul's existence.

Thus in a sense, the experienced world is one complex factor in the composition of many factors constituting the essence of the soul. We can phrase this shortly by saying that in one sense the world is in the soul.

But there is an antithetical doctrine balancing this primary truth. Namely, our experience of the world involves the exhibition of the soul itself as one of the components within the world. Thus there is a dual aspect to the relationship of an occasion of experience as one relatum and the experienced world as another relatum. The world is included within the occasion in one sense, and the occasion is included in the world in another sense. For example, I am in the room, and the room is an item in my present experience. But my present experience is what I now am.

But this baffling antithetical relation extends to all the connections which we have been discussing. For example, consider the enduring self-identity of the soul. The soul is nothing else than the succession of my occasions of experience, extending from birth to the present moment. Now, at this instant, I am the complete person embodying all these occasions. They are mine. On the other hand it is equally true that my immediate occasion of experience, at the present moment, is only one among the stream of occasions which constitutes my soul. Again, the world for me is nothing else than how the functionings of my body present it for my experience. The world is thus wholly to be discerned within those functionings. Knowledge of the world is nothing else than an analysis of the functionings. And yet, on the other hand, the body is merely one society of functionings within the universal society of the world. We have to construe the world in terms of the bodily society, and the bodily society in terms of the general functionings of the world.

Thus, as disclosed in the fundamental essence of our experience, the togetherness of things involves some doctrine of mutual immanence. In some sense or other, this community of the actualities of the world means that each happening is a factor in the nature of every other happening. After all, this is the only way in which we can understand notions habitually employed in daily life. Consider our notion of "causation." How can one event be the cause of another? In the first place, no event can be wholly and solely the cause of another event. The whole antecedent world conspires to produce a new occasion. But some one occasion in an important way conditions the formation of a successor. How can we understand this process of conditioning?

The mere notion of transferring a quality is entirely unintelligible. Suppose that two occurrences may be in fact detached so that one of them is comprehensible without reference to the other. Then all notion of causation between them, or of conditioning, becomes unintelligible. There is—with this supposition—no reason why the possession of any quality by one of them should in any way influence the possession of that quality, or of any other quality, by the other. With such a doctrine the play and interplay of qualitative succession in the world becomes a blank fact from which no conclusions can be drawn as to past, present, or future, beyond the range of direct observation. Such a positivistic belief is quite self-consistent, provided that we do not include in it any hopes for the future or regrets for the past. Science is then without any importance. Also effort is foolish, because it determines nothing. The only intelligible doctrine of causation is founded on the doctrine of immanence. Each occasion presupposes the antecedent world as active in its own nature. This is the reason why events have a determinate status relatively to each other. Also it is the reason why the qualitative energies of the past are combined into a pattern of qualitative energies in each present occasion. This is the doctrine of causation. It is the reason why it belongs to the essence of each occasion that it is *where* it is. It is the reason for the transference of character from occasion to occasion. It is the reason for the relative stability of laws of nature, some laws for a wider environment, some laws for a narrower environment. It is the reason why—as we have already noted—in our direct apprehension of the world around us we find that curious habit of claiming a two-fold unity with the observed data. We are in the world and the world is in us. Our immediate occasion is in the society of occasions forming the soul, and our soul is in our present occasion. The body is ours, and we are an activity within our body. This fact of observation, vague but imperative, is the foundation of the connexity of the world, and of the transmission of its types of order.

In this survey of the observational data in terms of which our philosophic cosmology must be founded, we have brought together the conclusions of physical science, and those habitual persuasions dominating the sociological functionings of mankind. These persuasions also guide the humanism of literature, of art, and of religion. Mere existence has never entered into the consciousness of man, except as the remote terminus of an abstraction in thought. Descartes' "Cogito, ergo sum" is wrongly translated, "I *think,* therefore I am." It is never bare thought or bare existence that we are aware of. I find myself as essentially a unity of emotions, enjoyments, hopes, fears, regrets, valuations of alternatives, decisions—all of them subjective reactions to the environment as active in my nature. My unity—which is Descartes' "I am"—is my process of shaping this welter of material into a consistent pattern of feelings. The individual enjoyment is what I am in my role of a natural activity, as I shape the activities of the environment into a new creation, which is myself at this moment; and yet, as being myself, it is a continuation of the antecedent world. If we stress the role of the environment, this process is causation. If we stress the role of my immediate pattern of active enjoyment, this process is self-creation. If we stress the role of the conceptual anticipation of the future whose existence is a necessity in the nature of the present, this process is the teleological aim at some ideal in the future. This aim, however, is not really beyond the present process. For the aim at the future is an enjoyment in the present. It thus effectively conditions the immediate self-creation of the new creature. . . .

Physical science has reduced nature to activity, and has discovered abstract mathematical formulae which are illustrated in these activities of Nature. But the fundamental question remains, How do we add content to the notion of bare activity? This question can only be answered by fusing life with nature.

In the first place, we must distinguish life from mentality. Mentality involves conceptual experience, and is only one variable ingredient in life. The sort of functioning here termed "conceptual experience" is the entertainment of possibilities for ideal realization in abstraction from any sheer physical realization. The most obvious example of conceptual experience is the entertainment of alternatives. Life lies below this grade of mentality. Life is the enjoyment of emotion, derived from the past and aimed at the future. It is the enjoyment of emotion which was then, which is now, and which will be then. This vector character is of the essence of such entertainment.

The emotion transcends the present in two ways. It issues from, and it issues towards. It is received, it is enjoyed, and it is passed along, from moment to moment. Each occasion is an activity of concern, in the Quaker sense of that term. It is the conjunction of transcendence and immanence. The occasion is concerned, in the way of feeling and aim, with things that in their own essence lie beyond it; although these things in their present functions are factors in the concern of that occasion. Thus each occasion, although engaged in its own immediate self-realization, is concerned with the universe.

The process is always a process of modification by reason of the numberless avenues of supply, and by reason of the numberless modes of qualitative texture. The unity of emotion, which is the unity of the present occasion, is a patterned texture of qualities, always shifting as it is passed into the future. The creative activity aims at preservation of the components and at preservation of intensity. The modifications of pattern, the dismissal into elimination, are in obedience to this aim.

In so far as conceptual mentality does not intervene, the grand patterns pervading the environment are passed on with the inherited modes of adjustment. Here we find the patterns of activity studied by the physicists and chemists. Mentality is merely latent in all these occasions as thus studied. In the case of inorganic nature any sporadic flashes are inoperative so far as our powers of discernment are concerned. The lowest stages of effective mentality, controlled by the inheritance of physical pattern, involve the faint direction of emphasis by unconscious ideal aim. The various examples of the higher forms of life exhibit the variety of grades of effectiveness of mentality. In the social habits of animals, there is evidence of flashes of mentality in the past which have degenerated into physical habits. Finally in the higher mammals and more particularly in mankind, we have clear evidence of mentality habitually effective. In our own experience, our knowledge consciously entertained and systematized can only mean such mentality, directly observed.

The qualities entertained as objects in conceptual activity are of the nature of catalytic agents, in the sense in which that phrase is used in chemistry. They modify the aesthetic process by which the occasion constitutes itself out of the many streams of feeling received from the past. It is not necessary to assume that conceptions introduce additional sources of measurable energy. They may do so; for the doctrine of the conservation of energy is not based upon exhaustive measurements. But the operation of mentality is primarily to be conceived as a diversion of the flow of energy.

In these lectures I have not entered upon systematic

metaphysical cosmology. The object of the lectures is to
indicate those elements in our experience in terms of which
such a cosmology should be constructed. The key notion
from which such construction should start is that the ener-
getic activity considered in physics is the emotional intensity entertained in life.

Philosophy begins in wonder. And, at the end, when
philosophic thought has done its best, the wonder remains.
There have been added, however, some grasp of the im-
mensity of things, some purification of emotion by understanding. Yet there is a danger in such reflections. An
immediate good is apt to be thought of in the degenerate
form of a passive enjoyment. Existence is activity ever
merging into the future. The aim at philosophic understanding is the aim at piercing the blindness of activity in respect
to its transcendent functions.]

CHAPTER VII

Phenomenology:

Edmund Husserl (1859–1938)

IN TURNING TO THE PHILOSOPHY OF EDMUND HUSSERL WE
take our leave of the philosophers of process but we certainly do not return to anything like the tradition of Moore.
Husserl is not easily classified in the loose scheme with
which we began because he not only inaugurates a philosophy which is passionately interested in the tiniest details of
experience, but he also thinks it provides a clue to art, religion, law, history, and all other aspects of culture and
the universe. (Perhaps, like Mr. Berlin's Tolstoi he is the
fox who wanted to be a hedgehog!) For this reason Husserl could have been hailed as an early ally of realism, then

to have become what is called a transcendental idealist, and ultimately a powerful influence on the existentialists.

Unlike Moore, Russell, and their teachers, Husserl never went through a hegelian period, partly because continental philosophy at the end of the nineteenth century was far less hegelian than British philosophy at that time. In his early days Husserl was influenced by an anti-idealistic movement led by his teacher Brentano, who has already been mentioned in the discussion of realism and who was very much interested in the doctrines of certain medieval scholastics. Under their influence Brentano held that *referring* or *intending* is the most important activity of the human soul, an activity in which we always experience something other than ourselves. Indeed, it is only when we are referring to other things that we can be acquainted with ourselves as well. His two most distinguished pupils were Meinong (of golden mountain fame and also previously mentioned in the discussion of realism) and Husserl, both of whom Brentano stimulated to inaugurate new philosophical disciplines devoted to studying objects of reference or "intentional objects." Meinong called his "The Theory of Objects"; Husserl called his "Transcendental Phenomenology," and it has had a far more prosperous career.

In spite of many differences between his view and those of Croce, Bergson, and Whitehead, Husserl insists with them that philosophy has its own peculiar method. He distinguishes transcendental phenomenology from all of the empirical sciences, and particularly from psychology, with which it might be confused for reasons that will soon be evident. It is worth pointing out that this sharp distinction between philosophy and the sciences is characteristic of most of the important philosophies of the twentieth century with the outstanding exceptions of certain varieties of realism and of Dewey's instrumentalism. Some realists have held that we must abandon the claim to a special philosophic method or a peculiar brand of knowledge to be obtained by its means. On this view philosophy differs from the special sciences simply by the generality of its problems and by the fact that it sometimes speculates on matters where conclusive evidence is absent. But most of the other influential movements of the twentieth century—even logical positivism—reserve a more distinctive role for philosophy, whether it be that of seeing the structure of things by intuition as in the case of Husserl, or that of analyzing rather than discovering truths of science as in the case of Carnap, or that of therapeutically eliminating what Wittgenstein's followers call mental cramps growing out of linguistically created puzzles. This has been one of the most striking responses of twentieth-century philosophy to the challenge of those nineteenth-century thinkers who had predicted the end of philosophy with the growth of science, with the progressive separation of physics, biology, social science, and finally psychology from the mother-discipline, philosophy.

Husserl, in the wake of Brentano and along with Meinong, opposed "psychologism" or the attempt to identify the youngest child, psychology, with philosophy—to think of abstract entities like numbers, essences, and characteristics as created by the mind or as in the mind. Husserl admitted that there was a study called "phenomenological psychology" that treated of mental phenomena, but said in the manner of Descartes that it was merely another empirical science that lacked the certainty of philosophy. When we reflect on our thinking, our observing, or our understanding, we discover what Husserl called "acts of experience" which are intentional in Brentano's sense and which therefore refer to "phenomena" that are not evident to us in unreflective moments—that is, in moments when we adopt what Husserl called the natural attitude. Thus when we reflect upon our perception of a cube from different angles it appears to us to have different shapes, and these appearances or phenomena (some of which seem to be *sense-data* in British terminology) are the primary objects of interest to the phenomenological psychologist. Each such phenomenon is said to have a structure that the phenomenological psychologist tries to discover by patient peering.

Now when we begin to reflect upon the various different appearances of the cube as we view it from different angles, we think of them as appearances *of that cube,* but we must give up this natural habit in order to concentrate on pure experience, on a pure phenomenon, on the appearance all by itself. It should be repeated here that in the case of the cube we can concentrate not only on the different *experiences* or appearances of the cube, but also on our different *experiencings* or acts of experience. It should be added that we can do something similar in the case of other selves: we can mentally blot out these other selves and then examine our own experiences and experiencings of them. In doing this sort of thing we suspend belief in the existence of the objects blotted out; we perform a "phenomenological reduction," in Greek an *epoché*. Husserl also speaks of this as a process of "bracketing" the external world; it consists in treating cubes and other objects as though they were not there, the better to concentrate on our experiences and experiencings themselves.

Having performed this first reduction we must then perform a second which consists in the description of the remainders of the first. We try to discover their essences or structures. Here Husserl uses the Greek word "eidos" for structure, so that he refers to this step as "eidetic reduction." These essences or forms or structures are said to "constrain psychical existence"; they are the possible structures that any psychical existent might have, and therefore Husserl holds that psychological phenomenology or phenomenological psychology—which is what we have been outlining—must rest on "eidetic phenomenology," the study of these forms and structures that do the constraining.

So far we have not considered the *I* in all of this looking at cubes. *I* see these appearances, *I* understand certain words, and *I* experience other selves, but so far I have performed reductions that yield only one kind of subject matter for phenomenological psychology, namely appearances of cubes, and other selves and corresponding acts. But the point is that *I* can also be experienced and treated as the result of a phenomenological reduction just as an appearance of a cube can be. It is just a matter of concentrating on the subject, rather than on the cube. But this *I* upon which one might concentrate is what Husserl calls *"psychical* subjectivity" and therefore is still a matter of mere empirical concern, of interest to phenomenological psychology. There is a deeper *I,* he says, "which for want of language we can only call . . . 'I myself.' " This is *transcendental* subjectivity and it is one of the main topics of transcendental phenomenology, i.e. philosophy. It is the hidden *I* to which the psychical *I* is present. It is the end product of the most stringent reduction of all, along with another product which Husserl calls *"transcendental* inter-subjectivity" and which this writer cannot understand well enough to expound—a fault which he shares with philosophers older and wiser and more trained in bracketing. Presumably by examining the structures of these obscure things we arrive at the most profound philosophical truths by "presuppositionless" methods.

Husserl has been extremely influential. Among others, Heidegger and Sartre have been strongly affected by his philosophy. He has had great influence in Germany, France, and Latin America and his followers have tried to bracket and reduce in many different fields. He has been an extremely controversial and productive writer. Like Bergson's, his life was clouded by the rise of the Nazis when he was deserted as an old man by "Aryan" scholars whom he had taught. "And we old people remain here," he wrote. "A singular turn of the times: it gives the philosopher—if it does not take away his breath—much to think of. But now: *Cogito ergo sum,* i.e. I prove *sub specie aeterni* my right to live. And this, the *aeternitas* in general, cannot be reached by any earthly powers."[1]

The following selection is the first chapter of the second section of Husserl's *Ideas: General Introduction to Pure Phenomenology* (1931). The title of the chapter is "The Thesis of the Natural Standpoint and its Suspension."[2]

[1] Quoted in Marvin Farber, *The Foundation of Phenomenology* (Harvard, 1943), p. 23.
[2] Acknowledgment is made to The Macmillan Co., New York, and to George Allen and Unwin, Ltd., London, for permission to reprint the chapter from *Ideas: General Introduction to Pure Phenomenology,* translated by W. R. Boyce Gibson. The original appeared in German in 1913 under the title *Ideen zu einer reinen Phänomenologie und phänomenologischen Philosophie.*

§ 27. The World of the Natural Standpoint: I and My World About Me

Our first outlook upon life is that of natural human beings, imaging, judging, feeling, willing, *"from the natural standpoint."* Let us make clear to ourselves what this means in the form of simple meditations which we can best carry on in the first person.

I am aware of a world, spread out in space endlessly, and in time becoming and become, without end. I am aware of it, that means, first of all, I discover it immediately, intuitively, I experience it. Through sight, touch, hearing, etc., in the different ways of sensory perception, corporeal things somehow spatially distributed are *for me simply there,* in verbal or figurative sense "present," whether or not I pay them special attention by busying myself with them, considering, thinking, feeling, willing. Animal beings also, perhaps men, are immediately there for me; I look up, I see them, I hear them coming towards me, I grasp them by the hand; speaking with them, I understand immediately what they are sensing and thinking, the feelings that stir them, what they wish or will. They too are present as realities in my field of intuition, even when I pay them no attention. But it is not necessary that they and other objects likewise should be present precisely in my *field of perception.* For me real objects are there, definite, more or less familiar, agreeing with what is actually perceived without being themselves perceived or even intuitively present. I can let my attention wander from the writing-table I have just seen and observed, through the unseen portions of the room behind my back to the verandah, into the garden, to the children in the summer-house, and so forth, to all the objects concerning which I precisely "know" that they are there and yonder in my immediate co-perceived surroundings—a knowledge which has nothing of conceptual thinking in it, and first changes into clear intuiting with the bestowing of attention, and even then only partially and for the most part very imperfectly.

But not even with the added reach of this intuitively clear or dark, distinct or indistinct *co-present* margin, which forms a continuous ring around the actual field of perception, does that world exhaust itself which in every waking moment is in some conscious measure "present" before me. It reaches rather in a fixed order of being into the limitless beyond. What is actually perceived, and what is more or less clearly co-present and determinate (to some extent at least), is partly pervaded, partly girt about with a *dimly apprehended depth or fringe of indeterminate reality*. I can pierce it with rays from the illuminating focus of attention with varying success. Determining representations, dim at first, then livelier, fetch me something out, a chain of such recollections takes shape, the circle of determinacy extends ever farther, and eventually so far that the connexion with the actual field of perception as the *immediate* environment is established. But in general the issue is a different one: an empty mist of dim indeterminacy gets studded over with intuitive possibilities or presumptions, and only the "form" of the world as "world" is foretokened. Moreover, the zone of indeterminacy is infinite. The misty horizon that can never be completely outlined remains necessarily there.

As it is with the world in its ordered being as a spatial present—the aspect I have so far been considering—so likewise is it with the world in respect to its *ordered being in the succession of time*. This world now present to me, and in every waking "now" obviously so, has its temporal horizon, infinite in both directions, its known and unknown, its intimately alive and its unalive past and future. Moving freely within the moment of experience which brings what is present into my intuitional grasp, I can follow up these connexions of the reality which immediately surrounds me. I can shift my standpoint in space and time, look this way and that, turn temporally forwards and backwards; I can provide for myself constantly new and more or less clear and meaningful perceptions and representations, and images also more or less clear, in which I make intuitable to myself whatever can possibly exist really or supposedly in the steadfast order of space and time.

In this way, when consciously awake, I find myself at all times, and without my ever being able to change this, set in relation to a world which, through its constant changes, remains one and ever the same. It is continually "present" for me, and I myself am a member of it. Therefore this world is not there for me as a mere *world of facts and affairs,* but, with the same immediacy, as a *world of values,* a *world of goods,* a *practical world.* Without further effort on my part I find the things before me furnished not only with the qualities that befit their positive nature, but with value-characters such as beautiful or ugly, agreeable or disagreeable, pleasant or unpleasant, and so forth. Things in their immediacy stand there as objects to be used, the "table" with its "books," the "glass to drink from," the "vase," the "piano," and so forth. These values and practicalities, they too belong to *the constitution of* the *"actually present" objects as such,* irrespective of my turning or not turning to consider them or indeed any other objects. The same considerations apply of course just as well to the men and beasts in my surroundings as to "mere things." They are my "friends" or my "foes," my "servants" or "superiors," "strangers" or "relatives," and so forth.

§ 28. THE "COGITO." MY NATURAL WORLD-ABOUT-ME AND THE IDEAL WORLDS-ABOUT-ME

It is then to this world, the *world in which I find myself and which is also my world-about-me,* that the complex forms of my manifold and shifting *spontaneities* of consciousness stand related: observing in the interests of research the bringing of meaning into conceptual form through description; comparing and distinguishing, collecting and counting, presupposing and inferring, the theorizing activity of consciousness, in short, in its different forms and stages. Related to it likewise are the diverse acts and states of sentiment and will: approval and disapproval, joy and sorrow, desire and aversion, hope and fear, decision and action. All these, together with the sheer acts of the Ego, in which I become acquainted with the world as *immediately* given me, through spontaneous tendencies to turn towards it and to grasp it, are included under the one Cartesian expression: *Cogito*. In the natural urge of life I live continually in *this fundamental form of all "wakeful" living,* whether in addition I do or do not assert the *cogito,* and whether I am or am not "reflectively" concerned with the Ego and the *cogitare*. If I am so concerned, a new *cogito* has become livingly active, which for its part is not reflected upon, and so not objective for me.

I am present to myself continually as someone who perceives, represents, thinks, feels, desires, and so forth; and *for the most part* herein I find myself related in present experience to the fact-world which is constantly about me. But I am not always so related, not every *cogito* in which I live has for its *cogitatum* things, men, objects or contents of one kind or another. Perhaps I am busied with pure numbers and the laws they symbolize: nothing of this sort is present in the world about me, this world of "real fact." And yet the world of numbers also is there for me, as the field of objects with which I am arithmetically busied; while I am thus occupied some numbers or constructions of a numerical kind will be at the focus of vision, girt by an arithmetical horizon partly defined, partly not; but obviously this being-there-for-me, like the being there at all, is something very different from this. *The arithmetical world is there for me only when and so long as I occupy the arithmetical standpoint.* But the *natural* world, the world in the ordinary sense of the word, is *constantly there for me,* so long as I live naturally and look in its direction. I am then at the *"natural standpoint,"* which is just another way of stating the same thing. And there is no need to modify these conclusions when I proceed to appropriate to myself the arithmetical world, and other similar "worlds," by adopting the corresponding standpoint. The natural world *still remains "present,"* I am at the natural standpoint after as well as before, and in this respect *undisturbed by the adoption of new standpoints*. If my *cogito* is active *only* in the worlds proper to the new standpoints, the natural world remains unconsidered; it is now the background for my consciousness as act, but it is *not the encircling sphere within which an arithmetical world finds its true and proper place.* The two worlds are present together but *disconnected,* apart, that is, from their relation to the Ego, in virtue of which I can freely direct my glance or my acts to the one or to the other.

§ 29. THE "OTHER" EGO-SUBJECT AND THE INTERSUBJECTIVE NATURAL WORLD-ABOUT-ME

Whatever holds good for me personally, also holds good, as I know, for all other men whom I find present in my world-about-me. Experiencing them as men, I understand and take them as Ego-subjects, units like myself, and re-lated to their natural surroundings. But this in such wise that I apprehend the world-about-them and the world-about-me objectively as one and the same world, which differs in each case only through affecting consciousness differently. Each has his place whence he sees the things that are present, and each enjoys accordingly different ap-pearances of the things. For each, again, the fields of per-ception and memory actually present are different, quite apart from the fact that even that which is here intersub-jectively known in common is known in different ways, is differently apprehended, shows different grades of clear-ness, and so forth. Despite all this, we come to under-standings with our neighbours, and set up in common an objective spatio-temporal fact-world as *the world about us that is there for us all, and to which we ourselves none the less belong.*

§ 30. THE GENERAL THESIS OF THE NATURAL STANDPOINT

That which we have submitted towards the characteriza-tion of what is given to us from the natural standpoint, and thereby of the natural standpoint itself, was a piece of pure description *prior to all "theory."* In these studies we stand bodily aloof from all theories, and by 'theories' we here mean anticipatory ideas of every kind. Only as facts of our environment, not as agencies for uniting facts validly to-gether, do theories concern us at all. But we do not set ourselves the task of continuing the pure description and raising it to a systematically inclusive and exhaustive char-acterization of the data, in their full length and breadth, discoverable from the natural standpoint (or from any standpoint, we might add, that can be knit up with the same in a common consent). A task such as this can and must —as scientific—be undertaken, and it is one of extraordinary importance, although so far scarcely noticed. Here it is not ours to attempt. For us who are striving towards the entrance-gate of phenomenology all the necessary work in this direction has already been carried out; the few features pertaining to the natural standpoint which we need are of a quite general character, and have already figured in our descriptions, and been sufficiently *and fully clarified* We even made a special point of securing this full measure of clearness.

We emphasize a most important point once again in the sentences that follow: I find continually present and standing over against me the one spatio-temporal fact-world to which I myself belong, as do all other men found in it and related in the same way to it. This "fact-world," as the word already tells us, I find to *be out there,* and also *take it just as it gives itself to me as something that exists out there.* All doubting and rejecting of the data of the natural world leaves standing the *general thesis of the natural standpoint.* "The" world is as fact-world always there; at the most it is at odd points "other" than I supposed, this or that under such names as "illusion," "hallucination," and the like, must be struck *out of it,* so to speak; but the "it" remains ever, in the sense of the general thesis, a world that has its being out there. To know it more comprehensively, more trustworthily, more perfectly than the naïve lore of experience is able to do, and to solve all the problems of scientific knowledge which offer themselves upon its ground, that is the goal of the *sciences* of *the natural standpoint.*

§ 31. RADICAL ALTERATION OF THE NATURAL THESIS: "DISCONNEXION," "BRACKETING"

Instead now of remaining at this standpoint, we propose to alter it radically. Our aim must be to convince ourselves of the possibility of this alteration on grounds of principle.

The General Thesis according to which the real world

about me is at all times known not merely in a general way as something apprehended, but as a fact-world *that has its being out there,* does *not* consist of course *in an act proper,* in an articulated judgment *about* existence. It is and remains something all the time the standpoint is adopted, that is, it endures persistently during the whole course of our life of natural endeavour. What has been at any time perceived clearly, or obscurely made present, in short everything out of the world of nature known through experience and prior to any thinking, bears in its totality and in all its articulated sections the character "present" "out there," a character which can function essentially as the ground of support for an explicit (predicative) existential judgment which is in agreement with the character it is grounded upon. If we express that same judgment, we know quite well that in so doing we have simply put into the form of a statement and grasped as a predication what already lay somehow in the original experience, or lay there as the character of something "present to one's hand."

We can treat the potential and unexpressed thesis exactly as we do the thesis of the explicit judgment. A procedure of this sort, *possible at any time,* is, for instance, *the attempt to doubt everything* which *Descartes,* with an entirely different end in view, with the purpose of setting up an absolutely indubitable sphere of Being, undertook to carry through. We link on here, but add directly and emphatically that this attempt to doubt everything should serve us *only as a device of method,* helping us to stress certain points which by its means, as though secluded in its essence, must be brought clearly to light.

The attempt to doubt everything has its place in the realm of our *perfect freedom.* We can *attempt to doubt* anything and everything, however convinced we may be concerning what we doubt, even though the evidence which seals our assurance is completely adequate.

Let us consider what is essentially involved in an act of this kind. He who attempts to doubt is attempting to doubt "Being" of some form or other, or it may be Being expanded into such predicative forms as "It is," "It is this or thus," and the like. The attempt does not affect the form of Being itself. He who doubts, for instance, whether an object, whose Being he does not doubt, is constituted in such and such a way, doubts *the way it is constituted.* We can obviously transfer this way of speaking from the doubting to the *attempt* at doubting. It is clear that we cannot doubt the Being of anything, and in the same act of consciousness (under the unifying form of simultaneity) bring what is substantive to this Being under the terms of the Natural Thesis, and so confer upon it the character of "being actually there" (*vorhanden*). Or to put the same in another way: we cannot at once doubt and hold for certain one and the same quality of Being. It is likewise clear that the *attempt* to doubt any object of awareness in respect of its *being actually there necessarily conditions a certain suspension* (*Aufhebung*) *of the thesis;* and it is precisely this that interests us. It is not a transformation of the thesis into antithesis, of positive into negative; it is also not a transformation into presumption, suggestion, indecision, doubt (in one or another sense of the word); such shifting indeed is not at our free pleasure. *Rather is it something quite unique. We do not abandon the thesis we have adopted, we make no change in our conviction,* which remains in itself what it is so long as we do not introduce new motives of judgment, which we precisely refrain from doing. And yet the thesis undergoes a modification—whilst remaining in itself what it is, *we set it as it were "out of action," we "disconnect it," "bracket it."* It still remains there like the bracketed in the bracket, like the disconnected outside the connexional system. We can also say: The thesis is experience as lived (*Erlebnis*), *but we make "no use" of it,* and by that, of course, we do not indicate privation (as when we say of the ignorant that he makes no use of a certain thesis); in this case rather, as with all parallel expressions, we are dealing with indicators that point to a definite but *unique form of consciousness,* which clamps on to the original simple thesis (whether it actually or even predicatively *posits* existence or not), and transvalues it in a quite peculiar way. *This transvaluing is a concern of our full freedom, and is opposed to all cognitive attitudes* that would set themselves up as co-ordinate with *the thesis,* and yet within the unity of "simultaneity" remain incompatible with it, as indeed it is in general with all attitudes whatsoever in the strict sense of the word.

In *the attempt to doubt* applied to a thesis which, as we presuppose, is certain and tenaciously held, the "disconnexion" takes place in and with a modification of the antithesis, namely, with the *"supposition"* (*Ansetzung*) *of Non-Being,* which is thus the partial basis of the attempt to doubt. With Descartes this is so markedly the case that one can say that his universal attempt at doubt is just an attempt at universal denial. We disregard this possibility here, we are not interested in every analytic component of the attempt to doubt, nor therefore in its exact and completely sufficing analysis. *We extract only the phenomenon of "bracketing" or "disconnecting,"* which is obviously not limited to that of the attempt to doubt, although it can be detached from it with special ease, but can appear *in other contexts also,* and with no less ease *independently.* In relation to *every* thesis and wholly uncoerced we can use this peculiar ἐποχή (*epoché*), *a certain refraining from judgment which is compatible with the unshaken and unshakable because self-evidencing conviction of Truth.* The thesis is "put out of action," bracketed, it passes off into the modified status of a "bracketed thesis," and the judgment *simpliciter* into *"bracketed judgment."*

Naturally one should not simply identify this consciousness with that of "mere supposal," that nymphs, for instance, are dancing in a ring; for thereby *no disconnecting* of a living conviction that goes on living takes place, although from another side the close relation of the two forms of consciousness lies clear. Again, we are not concerned here with supposal in the sense of *"assuming"* or *taking for granted,* which in the equivocal speech of current usage may also be expressed in the words: "I suppose (I make the assumption) that it is so and so."

Let us add further that nothing hinders us *from speaking of bracketing correlatively* also, in respect of *an objectivity to be posited,* whatever be the region or category to which it belongs. What is meant in this case is that *every thesis related to this objectivity* must be *disconnected* and changed into its bracketed counterpart. On closer view, moreover, the "bracketing" image is from the outset better suited to the sphere of the object, just as the expression "to put out of action" better suits the sphere of the Act or of Consciousness.

§ 32. THE PHENOMENOLOGICAL ἐποχή

We can now let the universal ἐποχή in the sharply defined and novel sense we have given to it step into the place of the Cartesian attempt at universal doubt. But on good grounds we *limit* the universality of this ἐποχή. For were it as inclusive as it is in general capable of being, then since every thesis and every judgment can be modified freely to any extent, and every objectivity that we can judge or criticize can be bracketed, no field would be left over for unmodified judgments, to say nothing of a science. But our design is just to discover a new scientific domain, such as might be won precisely *through the method of bracketing,* though only through a definitely limited form of it.

The limiting consideration can be indicated in a word. *We put out of action the general thesis which belongs to the essence of the natural standpoint,* we place in brackets whatever it includes respecting the nature of Being: *this entire natural world therefore* which is continually "there for us," "present to our hand," and will ever remain there, is a "fact-world" of which we continue to be conscious, even though it pleases us to put it in brackets.

If I do this, as I am fully free to do, I do *not* then *deny* this "world," as though I were a sophist, *I do not doubt that it is there* as though I were a sceptic; but I use the "phenomenological" ἐποχή, which *completely bars* me *from using any judgment that concerns spatio-temporal existence* (*Dasein*).

Thus *all sciences which relate to this natural world,* though they stand never so firm to me, though they fill me with wondering admiration, though I am far from any thought of objecting to them in the least degree, *I disconnect them* all, *I make absolutely no use of their standards, I do not appropriate a single one of the propositions that enter into their systems, even though their evidential value is perfect, I take none of them, no one of them serves me for a foundation*—so long, that is, as it is understood, in the way these sciences themselves understand it, as a truth *concerning the realities* of this world. *I may accept it only after I have placed it in the bracket.* That means: only in the modified consciousness of the judgment as it appears in disconnexion, and *not as it figures within the science as its proposition, a proposition which claims to be valid and whose validity I recognize and make use of.*

The ἐποχή here in question will not be confused with that which positivism demands, and against which, as we were compelled to admit, it is itself an offender. We are not concerned at present with removing the preconceptions which trouble the pure positivity (*Sachlichkeit*) of research, with the constituting of a science "free from theory" and "free from metaphysics" by bringing all the grounding back to the immediate data, nor with the means of reaching such ends, concerning whose value there is indeed no question. What *we* demand lies along another line. The whole world as placed within the nature-setting and presented in experience as real, taken completely "free from all theory," just as it is in reality experienced, and made clearly manifest in and through the linkings of our experiences, has now no validity for us, it must be set in brackets, untested indeed but also uncontested. Similarly all theories and sciences, positivistic or otherwise, which relate to this world, however good they may be, succumb to the same fate.]

CHAPTER VIII

Existentialism:

Jean-Paul Sartre (b. 1905)

THE PHILOSOPHERS PREVIOUSLY REPRESENTED IN THIS volume had established themselves as thinkers of first importance before the first world war; all of them were adult figures of great promise or distinction in 1905, the year in which Jean-Paul Sartre was born. I have said that my choice is sometimes dictated by the amount of influence exerted by the philosopher chosen and that is especially true of the present selection. Like Bergson, Sartre has achieved popular fame that far exceeds anything possible for an English-speaking philosopher today. He is a playwright, a novelist, and a critic, and has used all possible media in addition to the technical philosophical treatise for communicating his ideas. He may be criticized but he cannot be ignored.

Sartre tries to deal systematically with subjects that are more often treated by literary men and artists in the twentieth century. Like the romantic philosophers of the nineteenth century, he is interested in agonizing moral questions and in the notion of personal liberty. He refuses to drift along a stream which is not of his own choosing and eager to puncture all alibis invented by human beings to save themselves from the responsibility for their choices. Because of his deep moral concern, Sartre's interests diverge sharply from those of professional philosophers who, after Kant, Hegel, and J. S. Mill, abandon questions of ethics and moral psychology in order to concentrate on the methods and concepts of natural science and mathematics, and who, when they do deal with moral questions, choose their examples from too trivial and philistine a world and fail to analyze those disturbing questions which appear central to sensitive people of their time.

I have chosen Sartre as the representative of the movement known as *existentialism* mainly because he, along with a number of fellow-Parisians, has consciously adopted that name, while at least two German philosophers who are associated with this tradition, Martin Heidegger and Karl Jaspers, have rejected the label with its implication of a frozen, doctrinaire attitude or system. Moreover, in the (translated) selection that follows Sartre writes comparatively lucidly and comprehensibly, and this cannot be said of all passages from the existentialists. In this piece Sartre does not represent existentialism in the tortured and laboured style of dubious metaphysics and muddled logical theory, but primarily in the moods of literature and moral psychology, the very moods in which his forerunners Kierkegaard and Nietzsche excelled. It should be added that Sartre's chief philosophical work is called *Being and Nothingness* and is subtitled "An Essay in Phenomenological Ontology," so that Sartre aims to be far more than a *littérateur*. In that work he tries to lay the technical foundation for the philosophy of man at which he aims, while the selection that follows comes from an address in which he tries to sketch the connections between these fundamental views and his moral and personal attitudes.

These attitudes were widely shared by continental intellectuals living in a world devastated by the second world war; they had been given anticipatory expression in the nineteenth century by Dostoevski, Nietzsche, and Kierkegaard, and more recently by Franz Kafka, because of their interest in the dark emotions, in uncommon men, in underground men, in men who become insects. The taste for existentialism is related to the heightened taste for all of these writers during and after the fall of France, when understandable French absorption in the literature of despair, anguish, and forlornness resembled German interest in it directly after the first world war. It is one thing, however, to try to explain the social and cultural reasons for the popularity of a philosophy, and another to expound its content. Particularly because of its emphasis on freedom of choice, existentialism claims to be logically independent of the historical conditions that may have encouraged its wide acceptance, and furthermore those conditions have hardly disappeared. Whether or not the philosophy continues to be modish, it has had such powerful impact in our time that a historian of ideas in the twentieth century cannot avoid studying it carefully—nineteenth-century roots and twentieth-century branches. What follows is a very brief and necessarily superficial introduction to a complex subject, a subject for which the editor, like most English-speaking philosophers, is less fitted than he might be and toward which he feels not unlike those skeptical but curious Englishmen and Americans who began to pry into the secrets of Hegel and Kant in the nineteenth century. One way of looking at that episode has been dramatically expressed by a pair of contemporary English philosophers. The first had said that Kant was the greatest calamity ever to hit philosophy, to which the second replied that that was obviously an honor reserved for Hegel. Both Englishmen may have spoken too soon.

The Dane Sören Kierkegaard is probably the most important figure in the history of existentialism, to which he contributed at least three things. First of all his interest in feelings like boredom, dread, and anxiety, which he attempted to analyze psychologically; secondly, his Christian faith and his anti-clericalism; thirdly, and most important from our point of view, his ideas on existence. It is extremely difficult to disentangle these elements in his writing, which is deliberately anti-systematic and unscholastic, but it may help to begin with his ideas on existence and say something about their connection with the other elements mentioned.

The word "exists" is one of the most pivotal and controversial in philosophy. Some philosophers think of it as having one meaning: the sense in which we say that this book exists, that God does or does not exist, that there exist odd numbers between 8 and 20, that a characteristic like redness exists as well as things that are red, that the American government exists as well as the physical buildings in which the government is housed, that minds exist as well as bodies. And when the word "exists" is construed in this unambiguous way, many famous disputes in the history of philosophy and theology appear to be quite straightforward. Theists affirm that God exists while atheists deny the very same statement; materialists say that matter exists while some idealists think it is illusory; nominalists, as they are called, deny the existence of characteristics like redness while platonic realists affirm it; some kinds of behaviorists deny that there are minds inside bodies. There is, however, a tendency among some philosophers to insist that the word "exists" is ambiguous and therefore that some of these disputes are not disputes at all but merely the results of mutual misunderstanding, of a failure to see that certain things are said to exist in one sense while others exist in another. One of the outstanding efforts of this kind in the twentieth century occurs in the early writings of realists who maintained that only concrete things in space and time *exist,* while abstract characteristics of things or relations between them should be said to *subsist.* This is sometimes illustrated by pointing out that while Chicago and St. Louis both exist at definite places, the relation *more populous than* which holds between them exists neither in Chicago nor in St. Louis nor in the area between them, but is nevertheless *something* about which we can speak, something that is usually assigned to a timeless and spaceless realm like that of which Plato spoke. On this view, however, human minds or personalities are also said to *exist* in spite of being nonmaterial. In short, the great divide is between abstract subsistents and concrete existents, but both human personalities and physical objects are existents and do not share in the spacelessness and timelessness of platonic ideas.

So far as one can see, Kierkegaard too distinguishes different senses of "exists," except that he appears to need at least *three* distinct senses for which he should supply three distinct words. First of all he needs one for statements about God, and so he says that God *is.* Secondly, and by contrast, persons or personalities are said to *exist.* It would appear then that he needs some third term for physical objects, which on his view are very different from God and persons, but since existentialists don't seem to be very interested in physical objects or "mere" things, they

appear to get along with two. The great problem for
Kierkegaard is to relate God's *is-ness,* if I may use that term
for the moment, to human existence, and this he tries to
solve by appealing to the Incarnation. Christ's person is the
existent outgrowth of God who is. By what is admittedly a
mysterious process the abstract God enters a concrete
existent. We must accept this on faith and faith alone, for
clearly it cannot be like the process whereby one existent
is related to another; it involves a passage from one realm
to another which is not accessible to the human mind.
Christians who lacked this faith and who failed to live by it
were attacked by Kierkegaard; this was the theological root
of his violent criticism of the Established Church of Den-
mark. It is one source of his powerful influence on contemporary theology.

Sartre, as will appear in the selection from his writings,
calls himself an atheistic existentialist. There is no God, he
says, and therefore human beings are neither created nor
pervaded by anyone or anything that can have a plan or
idea of what they will be like before they come into
existence or before they develop by their own free action.
This is at least one meaning that I can give to his dictum:
existence is prior to essence. First of all that there is no
plan or idea of it before our personality appears, and
secondly that we make our own essence by our own free
choice, by developing as we will. Human personalities are
not made by anyone else. In the beginning they just *are;*
first they exist, and then they make themselves. It is in this
sense that some existentialists speak of the "absurdity" of
human existence, meaning that it is not explicable by reference to anything more fundamental.

I return now to Kierkegaard and the connection between
his theistic metaphysics and his preoccupation with boredom, dread, and anxiety, the subjects which have attracted
so many existentialist writers. Like Hegel, Comte, Marx,
Spencer, and so many thinkers of the nineteenth century,
Kierkegaard was captivated by the idea of development by
stages. But unlike Comte and Marx, who concentrated on
the development of society, Kierkegaard was interested in
the development of the existent, individual, concrete human

personality. Its chief Kierkegaardian stages are the esthetic, the moral, and the religious, and they form a striking contrast to Comte's trio: the theological, the metaphysical, and the scientific. For one thing Kierkegaard's highest stage of human existence is the religious, while Comte's is the scientific; for another, the Kierkegaardian personality's journey through its stages is absolutely free. A man can pass through them or not, depending on how he exercises his free will, but emotional turmoil is the price of failure to go to the very end. The route is marked by three signposts: esthetic indulgence in passing pleasures, ethical respect for the moral law, and religious worship of God. All along the way there are psychological terrors that can be escaped only by completing the journey, which is man's effort to transcend himself. This is the origin of the existentialist interest in man's inner life; it fits in with the concern with "subjectivity" that we have already seen in Husserl. It is the root of the existentialist insistence on the need for commitment and resolute decision. It is one of the more obvious links between existentialist philosophy and existentialist literature and also a source of the existentialists' comparative indifference to scientific psychology. Once again we observe a self-conscious effort to provide philosophy with a special function that will distinguish it from science, in this case the description and evaluation of man's condition by methods which are held to be peculiar to their subject matter: the inner life of active, free persons as opposed to passive, determined things.

Like every movement in philosophy, existentialism sponsors varying conceptions of its own ancestry, in part because of its internal differences and divisions. And so Nietzsche's writing is regarded as canonical and profoundly anticipatory in some histories of the movement but not in others; Husserl seems to have had more influence on Sartre than on others; Jaspers, Marcel, and Heidegger must be treated apart from Sartre and his friends in any serious study of the movement. Since this is hardly the place for a study of these more minute matters and since the selection from Sartre outlines some of them, we may turn to that, helped perhaps by this brief summary of the views of

Kierkegaard, who is universally accepted as the chief originator of the doctrine.

Sartre was trained as an academic philosopher and taught until 1942, when he resigned his post to give his full time to writing. He is the author of several distinguished novels, plays, and critical essays, and his views have been the subject of learned exposition and active debate. Like Croce, he is deeply interested in politics, literature, and philosophy. He was a prisoner of war in Germany and later active in the resistance movement. The passage that follows comes from an address in which Sartre answers some of his critics. It is an extract from *Existentialism and Humanism* (1948).[1]

[What, then, is this that we call existentialism? Most of those who are making use of this word would be highly confused if required to explain its meaning. For since it has become fashionable, people cheerfully declare that this musician or that painter is "existentialist." A columnist in *Clartés* signs himself "The Existentialist," and, indeed, the word is now so loosely applied to so many things that it no longer means anything at all. . . . All the same, it can easily be defined.

The question is only complicated because there are two kinds of existentialists. There are, on the one hand, the Christians, amongst whom I shall name Jaspers and Gabriel Marcel, both professed Catholics; and on the other the existential atheists, amongst whom we must place Heidegger as well as the French existentialists and myself. What they have in common is simply the fact that they believe that *existence* comes before *essence*—or, if you will, that we must begin from the subjective. What exactly do we mean by that? ·

If one considers an article of manufacture—as, for example, a book or a paper-knife—one sees that it has been made by an artisan who had a conception of it; and he has paid attention, equally, to the conception of a paper-knife

[1] Grateful acknowledgment is made to Methuen & Co., Ltd., London, and to Les Éditions Nagel, Paris, for permission to reprint pp. 25-42 of *Existentialism and Humanism* by Jean-Paul Sartre, translated by Philip Mairet from the French edition entitled *L'Existentialisme est un humanisme*.

and to the pre-existent technique of production which is a part of that conception and is, at bottom, a formula. Thus the paper-knife is at the same time an article producible in a certain manner and one which, on the other hand, serves a definite purpose, for one cannot suppose that a man would produce a paper-knife without knowing what it was for. Let us say, then, of the paper-knife that its essence—that is to say the sum of the formulae and the qualities which made its production and its definition possible—precedes its existence. The presence of such-and-such a paper-knife or book is thus determined before my eyes. Here, then, we are viewing the world from a technical standpoint, and we can say that production precedes existence.

When we think of God as the creator, we are thinking of him, most of the time, as a supernal artisan. Whatever doctrine we may be considering, whether it be a doctrine like that of Descartes, or of Leibniz himself, we always imply that the will follows, more or less, from the understanding or at least accompanies it, so that when God creates he knows precisely what he is creating. Thus, the conception of man in the mind of God is comparable to that of the paper-knife in the mind of the artisan: God makes man according to a procedure and a conception, exactly as the artisan manufactures a paper-knife, following a definition and a formula. Thus each individual man is the realisation of a certain conception which dwells in the divine understanding. In the philosophic atheism of the eighteenth century, the notion of God is suppressed, but not, for all that, the idea that essence is prior to existence; something of that idea we still find everywhere, in Diderot, in Voltaire and even in Kant. Man possesses a human nature; that "human nature," which is the conception of human being, is found in every man; which means that each man is a particular example of a universal conception, the conception of Man. In Kant, this universality goes so far that the wild man of the woods, man in the state of nature and the bourgeois are all contained in the same definition and have the same fundamental qualities. Here again, the essence of man precedes that historic existence which we confront in experience.

Atheistic existentialism, of which I am a representative, declares with greater consistency that if God does not exist there is at least one being whose existence comes before its essence, a being which exists before it can be defined by any conception of it. That being is man or, as Heidegger has it, the human reality. What do we mean by saying that existence precedes essence? We mean that man first of all exists, encounters himself, surges up in the world—and defines himself afterwards. If man as the existentialist sees him is not definable, it is because to begin with he is nothing. He will not be anything until later, and then he will be what he makes of himself. Thus, there is no human nature, because there is no God to have a conception of it. Man simply is. Not that he is simply what he conceives himself to be, but he is what he wills, and as he conceives himself after already existing—as he wills to be after that leap toward existence. Man is nothing else but that which he makes of himself. That is the first principle of existentialism. And this is what people call its "subjectivity," using the word as a reproach against us. But what do we mean to say by this, but that man is of a greater dignity than a stone or a table? For we mean to say that man primarily exists—that man is, before all else, something which propels itself towards a future and is aware that it is doing so. Man is, indeed, a project which possesses a subjective life, instead of being a kind of moss, or a fungus or a cauliflower. Before that projection of the self nothing exists; not even in the heaven of intelligence: man will only attain existence when he is what he purposes to be. Not, however, what he may wish to be. For what we usually understand by wishing or willing is a conscious decision taken—much more often than not—after we have made ourselves what we are. I may wish to join a party, to write a book or to marry—but in such a case what is usually called my will is probably a manifestation of a prior and more spontaneous decision. If, however, it is true that existence is prior to essence, man is responsible for what he is. Thus, the first effect of existentialism is that it puts every man in possession of himself as he is, and places the entire responsibility for his existence squarely upon his own shoulders. And, when we say that man is responsible for himself, we do not mean that he is responsible only for his own individuality, but that he is responsible for all men. The word "subjectivism" is to be understood in two senses, and our adversaries play upon only one of them. Subjectivism means, on the one hand, the freedom of the individual subject and, on the other, that man cannot pass beyond human subjectivity. It is the latter which is the deeper meaning of existentialism. When we say that man chooses himself, we do mean that every one of us must choose himself; but by that we also mean that in choosing for himself he chooses for all men. For in effect, of all the actions a man may take in order to create himself as he wills to be, there is not one which is not creative, at the same time, of an image of man such as he believes he ought to be. To choose between this or that is at the same time to affirm the value of that which is chosen; for we are unable ever to choose the worse. What we choose is always the better; and nothing can be better for us unless it is better for all. If, moreover, existence precedes essence and we will to exist at the same time as we fashion our image, that image is valid for all and for the entire epoch in which we find ourselves. Our responsibility is thus much greater than we had supposed, for it concerns mankind as a whole. If I am a worker, for instance, I may choose to join a Christian rather than a Communist trade union. And if, by that membership, I choose to signify that resignation is, after all, the attitude that best becomes a man, that man's kingdom is not upon this earth, I do not commit myself alone to that view. Resignation is my will for everyone, and my action is, in consequence, a commitment on behalf of all mankind. Or if, to take a more personal case, I decide to marry and to have children, even though this decision proceeds simply from my situation, from my passion or my desire, I am thereby committing not only myself, but humanity as a whole, to the practice of monogamy. I am thus responsible for myself and for all men, and I am creating a certain image of man as I would have him to be. In fashioning myself I fashion man.

This may enable us to understand what is meant by such terms—perhaps a little grandiloquent—as anguish, abandonment and despair. As you will soon see, it is very simple. First, what do we mean by anguish? The existentialist frankly states that man is in anguish. His meaning is as follows: When a man commits himself to anything, fully realising that he is not only choosing what he will be, but is thereby at the same time a legislator deciding for the whole of mankind—in such a moment a man cannot escape from the sense of complete and profound responsibility. There are many, indeed, who show no such anxiety. But we affirm that they are merely disguising their anguish or are in flight from it. Certainly, many people think that in what they are doing they commit no one but themselves to anything: and if you ask them, "What would happen if everyone did so?" they shrug their shoulders and reply, "Everyone does not do so." But in truth, one ought always to ask oneself what would happen if everyone did as one is doing; nor can one escape from that disturbing thought except by a kind of self-deception. The man who lies in self-excuse, by saying "Everyone will not do it," must be ill at ease in his conscience, for the act of lying implies the universal value which it denies. By its very disguise his anguish reveals itself. This is the anguish that Kierkegaard called "the anguish of Abraham." You know the story: An angel commanded Abraham to sacrifice his son: and obedience was obligatory, if it really was an angel who had appeared and said, "Thou, Abraham, shalt sacrifice thy son." But anyone in such a case would wonder, first, whether it was indeed an angel and secondly, whether I am really Abraham. Where are the proofs? A certain mad woman who suffered from hallucinations said that people were telephoning to her, and giving her orders. The doctor asked, "But who is it that speaks to you?" She replied: "He says it is God." And what, indeed, could prove to her that it was God? If an angel appears to me, what is the proof that it is an angel; or, if I hear voices, who can prove that they proceed from heaven and not from hell, or from my own subconsciousness or some pathological condition? Who can prove that they are really addressed to me?

Who, then, can prove that I am the proper person to impose, by my own choice, my conception of man upon mankind? I shall never find any proof whatever; there will be no sign to convince me of it. If a voice speaks to me, it is still I myself who must decide whether the voice is or is not that of an angel. If I regard a certain course of action as good, it is only I who choose to say that it is good and not bad. There is nothing to show that I am Abraham: nevertheless I also am obliged at every instant to perform actions which are examples. Everything happens to every man as though the whole human race had its eyes fixed upon what he is doing and regulated its conduct accordingly. So every man ought to say, "Am I really a man who has the right to act in such a manner that humanity regulates itself by what I do." If a man does not say that, he is dissembling his anguish. Clearly, the anguish with which we are concerned here is not one that could lead to quietism or inaction. It is anguish pure and simple, of the kind well known to all those who have borne responsibilities. When, for instance, a military leader takes upon himself the responsibility for an attack and sends a number of men to their death, he chooses to do it and at bottom he alone chooses. No doubt he acts under a higher command, but its orders, which are more general, require interpretation by him and upon that interpretation depends the life of ten, fourteen, or twenty men. In making the decision, he cannot but feel a certain anguish. . . .

And when we speak of "abandonment"—a favourite word of Heidegger—we only mean to say that God does not exist, and that it is necessary to draw the consequences of his absence right to the end. The existentialist is strongly opposed to a certain type of secular moralism which seeks to suppress God at the least possible expense. Towards 1880, when the French professors endeavoured to formulate a secular morality, they said something like this:— God is a useless and costly hypothesis, so we will do without it. However, if we are to have morality, a society and a law-abiding world, it is essential that certain values should be taken seriously; they must have an *a priori* existence ascribed to them. It must be considered obligatory *a priori* to be honest, not to lie, not to beat one's wife, to bring up children and so forth; so we are going to do a little work on this subject, which will enable us to show that these values exist all the same, inscribed in an intelligible heaven although, of course, there is no God. In other words—and this is, I believe, the purport of all that we in France call radicalism—nothing will be changed if God does not exist; we shall rediscover the same norms of honesty, progress and humanity, and we shall have disposed of God as an out-of-date hypothesis which will die away quietly of itself. The existentialist, on the contrary, finds it extremely embarrassing that God does not exist, for there disappears with Him all possibility of finding values in an intelligible heaven. There can no longer be any good *a priori*, since there is no infinite and perfect consciousness to think it. It is nowhere written that "the good" exists, that one must be honest or must not lie, since we are now upon the plane where there are only men. Dostoevski once wrote "If God did not exist, everything would be permitted"; and that, for existentialism, is the starting point. Everything is indeed permitted if God does not exist, and man is in consequence forlorn, for he cannot find anything to depend upon either within or outside himself. He discovers forthwith that he is without excuse. For if indeed existence precedes essence, one will never be able to explain one's action by reference to a given and specific human nature; in other words, there is no determinism—man is free, man *is* freedom. Nor, on the other hand, if God does not exist, are we provided with any values or commands that could legitimise our behaviour. Thus we have neither behind us, nor before us in a luminous realm of values, any means of justification or excuse. We are left alone, without excuse. That is what I mean when I say that man is condemned to be free. Condemned, because he did not create himself, yet is nevertheless at liberty, and from the moment that he is thrown into this world he is responsible for everything he does. The existentialist does not believe in the power of passion. He will never regard a grand passion as a destructive torrent upon which a man is swept into certain actions as by fate, and which, therefore, is an excuse for them. He thinks that man is responsible for his passion. Neither will an existentialist think that a man can find help through some sign being vouchsafed upon earth for his orientation: for he thinks that the man himself interprets the sign as he chooses. He thinks that every man, without any support or help whatever, is condemned at every instant to invent man. As Ponge has written in a very fine article, "Man is the future of man." That is exactly true. Only, if one took this to mean that the future is laid up in Heaven, that God knows what it is, it would be false, for then it would no longer even be a future. If, however, it means that, whatever man may now appear to be, there is a future to be fashioned, a virgin future that awaits him —then it is a true saying. But in the present one is forsaken.

As an example by which you may the better understand this state of abandonment, I will refer to the case of a pupil of mine, who sought me out in the following circumstances. His father was quarrelling with his mother and was also inclined to be a "collaborator"; his elder brother had been killed in the German offensive of 1940 and this young man, with a sentiment somewhat primitive but generous, burned to avenge him. His mother was living alone with him, deeply afflicted by the semi-treason of his father and by the death of her eldest son, and her one consolation was in this young man. But he, at this moment, had the choice between going to England to join the Free French Forces or of staying near his mother and helping her to live. He fully realised that this woman lived only for him and that his disappearance—or perhaps his death—would plunge her into despair. He also realised that, concretely and in fact, every action he performed on his mother's behalf would be sure of effect in the sense of aiding her to live, whereas anything he did in order to go and fight would be an ambiguous action which might vanish like water into sand and serve no purpose. For instance, to set out for England he would have to wait indefinitely in a Spanish camp on the way through Spain; or, on arriving in England or in Algiers he might be put into an office to fill up forms. Consequently, he found himself confronted by two very different modes of action; the one concrete, immediate, but directed towards only one individual; and the other an action addressed to an end infinitely greater, a national collectivity, but for that very reason ambiguous—and it might be frustrated on the way. At the same time, he was hesitating between two kinds of morality; on the one side the morality of sympathy, of personal devotion and, on the other side, a morality of wider scope but of more debatable validity. He had to choose between those two. What could help him to choose? Could the Christian doctrine? No. Christian doctrine says: Act with charity, love your neighbour, deny yourself for others, choose the way which is hardest, and so forth. But which is the harder road? To whom does one owe the more brotherly love, the patriot or the mother? Which is the more useful aim, the general one of fighting in and for the whole community, or the precise aim of helping one particular person to live? Who can give an answer to that *a priori*? No one. Nor is it given in any ethical scripture. The Kantian ethic says, Never regard another as a means, but always as an end. Very well; if I remain with my mother, I shall be regarding her as the end and not as a means: but by the same token I am in danger of treating as means those who are fighting on my behalf; and the converse is also true, that if I go to the aid of the combatants I shall be treating them as the end at the risk of treating my mother as a means.

If values are uncertain, if they are still too abstract to determine the particular, concrete case under consideration, nothing remains but to trust in our instincts. That is what this young man tried to do; and when I saw him he said, "In the end, it is feeling that counts; the direction in which it is really pushing me is the one I ought to choose. If I feel that I love my mother enough to sacrifice everything else for her—my will to be avenged, all my longings for action and adventure—then I stay with her.

If, on the contrary, I feel that my love for her is not enough, I go." But how does one estimate the strength of a feeling? The value of his feeling for his mother was determined precisely by the fact that he was standing by her. I may say that I love a certain friend enough to sacrifice such or such a sum of money for him, but I cannot prove that unless I have done it. I may say, "I love my mother enough to remain with her," if actually I have remained with her. I can only estimate the strength of this affection if I have performed an action by which it is defined and ratified. But if I then appeal to this affection to justify my action, I find myself drawn into a vicious circle.

Moreover, as Gide has very well said, a sentiment which is play-acting and one which is vital are two things that are hardly distinguishable one from another. To decide that I love my mother by staying beside her, and to play a comedy the upshot of which is that I do so—these are nearly the same thing. In other words, feeling is formed by the deeds that one does; therefore I cannot consult it as a guide to action. And that is to say that I can neither seek within myself for an authentic impulse to action, nor can I expect, from some ethic, formulae that will enable me to act. You may say that the youth did, at least, go to a professor to ask for advice. But if you seek counsel—from a priest, for example—you have selected that priest; and at bottom you already knew, more or less, what he would advise. In other words, to choose an adviser is nevertheless to commit oneself by that choice. If you are a Christian, you will say, Consult a priest; but there are collaborationists, priests who are resisters and priests who wait for the tide to turn: which will you choose? Had this young man chosen a priest of the resistance, or one of the collaboration, he would have decided beforehand the kind of advice he was to receive. Similarly, in coming to me, he knew what advice I should give him, and I had but one reply to make. You are free, therefore choose—that is to say, invent. No rule of general morality can show you what you ought to do: no signs are vouchsafed in this world. The Catholics will reply, "Oh, but they are!" Very well; still, it is I myself, in every case, who have to interpret the signs. Whilst I was imprisoned, I made the acquaintance of a somewhat remarkable man, a Jesuit, who had become a member of that order in the following manner. In his life he had suffered a succession of rather severe setbacks. His father had died when he was a child, leaving him in poverty, and he had been awarded a free scholarship in a religious institution, where he had been made continually to feel that he was accepted for charity's sake, and, in consequence, he had been denied several of those distinctions and honours which gratify children. Later, about the age of eighteen, he came to grief in a sentimental affair; and finally, at twenty-two—this was a trifle in itself, but it was the last drop that overflowed his cup—he failed in his military examination. This young man, then, could regard himself as a total failure: it was a sign—but a sign of what? He might have taken refuge in bitterness and despair. But he took it—very cleverly for him—as a sign that he was not intended for secular successes, and that only the attainments of religion, those of sanctity and of faith, were accessible to him. He interpreted his record as a message from God, and became a member of the Order. Who can doubt but that this decision as to the meaning of the sign was his, and his alone? One could have drawn quite different conclusions from such a series of reverses—as, for example, that he had better become a carpenter or a revolutionary. For the decipherment of the sign, however, he bears the entire responsibility. That is what "abandonment" implies, that we ourselves decide our being. And with this abandonment goes anguish.

As for "despair," the meaning of this expression is extremely simple. It merely means that we limit ourselves to a reliance upon that which is within our wills, or within the sum of the probabilities which render our action feasible. Whenever one wills anything, there are always these elements of probability. If I am counting upon a visit from a friend, who may be coming by train or by tram, I presuppose that the train will arrive at the appointed time, or that the tram will not be derailed. I remain in the realm of possibilities; but one does not rely upon any possibilities beyond those that are strictly concerned in one's action. Beyond the point at which the possibilities under consideration cease to affect my action, I ought to disinterest myself. For there is no God and no prevenient design, which can adapt the world and all its possibilities to my will. When Descartes said, "Conquer yourself rather than the world," what he meant was, at bottom, the same—that we should act without hope.

Marxists, to whom I have said this, have answered: "Your action is limited, obviously, by your death; but you can rely upon the help of others. That is, you can count both upon what the others are doing to help you elsewhere, as in China and in Russia, and upon what they will do later, after your death, to take up your action and carry it forward to its final accomplishment which will be the revolution. Moreover you must rely upon this; not to do so is immoral." To this I rejoin, first, that I shall always count upon my comrades-in-arms in the struggle, in so far as they are committed, as I am, to a definite, common cause; and in the unity of a party or a group which I can more or less control—that is, in which I am enrolled as a militant and whose movements at every moment are known to me. In that respect, to rely upon the unity and the will of the party is exactly like my reckoning that the train will run to time or that the tram will not be derailed. But I cannot count upon men whom I do not know, I cannot base my confidence upon human goodness or upon man's interest in the good of society, seeing that man is free and that there is no human nature which I can take as foundational. I do not know whither the Russian revolution will lead. I can admire it and take it as an example in so far as it is evident, to-day, that the proletariat plays a part in Russia which it has attained in no other nation. But I cannot affirm that this will necessarily lead to the triumph of the proletariat: I must confine myself to what I can see. Nor can I be sure that comrades-in-arms will take up my work after my death and carry it to the maximum perfection, seeing that those men are free agents and will freely decide, to-morrow, what man is then to be. To-morrow, after my death, some men may decide to establish Fascism, and the others may be so cowardly or so slack as to let them do so. If so, Fascism will then be the truth of man, and so much the worse for us. In reality, things will be such as men have decided they shall be. Does that mean that I should abandon myself to quietism? No. First I ought to commit myself and then act my commitment, according to the time-honoured formula that "one need not hope in order to undertake one's work." Nor does this mean that I should not belong to a party, but only that I should be without illusion and that I should do what I can. For instance, if I ask myself "Will the social ideal as such, ever become a reality?" I cannot tell, I only know that whatever may be in my power to make it so, I shall do; beyond that, I can count upon nothing.

Quietism is the attitude of people who say, "let others do what I cannot do." The doctrine I am presenting before you is precisely the opposite of this, since it declares that there is no reality except in action. It goes further, indeed, and adds, "Man is nothing else but what he purposes, he exists only in so far as he realises himself, he is therefore nothing else but the sum of his actions, nothing else but what his life is." Hence we can well understand why some people are horrified by our teaching. For many have but one resource to sustain them in their misery, and that is to think, "Circumstances have been against me, I was worthy to be something much better than I have been. I admit I have never had a great love or a great friendship; but that is because I never met a man or a woman who were worthy of it; if I have not written any very good books, it is because I had not the leisure to do so; or, if I have had no children to whom I could devote myself it is because I did not find the man I could have lived with. So there remains within me a wide range of abilities, inclinations and potentialities, unused but perfectly viable, which endow me with a worthiness that could never be inferred from the mere history of my actions." But in reality and for the existentialist, there is no love apart from the deeds of love; no potentiality of love other than that which is manifested in loving; there is no genius other than that which is expressed in works of art. The genius of Proust is the totality of the works of Proust; the genius of Racine is the series of his tragedies, outside of which there is nothing. Why should we attribute to Racine the capacity to write yet another tragedy when that is precisely what he did not write? In life, a man commits himself, draws his own portrait and there is nothing but that portrait. No doubt this thought may seem comfortless to one who has not made a success of his life. On the other hand, it puts everyone in a position to understand that reality alone is reliable; that dreams, expectations and hopes serve to define a man only as deceptive dreams, abortive hopes, expectations unfulfilled; that is to say, they define him negatively, not positively. Nevertheless, when one says, "You are nothing else but what you live," it does not imply that an artist is to be judged solely by his works of art, for a thousand other things contribute no less to his definition as a man. What we mean to say is that a man is no other than a series of undertakings, that he is the sum, the organisation, the set of relations that constitute these undertakings.]

CHAPTER IX

Pragmatism and Meaning:

Charles Sanders Peirce (1839–1914)

I HAVE ALREADY INDICATED WHY I SHALL CHOOSE PASSAGES from the writings of American pragmatists for the middle part of this volume, the point being that in certain respects pragmatism mediates between the extremes represented by the philosophers dealt with in the first and third parts, between the bold, speculative brush strokes of Whitehead, Bergson, and Croce, and the minute, pointillist philosophizing of Moore and Wittgenstein, between the coursing spirit of time-conscious metaphysicians and the placid *mots justes* of logicians. William James gave classic expression to the view of pragmatism as a mediating philosophy when he spoke of its reconciliation of his famous two extremes, the tender- and the tough-minded. In his *Pragmatism* of 1907 James formulated a sort of philosophical box score in which he divided philosophers, in fact, all mankind, into two spiritual teams:

THE TENDER-MINDED	THE TOUGH-MINDED
Rationalistic (going by "principles")	Empiricist (going by "facts")
Intellectualistic	Sensationalistic
Idealistic	Materialistic
Optimistic	Pessimistic
Religious	Irreligious
Free-Willist	Fatalistic
Monistic	Pluralistic
Dogmatical	Sceptical

James tried to mediate between these two sets of doctrinal attitudes by offering, as he said, "the oddly-named thing pragmatism as a philosophy that can satisfy both kinds of demands. It can remain religious like the rationalisms, but at the same time, like the empiricisms, it can preserve the richest intimacy with facts." James's contrast between tender religion and tough science must be read in the light of the divided legacy of the nineteenth century, which had presented him with an athletic materialism and an idealism permeated by the teatime atmosphere of Oxford or the evangelical bravado of his colleague Josiah Royce. A similar contrast had dominated American thought from the beginning.

The most conspicuous thing about the development of American philosophy is its oscillation between doctrines that are essentially religious, idealistic, or supernatural on the one hand, and scientific, secular, or naturalistic on the other. The usual, substantially accurate, textbook account begins with a period of philosophical theology that reaches its most striking expression in Jonathan Edwards' angry

God and subjective idealism. The next part of the history is usually given over to the Enlightenment, with its devotion to science in the case of Benjamin Franklin, to what John Dewey has called the experimentalism of Thomas Jefferson, and to popular expressions of Deism in the case of Tom Paine. Then we come to transcendentalism in the early part of the nineteenth century. It is the spiral nebula of our intellectual history, a spinning literary revolt against British empiricism which was led by Ralph Waldo Emerson. It is anti-lockeian, anti-humeian, anti-materialistic, and in all of this it converges with American versions of the Scottish philosophy, however different the Scots and the transcendentalists may be in other respects. The Scottish philosophy tried to meet Hume's skepticism with dogmatism of the driest, dullest kind, as might be expected from a philosophy partly derived from the learned but deadly Sir William Hamilton. Transcendentalist philosophy leaned heavily on Coleridge's garbled versions of post-kantian idealism.

The ideological curve that runs from Edwards to Jefferson to Emerson and the Scottish philosophy, therefore, is tender, tough, and tender again. But then at the height of what John Stuart Mill called "Germano-Coleridgean" and Scottish power, Darwin and Spencer initiated a new period of toughness in English and American philosophy. The *Origin of Species* appeared in 1859 and its impact on American and English thinking was almost instantaneous. It not only stimulated and supported a biologically oriented philosophy like that of the Americans Chauncey Wright and Charles Peirce, but it stiffened the resistance of the tender-minded as well. Those who fought the wave of Spencerian evolutionism and agnosticism at the end of the nineteenth century became much more hardened philosophically than the sweet singers of transcendental airs. The later idealists in Britain, like T. H. Green, John and Edward Caird, and then Bradley and McTaggart whom we have already mentioned, had to defend their concern for the inner life and spiritual values in the face of the great prestige of science; they had to show that the achievements of physics, biology, and technology were not merely grist for naturalistic, positivistic, materialistic, and agnostic mills. Idealism and the more traditionally religious philosophies were forced to show that their views were consistent with evolutionary doctrine. Some idealists like Royce and the young John Dewey did this with a vengeance. They argued that far from being inconsistent with evolution, idealism was vindicated by it, that evolution was the scientific confirmation of a truth which historically minded idealists had originated and seen, perhaps through a glass darkly.

This backward glance makes it easier to explain William James's important role in American philosophy. He came upon the scene when philosophy was being bullied by a tough and militant scientism, but the only organized alternative seemed to be the absolute idealism of the neo-hegelians which he could not stomach. He was the son of Henry James, Sr., a transcendentalist friend of Emerson and interpreter of Swedenborg the ghost-seer; he was the brother of the great novelist Henry James. He wanted facts but he also wanted a religion. But with Herbert Spencer the custodian of facts and Francis Herbert Bradley the custodian of The Absolute, James felt obliged to apply elsewhere. He thought of himself as an empiricist in the tradition of Locke, Berkeley, Hume, and Mill, but he was upset by the strident materialism and agnosticism into which empiricism had developed at the end of the nineteenth century. And so he looked for some device that would limit the sovereignty of science, something that would silence the bark of "Darwin's bull-dog," T. H. Huxley, and calm that *enfant terrible* of agnosticism, W. K. Clifford.

In 1877 Clifford had said "It is wrong in all cases to believe on insufficient evidence; and where it is presumption to doubt and to investigate, there it is worse than presumption to believe." Partly in response to this James produced what is perhaps his most famous essay on religious matters, "The Will to Believe" (of 1896), which he later said he should have called "The *Right* to Believe" simply because it defended a right that Clifford and other agnostics had denied. One year later James brought out a volume which featured this piece as title essay and carried a dedication to Charles Sanders Peirce. This publicly dates the beginning of one of the most important chapters in recent philosophy, for another year later in 1898 James delivered a lecture called "Philosophical Conceptions and Practical Results" in which he reminded the philosophical world of Peirce's founding of pragmatism in 1878.

By a number of moves which we shall observe later James transformed Peirce's pragmatism and what may be called his semantical agnosticism into a much more tender and tendentious thing. James, as we shall see, was not up to the austerity and the forbearance that Peirce's doctrine entailed. He was not satisfied with a logical principle that merely helped explicate or analyze the concepts of science; he wanted a device that would resolve his own spiritual turmoil and that of the age. To understand the pattern of his thinking and the development of pragmatism we must turn to Peirce, who is a very important philosopher in his own right and according to some the greatest philosopher America has ever produced.

Peirce was born in Cambridge, Massachusetts, in 1839, the son of the distinguished mathematician Benjamin Peirce. His father encouraged his early interests in mathematics, science, philosophy, and even more esoteric matters. It is reported that the father tried to teach the son the art of concentration "at a tender age" by playing rapid games of double dummy with him that lasted from 10 P.M. to dawn; that when Charles began to read philosophers in his teens his father would get him to repeat their proofs "and in a very few words would usually rip them up and show them empty"; that his father encouraged his "sensory discrimination" to the point where the young man studied to be a semi-professional winetaster. In other respects the relation between them is said to have been "idyllic," but one wonders whether Peirce's later unhappiness and chaotic personal life may have been connected with his life with father; one cannot avoid thinking of John Stuart Mill's life with his.

During his life Peirce never published a book on philosophy and it was left to admiring editors to produce six posthumous volumes of *Collected Papers* (1931-35) in which most of his scattered contributions were brought into some kind of pattern. He has experienced several revivals and pilgrimages since James revived him in 1898 (when he was still alive and able to defend himself). Logicians and philosophers under the influence of logical positivism hailed him as a forerunner in the thirties, and more recently it has become fashionable to remind the world that he was not merely a great logician and philosopher of science but also a transcendental metaphysician of immense stature.

Glimpses of Peirce's life suggest a romantic novel or a nineteenth-century opera: financial difficulties, marital difficulties, professional difficulties, pleading letters, nagging controversies, unfinished plans. He never received the academic recognition his brilliance merited and he died without the literary fame that is sometimes compensatory. His work as a mathematical logician was known to tiny European audiences when he was unknown in America, much as the great Yale physicist Willard Gibbs was more famous abroad than in his own New Haven. For most of his life Peirce was treated as a skeleton in a Cambridge closet, a brilliant unemployable who had to be befriended by saintly people like William James; he was thought to be incapable of making himself intelligible or attractive to Victorian academic audiences.

After Peirce's death in 1914 and the publication of his *Collected Papers* twenty years later, the pendulum swung far in the other direction. Adulation without complete understanding followed the first exhibition of his pragmatic and logical nuggets, but we are now on the verge of a full and sober evaluation of his more technical contributions as well as of the larger architectonic system into which Peirce tried so unsuccessfully to fit them. For our present purposes he is best viewed as the founder of pragmatism, since that is a doctrine which made him famous and a doctrine which should have made him famous. I select from his classic paper "How to Make Our Ideas Clear" in spite of its nineteenth century date (1878), taking the liberty of interpreting the phrase "twentieth century" ideologically, as it were, and not chronologically, since

pragmatism is spiritually of the twentieth century. There
are formulations of it which Peirce wrote after 1900 but
numerology should not keep from the reader one of the
most readable and influential expressions of his doctrine.

The main purpose of Peirce's pragmatism is to help us
explain the meanings of general terms, that is, common
nouns or adjectives as they are used by scientists, with the
implication that if we cannot assign a meaning by this
method, the term in question is meaningless from a scientific point of view. Take, for example, the predicate or
general term "hard." To specify its pragmatic meaning,
Peirce said, we must translate the sentence "This is hard"
into something like "If one were to try to scratch this, one
would not succeed." In general Peirce recommends that we
take an ordinary categorical singular statement in which we
apply a predicate to an object (like "This is hard") and
translate it into a conditional or hypothetical statement,
that is to say, an "if-then" statement of the following form:
"If operation O were to be performed on this, then E
would be experienced." On this view "This book is heavy"
is to be translated as "If all opposing forces on this book
were to be removed (like the force one exerts by holding it
in one's hand), this book would fall." Sometimes one gets
the impression that a single "if-then" statement can suffice
for such a translation, sometimes very many are needed,
sometimes an indefinite number, but that is a complicated
matter into which we cannot enter here. It has been carefully studied by a number of logicians under Peirce's influence—notably by C. I. Lewis in his *Mind and the World-
Order* (1929) and *An Analysis of Knowledge and Valuation* (1946)—and many subtleties and difficulties in the
formulation have been revealed.

The doctrine as Peirce presented it is compounded of
three prime elements that deserve labeling. First of all its
hypotheticalism, that is to say, its insistence on our translat-
ing singular statements into hypothetical form before we
can discover their pragmatic meanings. Secondly, its
operationalism, or insistence that the "if"-clause mention
a human operation, something that an experimenter does.
Thirdly, its *experientialism,* or its insistence that the

"then"-clause mention something experienced or observed by the experimenter after the test conditions have been instituted.

Two important consequences of this approach must be mentioned. First of all, if a general term resists, or if the person using it does not supply such a translation upon demand, the term must be regarded as meaningless. Naturally, it may evoke images or stimulate emotion but it is scientifically meaningless. Secondly, if the pragmatic translations or definitions of two general terms are the same, then the two terms are pragmatically or scientifically synonymous no matter how different they are in other respects. In particular, the disregard of the images called up by the term represents Peirce's opposition to the tradition of Descartes and Berkeley on the subject of meaning. These two consequences give rise to what I have called Peirce's "semantical agnosticism" for they require a noncommittal attitude toward a good deal of traditional metaphysics and theology. Peirce thought that serious application of the first consequence might show many metaphysical and theological terms meaningless; serious application of the second might show certain disputes to be pseudo disputes, merely arguments about what words to use in reports of the same experiment. Instead of saying as an ordinary agnostic might that one did not have sufficient evidence for a theological statement or its opposite, and therefore that one would have to suspend judgment, the semantic agnostic achieves a similar practical effect by calling the statement meaningless or deciding that the supposedly opposed statements mean the same thing. In physics this pragmatic attitude later converged with the kind of *operationalism* which many philosophical physicists based on Einstein's theory of relativity, chiefly because Einstein urged the need for a definition of simu'taneity which would supply an experimental method for testing whether or not two events occurred simultaneously.

In spite of the obscurity in which Peirce wrapped a good deal of his advice about clarity, most students of his philosophy regard the view just formulated as the kernel of his pragmatism. They frequently call it "the pragmatic theory

of meaning" which they identify with Peirce, as opposed
to the "pragmatic theory of truth" which is usually associated with James. Some go so far as to say that James's
great misunderstanding of Peirce arose from his failure
to see that Peirce's pragmatism was merely concerned with
meaning, and that James *added* a questionable theory of
truth. I shall have something to say about the justice of this
when we consider James's pragmatism in the next chapter,
but it should be realized already that Peirce's doctrine cannot be used automatically for the kind of reconciliation that
James so ardently desired. By itself Peirce's pragmatism
could not have bridged the gaps between opposite members
of the tender-minded and the tough-minded teams, and
used aggressively it might have even led to the un-Jamesian
conclusion that they were all saying the same thing or all
saying nothing. That would have plagued both their houses
rather than have reconciled them; in fact it was one of the
things that logical positivists of a later generation admired
in Peirce—his attack on "ontological metaphysics." His
effect on James was very, very different.

The following selection is an extract from Peirce's essay,
"How to Make Our Ideas Clear." [1]

[What . . . is belief? It is the demi-cadence which closes
a musical phrase in the symphony of our intellectual life.
We have seen that it has just three properties: First, it is
something that we are aware of; second, it appeases the
irritation of doubt; and, third, it involves the establishment
in our nature of a rule of action, or say for short, a *habit*.
As it appeases the irritation of doubt, which is the motive
for thinking, thought relaxes, and comes to rest for a
moment when belief is reached. But, since belief is a rule
for action, the application of which involves further doubt
and further thought, at the same time that it is a stopping-
place, it is also a new starting-place for thought. That is
why I have permitted myself to call it thought at rest, although thought is essentially an action. The *final* upshot of
thinking is the exercise of volition, and of this thought no
longer forms a part; but belief is only a stadium of mental

action, an effect upon our nature due to thought, which will influence future thinking.

The essence of belief is the establishment of a habit, and different beliefs are distinguished by the different modes of action to which they give rise. If beliefs do not differ in this respect, if they appease the same doubt by producing the same rule of action, then no mere differences in the manner of consciousness of them can make them different beliefs, any more than playing a tune in different keys is playing different tunes. Imaginary distinctions are often drawn between beliefs which differ only in their mode of expression;—the wrangling which ensues is real enough, however. . . . Such false distinctions do as much harm as the confusion of beliefs really different, and are among the pitfalls of which we ought constantly to beware, especially when we are upon metaphysical ground. One singular deception of this sort, which often occurs, is to mistake the sensation produced by our own unclearness of thought for a character of the object we are thinking. Instead of perceiving that the obscurity is purely subjective, we fancy that we contemplate a quality of the object which is essentially mysterious; and if our conception be afterward presented to us in a clear form we do not recognize it as the same, owing to the absence of the feeling of unintelligibility. So long as this deception lasts, it obviously puts an impassable barrier in the way of perspicuous thinking; so that it equally interests the opponents of rational thought to perpetuate it, and its adherents to guard against it.

Another such deception is to mistake a mere difference in the grammatical construction of two words for a distinction between the ideas they express. In this pedantic age, when the general mob of writers attend so much more to words than to things, this error is common enough. When I just said that thought is an *action*, and that it consists in a *relation*, although a person performs an action but not a relation, which can only be the result of an action, yet there was no inconsistency in what I said, but only a grammatical vagueness.

From all these sophisms we shall be perfectly safe so long as we reflect that the whole function of thought is to produce habits of action; and that whatever there is connected with a thought, but irrelevant to its purpose, is an accretion to it, but no part of it. If there be a unity among our sensations which has no reference to how we shall act on a given occasion, as when we listen to a piece of music, why we do not call that thinking. To develop its meaning we have, therefore, simply to determine what habits it produces, for what a thing means is simply what habits it involves. Now, the identity of a habit depends on how it might lead us to act, not merely under such circumstances as are likely to arise, but under such as might possibly occur, no matter how improbable they may be. What the habit is depends on *when* and *how* it causes us to act. As for the *when,* every stimulus of action is derived from perception; as for the *how,* every purpose of action is to produce some sensible result. Thus, we come down to what is tangible and practical, as the root of every real distinction of thought, no matter how subtle it may be; and there is no distinction of meaning so fine as to consist in anything but a possible difference of practice.

To see what this principle leads to, consider in the light of it such a doctrine as that of transubstantiation. The Protestant churches generally hold that the elements of the sacrament are flesh and blood only in a tropical sense; they nourish our souls as meat and the juice of it would our bodies. But the Catholics maintain that they are literally just that; although they possess all the sensible qualities of wafer-cakes and diluted wine. But we can have no conception of wine except what may enter into a belief, either—

1. That this, that, or the other, is wine; or,
2. That wine possesses certain properties.

Such beliefs are nothing but self-notifications that we should, upon occasion, act in regard to such things as we believe to be wine according to the qualities which we believe wine to possess. The occasion of such action would be some sensible perception, the motive of it to produce some sensible result. Thus our action has exclusive reference to what affects the senses, our habit has the same bearing as our action, our belief the same as our habit, our

conception the same as our belief; and we can consequently
mean nothing by wine but what has certain effects, direct
or indirect, upon our senses; and to talk of something as
having all the sensible characters of wine, yet being in
reality blood, is senseless jargon. Now, it is not my object
to pursue the theological question; and having used it as
a logical example I drop it, without caring to anticipate
the theologian's reply. I only desire to point out how impossible it is that we should have an idea in our minds
which relates to anything but conceived sensible effects of
things. Our idea of anything *is* our idea of its sensible
effects; and if we fancy that we have any other we deceive
ourselves, and mistake a mere sensation accompanying the
thought for a part of the thought itself. It is absurd to say
that thought has any meaning unrelated to its only function. It is foolish for Catholics and Protestants to fancy
themselves in disagreement about the elements of the sacrament, if they agree in regard to all their sensible effects,
here or hereafter.

It appears, then, that the rule for attaining the third
grade of clearness of apprehension is as follows: Consider
what effects, which might conceivably have practical bear-
ings, we conceive the object of our conception to have.
Then, our conception of these effects is the whole of our
conception of the object.

Let us illustrate this rule by some examples; and, to
begin with the simplest one possible, let us ask what we
mean by calling a thing *hard*. Evidently that it will not be
scratched by many other substances. The whole conception of this quality, as of every other, lies in its conceived
effects. There is absolutely no difference between a hard
thing and a soft thing so long as they are not brought to the
test. Suppose, then, that a diamond could be crystallized
in the midst of a cushion of soft cotton, and should remain
there until it was finally burned up. Would it be false to say
that that diamond was soft? This seems a foolish question,
and would be so, in fact, except in the realm of logic.
There such questions are often of the greatest utility as
serving to bring logical principles into sharper relief than

real discussions ever could. In studying logic we must not put them aside with hasty answers, but must consider them with attentive care, in order to make out the principles involved. We may, in the present case, modify our question, and ask what prevents us from saying that all hard bodies remain perfectly soft until they are touched, when their hardness increases with the pressure until they are scratched. Reflection will show that the reply is this: there would be no *falsity* in such modes of speech. They would involve a modification of our present usage of speech with regard to the words hard and soft, but not of their meanings. For they represent no fact to be different from what it is; only they involve arrangements of facts which would be exceedingly maladroit. This leads us to remark that the question of what would occur under circumstances which do not actually arise is not a question of fact, but only of the most perspicuous arrangement of them. For example, the question of free-will and fate in its simplest form, stripped of verbiage, is something like this: I have done something of which I am ashamed; could I, by an effort of the will, have resisted the temptation, and done otherwise? The philosophical reply is, that this is not a question of fact, but only of the arrangement of facts. Arranging them so as to exhibit what is particularly pertinent to my question—namely, that I ought to blame myself for having done wrong—it is perfectly true to say that, if I had willed to do otherwise than I did, I should have done otherwise. On the other hand, arranging the facts so as to exhibit another important consideration, it is equally true that, when a temptation has once been allowed to work, it will, if it has a certain force, produce its effect, let me struggle how I may. There is no objection to a contradiction in what would result from a false supposition. The *reductio ad absurdum* consists in showing that contradictory results would follow from a hypothesis which is consequently judged to be false. Many questions are involved in the free-will discussion, and I am far from desiring to say that both sides are equally right. On the contrary, I am of opinion that one side denies important facts, and that the other does not. But what I do say is, that the above single question was the origin of the whole doubt; that, had it not been for this question, the controversy would never have arisen; and that this question is perfectly solved in the manner which I have indicated.

Let us next seek a clear idea of Weight. This is another very easy case. To say that a body is heavy means simply that, in the absence of opposing force, it will fall. This (neglecting certain specifications of how it will fall, etc., which exist in the mind of the physicist who uses the word) is evidently the whole conception of weight. It is a fair question whether some particular facts may not *account* for gravity; but what we mean by the force itself is completely involved in its effects. . . .

Let us now approach the subject of logic, and consider a conception which particularly concerns it, that of *reality*. Taking clearness in the sense of familiarity, no idea could be clearer than this. Every child uses it with perfect confidence, never dreaming that he does not understand it. As for clearness in its second grade, however, it would probably puzzle most men, even among those of a reflective turn of mind, to give an abstract definition of the real. Yet such a definition may perhaps be reached by considering the points of difference between reality and its opposite, fiction. A figment is a product of somebody's imagination; it has such characters as his thought impresses upon it. That those characters are independent of how you or I think is an external reality. There are, however, phenomena within our own minds, dependent upon our thought, which are at the same time real in the sense that we really think them. But though their characters depend on how we think, they do not depend on what we think those characters to be. Thus, a dream has a real existence as a mental phenomenon, if somebody has really dreamt it; that he dreamt so and so, does not depend on what anybody thinks was dreamt, but is completely independent of all opinion on the subject. On the other hand, considering not the fact of dreaming, but the thing dreamt, it retains its peculiarities by virtue of no other fact than that it was dreamt to possess them. Thus we may define the real as that whose characters are independent of what anybody may think them to be.

But, however satisfactory such a definition may be found, it would be a great mistake to suppose that it makes the idea of reality perfectly clear. Here, then, let us apply our rules. According to them, reality, like every other quality, consists in the peculiar sensible effects which things partaking of it produce. The only effect which real things have is to cause belief, for all the sensations which they excite emerge into consciousness in the form of beliefs. The question, therefore, is, how is true belief (or belief in the real) distinguished from false belief (or belief in fiction). Now, as we have seen in the former paper, the ideas of truth and falsehood, in their full development, appertain exclusively to the scientific method of settling opinion. A person who arbitrarily chooses the propositions which he will adopt can use the word truth only to emphasize the expression of his determination to hold on to his choice. Of course, the method of tenacity never prevailed exclusively; reason is too natural to men for that. But in the literature of the dark ages we find some fine examples of it. When Scotus Erigena is commenting upon a poetical passage in which hellebore is spoken of as having caused the death of Socrates, he does not hesitate to inform the inquiring reader that Helleborus and Socrates were two eminent Greek philosophers, and that the latter having been overcome in argument by the former took the matter to heart and died of it! What sort of idea of truth could a man have who could adopt and teach, without the qualification of a perhaps, an opinion taken so entirely at random? The real spirit of Socrates, who I hope would have been delighted to have been "overcome in argument," because he would have learned something by it, is in curious contrast with the naïve idea of the glossist, for whom discussion would seem to have been simply a struggle. When philosophy began to awake from its long slumber, and before theology completely dominated it, the practice seems to have been for each professor to seize upon any philosophical position he found unoccupied and which seemed a strong one, to intrench himself in it, and to sally forth from time to time to give battle to the others. Thus, even the scanty records we possess of those disputes enable us to make out a dozen or more opinions held by different teachers at one time concerning the question of nominalism and realism. Read the opening part of the *Historia Calamitatum* of Abélard, who was certainly as philosophical as any of his contemporaries, and see the spirit of combat which it breathes. For him, the truth is simply his particular stronghold. When the method of authority prevailed, the truth meant little more than the Catholic faith. All the efforts of the scholastic doctors are directed toward harmonizing their faith in Aristotle and their faith in the Church, and one may search their ponderous folios through without finding an argument which goes any further. It is noticeable that where different faiths flourish side by side, renegades are looked upon with contempt even by the party whose belief they adopt; so completely has the idea of loyalty replaced that of truth-seeking. Since the time of Descartes, the defect in the conception of truth has been less apparent. Still, it will sometimes strike a scientific man that the philosophers have been less intent on finding out what the facts are, than on inquiring what belief is most in harmony with their system. It is hard to convince a follower of the *a priori* method by adducing facts; but show him that an opinion he is defending is inconsistent with what he has laid down elsewhere, and he will be very apt to retract it. These minds do not seem to believe that disputation is ever to cease; they seem to think that the opinion which is natural for one man is not so for another, and that belief will, consequently, never be settled. In contenting themselves with fixing their own opinions by a method which would lead another man to a different result, they betray their feeble hold of the conception of what truth is.

On the other hand, all the followers of science are fully persuaded that the processes of investigation, if only pushed far enough, will give one certain solution to every question to which they can be applied. One man may investigate the velocity of light by studying the transits of Venus and the aberration of the stars; another by the oppositions of Mars and the eclipses of Jupiter's satellites; a third by the method of Fizeau; a fourth by that of Foucault; a fifth by the motions of the curves of Lissajoux; a sixth, a seventh, an eighth, and a ninth, may follow the different methods of comparing the measures of statical and dynamical electricity. They may at first obtain different results, but, as each perfects his method and his processes, the results will move steadily together toward a destined center. So with all scientific research. Different minds may set out with the most antagonistic views, but the progress of investigation carries them by a force outside of themselves to one and the same conclusion. This activity of thought by which we are carried, not where we wish, but to a foreordained goal, is like the operation of destiny. No modification of the point of view taken, no selection of other facts for study, no natural bent of mind even, can enable a man to escape the predestinate opinion. This great law is embodied in the conception of truth and reality. The opinion which is fated* to be ultimately agreed to by all who investigate, is what we mean by the truth, and the object represented in this opinion is the real. That is the way I would explain reality.

But it may be said that this view is directly opposed to the abstract definition which we have given of reality, inasmuch as it makes the characters of the real depend on what is ultimately thought about them. But the answer to this is that, on the one hand, reality is independent, not necessarily of thought in general, but only of what you or I or any finite number of men may think about it; and that, on the other hand, though the object of the final opinion depends on what that opinion is, yet what that opinion is does not depend on what you or I or any man thinks. Our perversity and that of others may indefinitely postpone the settlement of opinion; it might even conceivably cause an arbitrary proposition to be universally accepted as long as the human race should last. Yet even that would not change the nature of the belief, which alone could be the result of

* Fate means merely that which is sure to come true, and can nohow be avoided. It is a superstition to suppose that a certain sort of events are ever fated, and it is another to suppose that the word fate can never be freed from its superstitious taint. We are all fated to die. AUTHOR'S NOTE.

investigation carried sufficiently far; and if, after the extinction of our race, another should arise with faculties and disposition for investigation, that true opinion must be the one which they would ultimately come to. "Truth crushed to earth shall rise again," and the opinion which would finally result from investigation does not depend on how anybody may actually think. But the reality of that which is real does depend on the real fact that investigation is destined to lead, at last, if continued long enough, to a belief in it.

But I may be asked what I have to say to all the minute facts of history, forgotten never to be recovered, to the lost books of the ancients, to the buried secrets.

> "Full many a gem of purest ray serene
>   The dark, unfathomed caves of ocean bear;
> Full many a flower is born to blush unseen,
>   And waste its sweetness on the desert air."

Do these things not really exist because they are hopelessly beyond the reach of our knowledge? And then, after the universe is dead (according to the prediction of some scientists), and all life has ceased forever, will not the shock of atoms continue though there will be no mind to know it? To this I reply that, though in no possible state of knowledge can any number be great enough to express the relation between the amount of what rests unknown to the amount of the known, yet it is unphilosophical to suppose that, with regard to any given question (which has any clear meaning), investigation would not bring forth a solution of it, if it were carried far enough. Who would have said, a few years ago, that we could ever know of what substances stars are made whose light may have been longer in reaching us than the human race has existed? Who can be sure of what we shall not know in a few hundred years? Who can guess what would be the result of continuing the pursuit of science for ten thousand years, with the activity of the last hundred? And if it were to go on for a million, or a billion, or any number of years you please, how is it possible to say that there is any question which might not ultimately be solved?

But it may be objected, "Why make so much of these remote considerations, especially when it is your principle that only practical distinctions have a meaning?" Well, I must confess that it makes very little difference whether we say that a stone on the bottom of the ocean, in complete darkness, is brilliant or not—that is to say, that it *probably* makes no difference, remembering always that that stone *may* be fished up to-morrow. But that there are gems at the bottom of the sea, flowers in the untraveled desert, etc., are propositions which, like that about a diamond being hard when it is not pressed, concern much more the arrangement of our language than they do the meaning of our ideas.

It seems to me, however, that we have, by the application of our rule, reached so clear an apprehension of what we mean by reality, and of the fact which the idea rests on, that we should not, perhaps, be making a pretension so presumptuous as it would be singular, if we were to offer a metaphysical theory of existence for universal acceptance among those who employ the scientific method of fixing belief. However, as metaphysics is a subject much more curious thán useful, the knowledge of which, like that of a sunken reef, serves chiefly to enable us to keep clear of it, I will not trouble the reader with any more Ontology at this moment. I have already been led much further into that path than I should have desired; and I have given the reader such a dose of mathematics, psychology, and all that is most abstruse, that I fear he may already have left me, and that what I am now writing is for the compositor and proofreader exclusively. I trusted to the importance of the subject. There is no royal road to logic, and really valuable ideas can only be had at the price of close attention. But I know that in the matter of ideas the public prefer the cheap and nasty; and in my next paper I am going to return to the easily intelligible, and not wander from it again. The reader who has been at the pains of wading through this paper, shall be rewarded in the next one by seeing how beautifully what has been developed in this tedious way can be applied to the ascertainment of the rules of scientific reasoning.]

CHAPTER X

Truth and Practice:

William James (1842–1910)

ENOUGH HAS BEEN SAID ABOUT THE BACKGROUND OF William James's philosophy in the last chapter, including the doctrine of Peirce to which he was so indebted, so that we may now turn to James's peculiar contribution to the pragmatic tradition. Peirce is the pragmatic philosopher of science, James the pragmatic philosopher of religion, and Dewey the pragmatic philosopher of morals, only it must be clear by now that it is not always the same pragmatism that they apply to these different problems. I present their views on these vital subjects not only because they are interesting, influential, and typical, but also to show more concretely that pragmatism is a kind of intellectual halfway house between our first group of philosophers and our last, that it is a philosophy which seeks contact with science, life, and culture while it maintains certain logical and analytical standards.

I should point out, therefore, that the twentieth-century contrast I have identified with the struggle between hedgehogs and foxes is less a matter of doctrine than of method. Unlike James's distinction between the tender and the tough, it is less influenced by the specific religious beliefs, the specific moral beliefs, and the specific emotional attitudes of the contending parties, and more influenced by the difference between those who try to tie all of these together and those who don't. For plainly Sartre is atheistic and pessimistic while being a free-willist (as he should not be on James's diagnosis); Croce is an idealist and yet not dogmatical; Bergson is anti-intellectualistic without being a fatalist or an empiricist. James's contrast, as I have suggested, was the product of the nineteenth century and cannot be mechanically translated to the later philosophy of the twentieth century. Of course, something of it remains, just as something remains of the nineteenth-century struggle between Democrats and Republicans, but in a time of crisis old party lines are broken, party whips are far less effective in producing parliamentary unity just as party hacks fail to deliver a solid vote. What remains is something that comes closest to the seventh opposition on James's two tickets, that between monist and pluralist— meaning by that, however, not a substantive metaphysical difference but a procedural difference between those who prefer a large, even a fuzzy composite of the universe or a guide to life, to the piecemeal, detailed, side-views, back-views, front-views, and noncommittal reportage of more analytic and positivistic thinkers.

Whether he agrees with William James or not, every reader of the history of American philosophy sighs with relief when, after starting from the beginning, he reaches James's writing. James is original, exciting, and cosmo-politan, and very soon he makes you forget the cracker-barrel atmosphere of the previous history of American philosophy. (I do not think of the Emersonian transcen-dentalists as philosophers.) James (like Peirce) was no second-rate imitator or satellite of British or continental philosophy; he was a major philosophical planet who whirled on his own axis and drew all of the other pragma-tic luminaries into his powerful field. His pragmatism was anticipated by Peirce and revised by John Dewey, but he was unquestionably the central literary figure in the prag-matic movement, an "adorable genius" as Whitehead called him, and the man of whom Russell said: "No degree of democratic feeling and of desire to identify himself with the common herd could make him anything but a natural aristocrat, a man whose personal distinction commanded respect."[1] Even his fastidious brother Henry agreed (or said he agreed) with his pragmatism; Henry didn't fall into a cheap interpretation of it as the ideology of American capitalism, opportunism, and smugness.

[1] *Unpopular Essays* (Simon and Schuster, New York, 1950), p. 167.

James began his career as a physician, moved on to psychology, in 1890 produced one of the most famous works in that field, his *Principles of Psychology,* and finally turned to philosophy. His *Pragmatism,* from which the following selection is made, appeared in 1907 when he was at the height of his great international reputation and three years before his death. It is one of his most sustained attempts to mediate the claims of science and religion by reinterpreting their foundations.

Our discussion of Peirce and the selection from his writings make it easier to introduce James's view of truth and his conception of the relation between science and religion. It is best to begin by considering the relationship between Peirce's pragmatic approach to meaning and James's pragmatic theory of truth. We have already illustrated Peirce's doctrine by using examples like "heavy" and "hard," and we have seen that the peculiarity of the pragmatic theory of meaning lies in the fact that it recommends translation of statements like "This is heavy" into statements of the form "If operation O is performed on this, then E is experienced." The theory tells us merely how to translate one kind of statement into another of *a very special kind.* And although the original can also be translated into statements which are *not* hypothetical, operational, or experimental as we explained these terms in the last chapter, such translations are not helpful to the scientist from Peirce's point of view. He says:

"If you look into a textbook of chemistry for a definition of *lithium,* you may be told that it is that element whose atomic weight is 7 very nearly. But if the author has a more logical mind he will tell you that if you search among minerals that are vitreous, translucent, grey or white, very hard, brittle, and insoluble, for one which imparts a crimson tinge to an unluminous flame, this mineral being triturated with lime of witherite's rats-bane, and then fused, can be partly dissolved with muriatic acid; and if this solution can be evaporated, and the residue be extracted with sulphuric acid, and duly purified, it can be converted by ordinary methods into a chloride, which being obtained in the solid state, fused, and electrolyzed with half a dozen powerful cells, will yield a globule of a pinkish silvery metal that will float on gasolene; and the material of *that* is a specimen of lithium. The peculiarity of this definition —or rather this precept that is more serviceable than a definition—is that it tells you what the word lithium denotes by prescribing what you are to *do* in order to gain a perceptual acquaintance with the object of the word."[2]

The progress in such translation is in the direction of clarity, Peirce says. It's a little like telling an American who knows no French what a French sentence means in English as opposed to telling him its meaning in a language that he doesn't know and can't use. But in this kind of translation as well as in pragmatic translation nothing is said about the *truth* of a statement like "This is a specimen of lithium." On the other hand, if I should point to a book and say: "If you let it go, you will see it on the floor in a second," you might agree with me and say "That's true." If you did, you would be applying the predicate "true" to my statement, and this predicate or general term is somewhat different from the predicates "lithium," "hard," and "heavy" just because it is applied to linguistic expressions like statements rather than to blocks or stones. The question arises: Is there some pragmatic way of explaining the meaning of "true" in spite of the fact that it is a predicate which is applied to linguistic expressions? Naturally, one sensible reply is "It all depends on what is meant by 'pragmatic.' "

It is obvious that you won't find out whether a statement is true by poking *it* or swallowing *it* and then waiting to see what happens, so that if the heart of pragmatism is its operationalism and its experientialism narrowly conceived, it *won't* be applicable to the notion of truth. But if we broaden the notions of operation and experience somewhat, it seems possible at least to deal with the notion of truth in a way that is analogous to Peirce's treatment of "hard," "heavy," and "lithium." Remembering the pattern "If operation O, then experience E," we allow *acceptance* or *belief* of a statement as an admissible operation, and a

[2] *Collected Papers* (Harvard University Press, 1931-35), Vol. II, Section 330.

consequent experience of *satisfaction* as admissible, and
the formula: "If you believe or accept statement *S,* then
certain satisfactory experiences ensue" becomes the pragmatic translation of "*S* is true." In this way we reach the
outline of a pragmatic theory of truth which is as much an
application of the pragmatic theory of meaning as Peirce's
pragmatic definition of lithium. It may be argued whether
it is an *adequate* definition of truth, just as it may be argued whether Peirce's definition of lithium is adequate,
but such arguments are far more interesting and fruitful
than arguing about whether they are pragmatic.

I cannot enter all of the details of this extremely difficult
and historically complex subject, but it is fair to say that
James's pragmatic theory of truth proceeds along the lines
indicated. It involved him in difficulties over the notion
of belief and the notion of satisfaction—his *O* and his *E*—
but by construing them loosely enough he was able to
invite back into respectability many speculative, metaphysical, and theological statements that seemed to be meaningless by Peirce's criterion of meaning. Moreover, the test
of scientific, metaphysical, and theological truth was made
uniform by James. If you want to know whether a theory
of any kind is true, try believing it and see whether satisfactory results ensue: that is the brief summary that led
some to hail James as a savior and others to caricature him
brutally. It is the key to his attempted reconciliation of
science and religion, and the origin of Peirce's decision to
disassociate himself from the doctrine by rebaptizing his
own view "pragmaticism," a term which he described as
"ugly enough to be safe from kidnappers."

Rather than spend the rest of my space on the many
other differences and similarities between Peirce and
James, it might be more illuminating to say something further about the philosophical reasons for James's approach
to truth, lest it be thought that he was merely sentimentally
motivated by a desire to tenderize the tough and vice versa.
The fact is that James saw more deeply than a number of
his glib critics did. A good insight into his motivation may
be gotten from his statement that pragmatism agrees with
"nominalism . . . in always appealing to particulars; with

utilitarianism in emphasizing practical aspects; with positivism in its disdain for verbal solutions." As a nominalist he was unable to say that a true statement expressed a "proposition" that corresponds to the "facts," because "facts" and "propositions" are abstract entities which consistent nominalists must not postulate. As a sympathizer of nineteenth-century positivism he regarded the correspondence theory of truth—the theory that a statement is true because it expresses a proposition that corresponds to the facts—as no more helpful than saying that sleeping pills put us to sleep because they have the dormitive virtue. These two sympathies led him to become an epistemological utilitarian. *Pragmatism* was warmly dedicated to the memory of John Stuart Mill, whose treatment of right moral conduct James tried to emulate in his theory of truth. James's argument may be put succinctly in three sentences. The true is that which we ought to believe. That which we ought to believe is what is best for us to believe. Therefore, the true is that which is best for us to believe.

By putting it all so baldly he exposed himself to a host of objections that were closely related to those which had been brewing over utilitarianism throughout the nineteenth century. His second premise raised the old question "Good for whom?" and James sometimes answered characteristically "For the individual!" On other occasions he protested that he was not leaving truth to individual taste. His ambiguity reflected an ambiguity in utilitarian ethics, and it was not surprising that Peirce should have concluded a letter to James by writing "What is utility, if it is confined to a single person? Truth is public." This was the theme which John Dewey emphasized more than any other pragmatist. But we cannot leave James without remembering that no matter how ambiguous his statements on truth were, they did stress certain important similarities between the notion of warranted belief or scientific acceptability and those of ethics. They constitute an extremely important contribution to philosophy whose full significance is yet to be widely appreciated.

Because I have concentrated on his pragmatism, it should be said that a fuller study of James's philosophy would require analysis of his metaphysical pluralism, which linked him to the realists, and his radical empiricism, which brought him so close to Bergson. They are expounded in other works, notably in *A Pluralistic Universe* of 1909 and *Essays in Radical Empiricism,* which appeared posthumously in 1912. The latter was edited by Ralph Barton Perry, who in 1935 produced *The Thought and Character of William James,* one of the greatest philosophical biographies ever written and an inexhaustible source of information about James, his ideas, and his times.

The following is an abridgment of Lecture II of James's *Pragmatism* (1907), "What Pragmatism Means," with indications of omissions.[3]

[The pragmatic method is primarily a method of settling metaphysical disputes that otherwise might be interminable. Is the world one or many?—fated or free?—material or spiritual?—here are notions either of which may or may not hold good of the world; and disputes over such notions are unending. The pragmatic method in such cases is to try to interpret each notion by tracing its respective practical consequences. What difference would it practically make to anyone if this notion rather than that notion were true? If no practical difference whatever can be traced, then the alternatives mean practically the same thing, and all dispute is idle. Whenever a dispute is serious, we ought to be able to show some practical difference that must follow from one side or the other's being right.

A glance at the history of the idea will show you still better what pragmatism means. The term is derived from the same Greek word πράγμα (*prágma*), meaning action, from which our words "practice" and "practical" come. It was first introduced into philosophy by Mr. Charles Peirce in 1878. In an article entitled "How to Make Our Ideas Clear," in the *Popular Science Monthly* for January of that year.* Mr. Peirce, after pointing out that our beliefs

[3] I wish to thank Paul R. Reynolds & Son, New York, for their very generous permission to reprint this section from *Pragmatism* by William James. Copyright, 1907, by William James.

* Translated in the *Revue Philosophique* for January, 1879 (vol. vii). AUTHOR'S NOTE.

are really rules for action, said that, to develop a thought's meaning, we need only determine what conduct it is fitted to produce; that conduct is for us its sole significance. And the tangible fact at the root of all our thought-distinctions, however subtle, is that there is no one of them so fine as to consist in anything but a possible difference of practice. To attain perfect clearness in our thoughts of an object, then, we need only consider what conceivable effects of a practical kind the object may involve—what sensations we are to expect from it, and what reactions we must prepare. Our conception of these effects, whether immediate or remote, is then for us the whole of our conception of the object, so far as that conception has positive significance at all. . . .

To take in the importance of Peirce's principle, one must get accustomed to applying it to concrete cases. I found a few years ago that Ostwald, the illustrious Leipzig chemist, had been making perfectly distinct use of the principle of pragmatism in his lectures on the philosophy of science, though he had not called it by that name.

"All realities influence our practice," he wrote me, "and that influence is their meaning for us. I am accustomed to put questions to my classes in this way: In what respects would the world be different if this alternative or that were true? If I can find nothing that would become different, then the alternative has no sense."

That is, the rival views mean practically the same thing, and meaning, other than practical, there is for us none. Ostwald in a published lecture gives this example of what he means. Chemists have long wrangled over the inner constitution of certain bodies called "tautomerous." Their properties seemed equally consistent with the notion that an instable hydrogen atom oscillates inside of them, or that they are instable mixtures of two bodies. Controversy raged, but never was decided. "It would never have begun," says Ostwald, "if the combatants had asked themselves what particular experimental fact could have been made different by one or the other view being correct. For it would then have appeared that no difference of fact could possibly ensue; and the quarrel was as unreal as if, theorizing in primitive times about the raising of dough by yeast, one party should have invoked a 'brownie,' while another insisted on an 'elf,' as the true cause of the phenomenon." *

It is astonishing to see how many philosophical disputes collapse into insignificance the moment you subject them to this simple test of tracing a concrete consequence. There can *be* no difference anywhere that doesn't *make* a difference elsewhere—no difference in abstract truth that doesn't express itself in a difference in concrete fact and in conduct consequent upon that fact, imposed on somebody, somehow, somewhere, and somewhen. The whole function of philosophy ought to be to find out what definite difference it will make to you and me, at definite instants of our life, if this world-formula or that world-formula be the true one. . . .

Pragmatism represents a perfectly familiar attitude in philosophy, the empiricist attitude, but it represents it, as it seems to me, both in a more radical and in a less objectionable form than it has ever yet assumed. A pragmatist turns his back resolutely and once for all upon a lot of inveterate habits dear to professional philosophers. He turns away from abstraction and insufficiency, from verbal solutions, from bad *a priori* reasons, from fixed principles, closed systems, and pretended absolutes and origins. He turns towards concreteness and adequacy, towards facts, towards action and towards power. That means the empiricist temper regnant and the rationalist temper sincerely given up. It means the open air and possibilities of nature, as against dogma, artificiality, and the pretence of finality in truth.

At the same time it does not stand for any special results. It is a method only. But the general triumph of

* "Theorie und Praxis," *Zeitsch. des Oesterreichischen Ingenieur u. Architecten-Vereines,* 1905, Nr. 4 u. 6. I find a still more radical pragmatism than Ostwald's in an address by Professor W. S. Franklin: "I think that the sickliest notion of physics, even if a student gets it, is that it ıs 'the science of masses, molecules, and the ether.' And I think that the healthiest notion, even if a student does not wholly get it, is that physics is the science of the ways of taking hold of bodies and pushing them!" (*Science,* January 2, 1903.) AUTHOR'S NOTE.

that method would mean an enormous change in what I called in my last lecture the "temperament" of philosophy. Teachers of the ultra-rationalistic type would be frozen out, much as the courtier type is frozen out in republics, as the ultramontane type of priest is frozen out in protestant lands. Science and metaphysics would come much nearer together, would in fact work absolutely hand in hand. . . .

Theories thus become instruments, not answers to enigmas, in which we can rest. We don't lie back upon them, we move forward, and, on occasion, make nature over again by their aid. Pragmatism unstiffens all our theories, limbers them up and sets each one at work. Being nothing essentially new, it harmonizes with many ancient philosophic tendencies. It agrees with nominalism, for instance, in always appealing to particulars; with utilitarianism in emphasizing practical aspects; with positivism in its disdain for verbal solutions, useless questions and metaphysical abstractions.

All these, you see, are *anti-intellectualist* tendencies. Against rationalism as a pretension and a method pragmatism is fully armed and militant. But, at the outset, at least, it stands for no particular results. . . .

No particular results then, so far, but only an attitude of orientation, is what the pragmatic method means. *The attitude of looking away from first things, principles, "categories," supposed necessities; and of looking towards last things, fruits, consequences, facts.*

So much for the pragmatic method! You may say that I have been praising it rather than explaining it to you, but I shall presently explain it abundantly enough by showing how it works on some familiar problems. Meanwhile the word pragmatism has come to be used in a still wider sense, as meaning also a certain *theory of truth.* I mean to give a whole lecture to the statement of that theory, after first paving the way, so I can be very brief now. . . .

One of the most successfully cultivated branches of philosophy in our time is what is called inductive logic, the study of the conditions under which our sciences have evolved. Writers on this subject have begun to show a singular unanimity as to what the laws of nature and elements of fact mean, when formulated by mathematicians, physicists and chemists. When the first mathematical, logical, and natural uniformities, the first *laws,* were discovered, men were so carried away by the clearness, beauty and simplification that resulted, that they believed themselves to have deciphered authentically the eternal thoughts of the Almighty. His mind also thundered and reverberated in syllogisms. He also thought in conic sections, squares and roots and ratios, and geometrized like Euclid. He made Kepler's laws for the planets to follow; he made velocity increase proportionally to the time in falling bodies; he made the law of the sines for light to obey when refracted; he established the classes, orders, families and genera of plants and animals, and fixed the distances between them. He thought the archetypes of all things, and devised their variations; and when we rediscover any one of these his wondrous institutions, we seize his mind in its very literal intention.

But as the sciences have developed farther, the notion has gained ground that most, perhaps all, of our laws are only approximations. The laws themselves, moreover, have grown so numerous that there is no counting them; and so many rival formulations are proposed in all the branches of science that investigators have become accustomed to the notion that no theory is absolutely a transcript of reality, but that any one of them may from some point of view be useful. Their great use is to summarize old facts and to lead to new ones. They are only a man-made language, a conceptual shorthand, as some one calls them, in which we write our reports of nature; and languages, as is well known, tolerate much choice of expression and many dialects. . . .

Riding now on the front of this wave of scientific logic Messrs. Schiller and Dewey appear with their pragmatistic account of what truth everywhere signifies. Everywhere, these teachers say, "truth" in our ideas and beliefs means the same thing that it means in science. It means, they say, nothing but this, *that ideas (which themselves are but parts of our experience) become true just in so far as they help us to get into satisfactory relation with other parts of our experience,* to summarize them and get about among them by conceptual short-cuts instead of following the interminable succession of particular phenomena. Any idea upon which we can ride, so to speak; any idea that will carry us prosperously from any one part of our experience to any other part, linking things satisfactorily, working securely, simplifying, saving labor; is true for just so much, true in so far forth, true *instrumentally.* This is the "instrumental" view of truth taught so successfully at Chicago, the view that truth in our ideas means their power to "work," promulgated so brilliantly at Oxford. . . .

The observable process which Schiller and Dewey particularly singled out for generalization is the familiar one by which any individual settles into *new opinions.* The process here is always the same. The individual has a stock of old opinions already, but he meets a new experience that puts them to a strain. Somebody contradicts them; or in a reflective moment he discovers that they contradict each other; or he hears of facts with which they are incompatible; or desires arise in him which they cease to satisfy. The result is an inward trouble to which his mind till then had been a stranger, and from which he seeks to escape by modifying his previous mass of opinions. He saves as much of it as he can, for in the matter of belief we are all extreme conservatives. So he tries to change first this opinion, and then that (for they resist change very variously), until at last some new idea comes up which he can graft upon the ancient stock with a minimum of disturbance of the latter, some idea that mediates between the stock and the new experience and runs them into one another most felicitously and expediently.

This new idea is then adopted as the true one. It preserves the older stock of truths with a minimum of modification, stretching them just enough to make them admit the novelty, but conceiving that in ways as familiar as the case leaves possible. An *outrée* explanation, violating all our preconceptions, would never pass for a true account of a novelty. We should scratch round industriously till we found something less excentric. The

most violent revolutions in an individual's beliefs leave
most of his old order standing. Time and space, cause and
effect, nature and history, and one's own biography remain untouched. New truth is always a go-between, a
smoother-over of transitions. It marries old opinion to new
fact so as ever to show a minimum of jolt, a maximum of
continuity. We hold a theory true just in proportion to its
success in solving this "problem of maxima and minima."
But success in solving this problem is eminently a matter
of approximation. We say this theory solves it on the whole
more satisfactorily than that theory; but that means more
satisfactorily to ourselves, and individuals will emphasize
their points of satisfaction differently. To a certain degree,
therefore, everything here is plastic.

The point I now urge you to observe particularly is the
part played by the older truths. Failure to take account of
it is the source of much of the unjust criticism levelled
against pragmatism. Their influence is absolutely control-
ling. Loyalty to them is the first principle—in most cases
it is the only principle; for by far the most usual way of
handling phenomena so novel that they would make for a
serious rearrangement of our preconception is to ignore
them altogether, or to abuse those who bear witness for
them.

You doubtless wish examples of this process of truth's
growth, and the only trouble is their superabundance. The
simplest case of new truth is of course the mere numerical
addition of new kinds of facts, or of new single facts of
old kinds, to our experience—an addition that involves no
alteration in the old beliefs. Day follows day, and its contents are simply added. The new contents themselves are
not true, they simply *come* and *are*. Truth is *what we say
about* them, and when we say that they have come, truth
is satisfied by the plain additive formula.

But often the day's contents oblige a rearrangement. If
I should now utter piercing shrieks and act like a maniac
on this platform, it would make many of you revise your
ideas as to the probable worth of my philosophy. "Radium"
came the other day as part of the day's content, and seemed
for a moment to contradict our ideas of the whole order

of nature, that order having come to be identified with what is called the conservation of energy. The mere sight of radium paying heat away indefinitely out of its own pocket seemed to violate that conservation. What to think? If the radiations from it were nothing but an escape of unsuspected "potential" energy, pre-existent inside of the atoms, the principle of conservation would be saved. The discovery of "helium" as the radiation's outcome, opened a way to this belief. So Ramsay's view is generally held to be true, because, although it extends our old ideas of energy, it causes a minimum of alteration in their nature.

I need not multiply instances. A new opinion counts as "true" just in proportion as it gratifies the individual's desire to assimilate the novel in his experience to his beliefs in stock. It must both lean on old truth and grasp new fact; and its success (as I said a moment ago) in doing this, is a matter for the individual's appreciation. When old truth grows, then, by new truth's addition, it is for subjective reasons. We are in the process and obey the reasons. That new idea is truest which performs most felicitously its function of satisfying our double urgency. It makes itself true, gets itself classed as true, by the way it works; grafting itself then upon the ancient body of truth, which thus grows much as a tree grows by the activity of a new layer of cambium.

Now Dewey and Schiller proceed to generalize this observation and to apply it to the most ancient parts of truth. They also once were plastic. They also were called true for human reasons. They also mediated between still earlier truths and what in those days were novel observations. Purely objective truth, truth in whose establishment the function of giving human satisfaction in marrying previous parts of experience with newer parts played no role whatever, is nowhere to be found. The reasons why we call things true is the reason why they *are* true, for "to be true" *means* only to perform this marriage-function.

The trail of the human serpent is thus over everything. Truth independent; truth that we *find* merely; truth no longer malleable to human need; truth incorrigible, in a word; such truth exists indeed superabundantly—or is supposed to exist by rationalistically minded thinkers; but then it means only the dead heart of the living tree, and its being there means only that truth also has its paleontology, and its "prescription," and may grow stiff with years of veteran service and petrified in men's regard by sheer antiquity. . . .

You will probably be surprised to learn, then, that Messrs. Schiller's and Dewey's theories have suffered a hailstorm of contempt and ridicule. All rationalism has risen against them. In influential quarters Mr. Schiller, in particular, has been treated like an impudent schoolboy who deserves a spanking. I should not mention this, but for the fact that it throws so much sidelight upon that rationalistic temper to which I have opposed the temper of pragmatism. Pragmatism is uncomfortable away from facts. Rationalism is comfortable only in the presence of abstractions. This pragmatist talk about truths in the plural, about their utility and satisfactoriness, about the success with which they "work," etc., suggests to the typical intellectualist mind a sort of coarse lame second-rate make-shift article of truth. Such truths are not real truth. Such tests are merely subjective. As against this, objective truth must be something non-utilitarian, haughty, refined, remote, august, exalted. It must be an absolute correspondence of our thoughts with an equally absolute reality. It must be what we *ought* to think unconditionally. The conditioned ways in which we *do* think are so much irrelevance and matter for psychology. Down with psychology, up with logic, in all this question!

See the exquisite contrast of the types of mind! The pragmatist clings to facts and concreteness, observes truth at its work in particular cases, and generalizes. Truth, for him, becomes a class-name for all sorts of definite working-values in experience. For the rationalist it remains a pure abstraction, to the bare name of which we must defer. When the pragmatist undertakes to show in detail just *why* we must defer, the rationalist is unable to recognize the concretes from which his own abstraction is taken. He accuses us of *denying* truth; whereas we have only sought to trace exactly why people follow it and always ought to follow it. Your typical ultra-abstractionist fairly shudders at concreteness: other things equal, he positively prefers the pale and spectral. If the two universes were offered, he would always choose the skinny outline rather than the rich thicket of reality. It is so much purer, clearer, nobler.

I hope that as these lectures go on, the concreteness and closeness to facts of the pragmatism which they advocate may be what approves itself to you as its most satisfactory peculiarity. It only follows here the example of the sister-sciences, interpreting the unobserved by the observed. It brings old and new harmoniously together. It converts the absolutely empty notion of a static relation of "correspondence" (what that may mean we must ask later) between our minds and reality, into that of a rich and active commerce (that anyone may follow in detail and understand) between particular thoughts of ours, and the great universe of other experiences in which they play their parts and have their uses. . . .

Men who are strongly of the fact-loving temperament, you may remember me to have said, are liable to be kept at a distance by the small sympathy with facts which that philosophy from the present-day fashion of idealism offers them. It is far too intellectualistic. Old-fashioned theism was bad enough, with its notion of God as an exalted monarch, made up of a lot of unintelligible or preposterous "attributes"; but, so long as it held strongly by the argument from design, it kept some touch with concrete realities. Since, however, darwinism has once for all displaced design from the minds of the "scientific," theism has lost that foothold; and some kind of an immanent or pantheistic deity working *in* things rather than above them is, if any, the kind recommended to our contemporary imagination. Aspirants to a philosophic religion turn, as a rule, more hopefully nowadays towards idealistic pantheism than towards the older dualistic theism, in spite of the fact that the latter still counts able defenders.

But, as I said in my first lecture, the brand of pantheism offered is hard for them to assimilate if they are lovers of facts, or empirically minded. It is the absolutistic brand, spurning the dust and reared upon pure logic. It keeps no connexion whatever with concreteness. Affirming the Absolute Mind, which is its substitute for God, to be the rational presupposition of all particulars of fact, whatever they may be, it remains supremely indifferent to what the particular facts in our world actually are. . . .

Far be it from me to deny the majesty of this conception, or its capacity to yield religious comfort to a most respectable class of minds. But from the human point of view, no one can pretend that it doesn't suffer from the faults of remoteness and abstractness. It is eminently a product of what I have ventured to call the rationalistic temper. It disdains empiricism's needs. It substitutes a pallid outline for the real world's richness. It is dapper, it is noble in the bad sense, in the sense in which to be noble is to be inapt for humble service. In this real world of sweat and dirt, it seems to me that when a view of things is "noble," that ought to count as a presumption against its truth, and as a philosophic disqualification. The prince of darkness may be a gentleman, as we are told he is, but whatever the God of earth and heaven is, he can surely be no gentleman. His menial services are needed in the dust of our human trials, even more than his dignity is needed in the empyrean.

Now pragmatism, devoted though she be to facts, has no such materialistic bias as ordinary empiricism labors under. Moreover, she has no objection whatever to the realizing of abstractions, so long as you get about among particulars with their aid and they actually carry you somewhere. Interested in no conclusions but those which our minds and our experiences work out together, she has no *a priori* prejudice against theology. *If theological ideas prove to have a value for concrete life, they will be true, for pragmatism, in the sense of being good for so much. For how much more they are true, will depend entirely on their relations to the other truths that also have to be acknowledged.* . . .

I am well aware how odd it must seem to some of you to hear me say that an idea is "true" so long as to believe it is profitable to our lives. That it is *good,* for as much as it profits, you will gladly admit. If what we do by its aid is good, you will allow the idea itself to be good in so far forth, for we are the better for possessing it. But is it not a strange misuse of the word "truth," you will say, to call ideas also "true" for this reason?

To answer this difficulty fully is impossible at this stage of my account. . . . Let me now say only this, that truth is *one species of good,* and not, as is usually supposed, a category distinct from good, and co-ordinate with it. *The true is the name of whatever proves itself to be good in the way of belief, and good, too, for definite, assignable reasons.* Surely you must admit this, that if there were *no* good for life in true ideas, or if the knowledge of them were positively disadvantageous and false ideas the only useful ones, then the current notion that truth is divine and precious, and its pursuit a duty, could never have grown up or become a dogma. In a world like that, our duty would be to *shun* truth, rather. But in this world, just as certain foods are not only agreeable to our taste, but good for our teeth, our stomach, and our tissues; so certain ideas are not only agreeable to think about, or agreeable as supporting other ideas that we are fond of, but they are also helpful in life's practical struggles. If there be any life that it is really better we should lead, and if there be any idea which, if believed in, would help us to lead that life, then it would be really *better for us* to believe in that idea, *unless, indeed, belief in it incidentally clashed with other greater vital benefits.*

"What would be better for us to believe"! This sounds very like a definition of truth. It comes very near to saying "what we *ought* to believe": and in *that* definition none of you would find any oddity. Ought we ever not to believe what it is *better for us* to believe? And can we then keep the notion of what is better for us, and what is true for us, permanently apart?

Pragmatism says no, and I fully agree with her. Probably you also agree, so far as the abstract statement goes, but with a suspicion that if we practically did believe everything that made for good in our own personal lives, we should be found indulging all kinds of fancies about this world's affairs, and all kinds of sentimental superstitions about a world hereafter. Your suspicion here is undoubtedly well founded, and it is evident that something happens when you pass from the abstract to the concrete that complicates the situation.

I said just now that what is better for us to believe is true *unless the belief incidentally clashes with some other vital benefit*. Now in real life what vital benefits is any particular belief of ours most liable to clash with? What indeed except the vital benefits yielded by *other beliefs* when these prove incompatible with the first ones? In other words, the greatest enemy of any one of our truths may be the rest of our truths. Truths have once for all this desperate instinct of self-preservation and of desire to extinguish whatever contradicts them. My belief in the Absolute, based on the good it does me, must run the gauntlet of all my other beliefs. Grant that it may be true in giving me a moral holiday. Nevertheless, as I conceive it—and let me speak now confidentially, as it were, and merely in my own private person—it clashes with other truths of mine whose benefits I hate to give up on its account. It happens to be associated with a kind of logic of which I am the enemy, I find that it entangles me in metaphysical paradoxes that are inacceptable, etc., etc. But as I have enough trouble in life already without adding the trouble of carrying these intellectual inconsistencies, I personally just give up the Absolute. I just *take* my moral holidays; or else, as a professional philosopher, I try to justify them by some other principle. . . .

You see by this what I meant when I called pragmatism a mediator and reconciler and said, borrowing the word from Papini, that she "unstiffens" our theories. She has in fact no prejudices whatever, no obstructive dogmas, no rigid canons of what shall count as proof. She is completely genial. She will entertain any hypothesis, she will consider any evidence. It follows that in the religious field she is at a great advantage both over positivistic empiricism, with its anti-theological bias, and over religious rationalism, with its exclusive interest in the remote, the noble, the simple, and the abstract in the way of conception. . . .

Her only test of probable truth is what works best in the way of leading us, what fits every part of life best and combines with the collectivity of experience's demands, nothing being omitted. If theological ideas should do this, if the notion of God, in particular, should prove to do it, how could pragmatism possibly deny God's existence? She could see no meaning in treating as "not true" a notion that was pragmatically so successful. What other kind of truth could there be, for her, than all this agreement with concrete reality?]

CHAPTER XI

Science and Morals:

John Dewey (1859–1952)

IT IS SURPRISING TO FIND A MOVEMENT IN PHILOSOPHY led by three contemporaries as distinguished and different from each other as Peirce, James, and Dewey. After saying this one thinks immediately of the three great empiricists, Locke, Berkeley, and Hume, but Locke died before Hume was born and the three did not work as co-operating contemporaries. Then again, their most memorable contributions as empiricists are mainly in one field, epistemology, while Peirce, James, and Dewey exerted their pragmatic energies and revealed their different backgrounds and temperaments in widely separated subjects. Dewey was primarily a moral philosopher, an educator, and a political thinker, though he wrote in every branch of philosophy. This may reflect the fact that his serious entry into philosophy began with a study of Hegel who, as Dewey says, left a permanent influence on him by emphasizing the historical, cultural, social context of all human thought and activity. Dewey's introduction to philosophy contrasts dramatically with the predominantly empiricist background of James's thinking, with James's primary interest in individual rather than social psychology and his preoccupation with personal and emotional problems. It also contrasts with the Kantian background of Peirce's thinking, a fact whose general significance Peirce saw when he said that his own outlook, like Kant's, was that of a physicist who had entered philosophy. What links all of the pragmatists, nevertheless, is the fact that they are critical thinkers who also think of philosophy as an active force in civilization.

Quite apart from the way in which they reflect a typically American interest in relating the abstract to the concrete, they also reflect America's effort to absorb the best in European philosophy. A distinguished French philosopher has said that he understands American philosophers far better than he does the English, and Englishmen look across the channel with similar feelings. But American philosophers who learned from Peirce, James, Dewey, Royce, and Santayana became part of a more international, cosmopolitan tradition in philosophy which was less motivated by national concern and less burdened by xenophobia than any other group of philosophers in the world. This is not to say that they were detached from American life; on the contrary, many of them were dedicated to it and its problems in a way that prompted them to learn from and communicate with philosophers all over the Western world. For this reason American philosophy in the twentieth century has not been parochial, and while this does not necessarily indicate greatness it certainly refutes cliché generalizations about the spiritual uniformities produced by our pioneers, our engineers, and our capitalists. Hardly any great American university is dominated by pragmatism, "the national philosophy." Some have established reservations for dying philosophical races like idealism; some get to sound more and more like contemporary Oxford and others like Cambridge in the thirties. All over the land there are echoes of Vienna in the twenties, Paris in the thirteenth century, and even of existentialist cafés. It is true that America has produced no world figures in the twentieth century who have not been pragmatists, but this needs no more apologies than Englishmen were required to give in the early nineteenth century when their long philosophical history could boast only of great empiricists.

From this digression I return to John Dewey, the subject of this chapter. It should be said quickly that he did not remain a hegelian forever. Under the influence of Darwin and James he transformed the antitheses of the hegelian dialectic into the tensions of a biologically rooted and socially enveloped "problematic situation." He held that all thought is dedicated to resolving these tensions and therefore that scientific theories are to be measured by their contributions to this resolution. In this he reverts to the more social and public pragmatism of Peirce and criticizes the capriciousness of the Jamesian test of truth. He calls his philosophy instrumentalism or experimentalism.

In logical theory Dewey held that laws of deduction arise in the context of scientific inquiry and that they too are to be tested by their contribution to the over-all efficiency of science. In politics his view was that intelligence is man's chief weapon in his fight for a free society, and that all forms of totalitarianism, Communist or Fascist, are man's enemies. Dewey joined actively in the fight against Communist ideology and politics when active disapproval of it was less fashionable among American intellectuals than it is today. He was never a totalitarian liberal and he was one of the most respected intellectuals of his time. He earned scurrilous attacks from the Communists and bigoted enemies of his theory of progressive education. Even as an old man he was active in the fight for freedom throughout the world; from his defense of Sacco and Vanzetti to his attack on the Moscow Trials he was the conscience of American philosophy. It is hard to think of the American scene without him. Like Justice Holmes, who admired his work and with whom he shared so much, he lived into his nineties. And even though he was the youngest of the three pragmatists, one thinks of him as the father in the holy family of pragmatism—not so clever as Peirce in matters of logic and science, not as witty or as brilliant as James, but in many ways a more rugged and compelling figure than either of the others.

In the selection to follow Dewey presents his ethical views at length, but a discussion of their background and some of their implications may be illuminating. In a sense Dewey continues James's effort at mediation between the tough and the tender, except that he transfers it from theology to morals. The last lines of James's *Pragmatism* read: "Between the two extremes of crude naturalism on the one hand and transcendental absolutism on the other, you may find that what I take the liberty of calling the pragmatistic or melioristic type of theism is exactly what you require." In a similar spirit Dewey offered an ethical theory which, he hoped, would mediate between the remote ethics of "transcendental eternal values" and the view that value is constituted by mere liking, desire, or enjoyment. In the major ethical controversy of the first quarter of the twentieth century, that is to say, before the emergence of logical positivism, Dewey defended a position somewhere between the view of G. E. Moore that "good" is an indefinable predicate which is radically different from the descriptive, naturalistic terms of science, and the view of Ralph Barton Perry, that to have value is to be an object of interest.

Moore's view was closely associated with his own epistemological realism but it was not a logical consequence of it. Since I have stressed the fact that Moore led the rebellion against idealism, and since I have also stressed idealism's rejection of nineteenth-century naturalism, the reader should be warned that Moore's attack on idealism did not involve a reversion to the ethical naturalism the idealists attacked. On the contrary, his *Principia Ethica* (1903) contained a more devastating criticism of the ethics of Herbert Spencer and John Stuart Mill than did any idealist work of the nineteenth or twentieth century. Moore held that while ethical qualities like goodness are objective and real, independent of the mind, they cannot be defined by reference to descriptive predicates, on pain of committing what he called "the naturalistic fallacy." For this reason, Moore's realistic comrade in America, Perry, said in his *Present Philosophical Tendencies* (1912): "In discussing the nature of goodness or value, I find myself in disagreement with certain eminent realists with whom I should much prefer to agree. Mr. G. E. Moore and Mr. Bertrand Russell both contend that goodness is an indefinable quality which attaches to things independently of consciousness." Instead, Perry advanced the view that values are constituted by interest, which he later developed in his *General Theory of Value* (1926). Perry's view is the closest thing to what Dewey calls "the empirical theory" in the selection that follows, while Moore's view was regarded by instrumentalists as the most objectionable variety of ethical transcendentalism since the decline of idealism.

The solution that Dewey proposes is closely related to the pragmatic theory of meaning. His objection to "the empirical theory" is best stated in the passage "The objection is that the theory in question holds value down to objects *antecedently* enjoyed, apart from reference to the method by which they come into existence; it takes enjoyments which are casual because unregulated by intelligent operation to be values in and of themselves. Operational thinking needs to be applied to the judgment of values just as it has now finally been applied in conceptions of physical objects." If the reader will turn back to page 156 of this volume he will find a long quotation from Charles Peirce which may illuminate the point at issue. We may assume that Peirce was there illustrating the operational thinking Dewey had in mind, for Dewey has often identified his view with Peirce's in such matters. Dewey's point, as I understand it, is that something may be said to have value if and only if enjoying it or liking it is the outcome of an intelligently controlled experiment of the kind Peirce describes. To use an even simpler illustration, Dewey reminds us that when we judge the objective color of something, we do not conclude that it *is* red merely from the fact that it *looks* red, but we make sure that the light is good and that our eyes are in normal condition. In the same way, Dewey holds, our enjoyment must be more than "casual" before we can assign value to the things we like. The result is a theory of value which translates singular judgments like "This is good" into hypothetical, operational, and experiential judgments of the form "If operation O is performed on this, then E is experienced." In this way Dewey hopes to avoid what he thinks is "the empirical theory's" exclusive dependence on raw impulse (a parallel to the raw sensationalism of certain varieties of epistemological empiricism), and the transcendentalist's failure to make a contact with impulse altogether.

This concludes our necessarily limited discussion of pragmatism. Peirce's pragmatic theory of meaning was carried over to "true" by James and by Dewey to "good," and in this way pragmatism invaded fields far outside of Peirce's chemical laboratory. By the time Dewey's *Art as Experience* had appeared in 1934 the True, the Beautiful, and the Good had all received pragmatic treatment; the "normative" disciplines of logic, esthetics, and ethics had been brought closer to empirical science than at any previous moment in the history of philosophy. The implications of this rapprochement are still being actively debated in American philosophy, and the upshot cannot be predicted or understood without examining the development of the analytic tradition to which we turn in the third part. As we have already seen, analytic philosophy originated in reaction to idealism, and it too was deeply respectful of science, but it did not carry its admiration of science as far as Dewey did. This contrast between pragmatism and analytic philosophy underlies a great deal of division within philosophy today, just as it underlies so many other divisions in the world.

The passage below is extracted from Dewey's *Quest for Certainty* (1929). It comes from Chapter X: "The Construction of Good."[1]

[The attention which has been given to the fact that in its experimental procedure science has surrendered the separation between knowing and doing has its source in the fact that there is now provided within a limited, specialized and technical field the possibility and earnest, as far as theory is concerned, of effecting the needed integration in the wider field of collective human experience. Philosophy is called upon to be the theory of the practice,

[1] I wish to thank G. P. Putnam's Sons for allowing me to reprint pp. 255-68 from *Quest for Certainty* by John Dewey. Copyright, 1929, by John Dewey.

JOHN DEWEY   179

through ideas sufficiently definite to be operative in experimental endeavor, by which the integration may be
made secure in actual experience. Its central problem is
the relation that exists between the beliefs about the nature
of things due to natural science to beliefs about values—
using that word to designate whatever is taken to have
rightful authority in the direction of conduct. A philosophy which should take up this problem is struck first of
all by the fact that beliefs about values are pretty much
in the position in which beliefs about nature were before
the scientific revolution. There is either a basic distrust of
the capacity of experience to develop its own regulative
standards, and an appeal to what philosophers call eternal
values, in order to ensure regulation of belief and action;
or there is acceptance of enjoyments actually experienced
irrespective of the method or operation by which they are
brought into existence. Complete bifurcation between
rationalistic method and an empirical method has its final
and most deeply human significance in the ways in which
good and bad are thought of and acted for and upon.

As far as technical philosophy reflects this situation,
there is division of theories of values into two kinds. On
the one hand, goods and evils, in every region of life, as
they are concretely experienced, are regarded as characteristic of an inferior order of Being—intrinsically inferior.
Just because they are things of human experience, their
worth must be estimated by reference to standards and
ideals derived from ultimate reality. Their defects and per-
version are attributed to the same fact; they are to be cor-
rected and controlled through adoption of methods of
conduct derived from loyalty to the requirements of Supreme Being. This philosophic formulation gets actuality
and force from the fact that it is a rendering of the beliefs
of men in general as far as they have come under the influence of institutional religion. Just as rational conceptions
were once superimposed upon observed and temporal phenomena, so eternal values are superimposed upon experienced goods. In one case as in the other, the alternative is
supposed to be confusion and lawlessness. Philosophers

suppose these eternal values are known by reason; the mass of persons that they are divinely revealed.

Nevertheless, with the expansion of secular interests, temporal values have enormously multiplied; they absorb more and more attention and energy. The sense of transcendent values has become enfeebled; instead of permeating all things in life, it is more and more restricted to special times and acts. The authority of the church to declare and impose divine will and purpose has narrowed. Whatever men say and profess, their tendency in the presence of actual evils is to resort to natural and empirical means to remedy them. But in formal belief, the old doctrine of the inherently disturbed and unworthy character of the goods and standards of ordinary experience persists. This divergence between what men do and what they nominally profess is closely connected with the confusions and conflicts of modern thought.

It is not meant to assert that no attempts have been made to replace the older theory regarding the authority of immutable and transcendent values by conceptions more congruous with the practices of daily life. The contrary is the case. The utilitarian theory, to take one instance, has had great power. The idealistic school is the only one in contemporary philosophy, with the exception of one form of neo-realism, that makes much of the notion of a reality which is all one with ultimate moral and religious values. But this school is also the one most concerned with the conservation of "spiritual" life. Equally significant is the fact that empirical theories retain the notion that thought and judgment are concerned with values that are experienced independently of them. For these theories, emotional satisfactions occupy the same place that sensations hold in traditional empiricism. Values are constituted by liking and enjoyment; to be enjoyed and to be a value are two names for one and the same fact. Since science has extruded values from its objects, these empirical theories do everything possible to emphasize the purely subjective character of value. A psychological theory of desire and liking is supposed to cover the whole ground of the theory of values; in it, immediate feeling is the counterpart of immediate sensation.

I shall not object to this empirical theory as far as it connects the theory of values with concrete experiences of desire and satisfaction. The idea that there is such a connection is the only way known to me by which the pallid remoteness of the rationalistic theory, and the only too glaring presence of the institutional theory of transcendental values can be escaped. The objection is that the theory in question holds down value to objects *antecedently* enjoyed, apart from reference to the method by which they come into existence; it takes enjoyments which are casual because unregulated by intelligent operations to be values in and of themselves. Operational thinking needs to be applied to the judgment of values just as it has now finally been applied in conceptions of physical objects. Experimental empiricism in the field of ideas of good and bad is demanded to meet the conditions of the present situation.

The scientific revolution came about when material of direct and uncontrolled experience was taken as problematic; as supplying material to be transformed by reflective operations into known objects. The contrast between experienced and known objects was found to be a temporal one; namely, one between empirical subject-matters which were had or "given" prior to the acts of experimental variation and redisposition and those which succeeded these acts and issued from them. The notion of an act whether of sense or thought which supplied a valid measure of thought in immediate knowledge was discredited. Consequences of operations became the important thing. The suggestion almost imperatively follows that escape from the defects of transcendental absolutism is not to be had by setting up as values enjoyments that happen anyhow, but in defining value by enjoyments which are the consequences of intelligent action. Without the intervention of thought, enjoyments are not values but problematic goods, becoming values when they reissue in a changed form from intelligent behavior. The fundamental trouble with the current empirical theory of values is that it merely formulates and justifies the socially prevailing habit of regarding enjoyments as they are actually experienced as values in and of themselves. It completely sidesteps the question of regulation of these enjoyments. This issue involves nothing less than the problem of the directed reconstruction of economic, political and religious institutions.

There was seemingly a paradox involved in the notion that if we turned our backs upon the immediately perceived qualities of things, we should be enabled to form valid conceptions of objects, and that these conceptions could be used to bring about a more secure and more significant experience of them. But the method terminated in disclosing the connections or interactions upon which perceived objects, viewed as events, depend. Formal analogy suggests that we regard our direct and original experience of things liked and enjoyed as only *possibilities* of values to be achieved; that enjoyment becomes a value when we discover the relations upon which its presence depends. Such a causal and operational definition gives only a conception of a value, not a value itself. But the utilization of the conception in action results in an object having secure and significant value.

The formal statement may be given concrete content by pointing to the difference between the enjoyed and the enjoyable, the desired and the desirable, the satis*fying* and the satis*factory*. To say that something is enjoyed is to make a statement about a fact, something already in existence; it is not to judge the value of that fact. There is no difference between such a proposition and one which says that something is sweet or sour, red or black. It is just correct or incorrect and that is the end of the matter. But to call an object a value is to assert that it satisfies or fulfills certain conditions. Function and status in meeting conditions is a different matter from bare existence. The fact that something is desired only raises the *question* of its desirability; it does not settle it. Only a child in the degree of his immaturity thinks to settle the question of desirability by reiterated proclamation: "I want it, I want it, I want it." What is objected to in the current empirical theory of values is not connection of them with desire and enjoyment but failure to distinguish between enjoyments of radically different sorts. There are many common expressions in which the difference of the two kinds is clearly recognized. Take for example the difference between the ideas of "satisfying" and "satisfactory." To say that something satisfies is to report something as an isolated finality. To assert that it is satis*factory* is to define it in its connections and interactions. The fact that it pleases or is immediately congenial poses a problem to judgment. How shall the satisfaction be rated? Is it a value or is it not? Is it something to be prized and cherished, *to be* enjoyed? Not stern moralists alone but everyday experience informs us that finding satisfaction in a thing may be a warning, a summons to be on the lookout for consequences. To declare something satis*factory* is to assert that it meets specifiable conditions. It is, in effect, a judgment that the thing "will do." It involves a prediction; it contemplates a future in which the thing will continue to serve; it *will* do. It asserts a consequence the thing will actively institute; it will *do*. That it is satisfying is the content of a proposition of fact; that it is satisfactory is a judgment, an estimate, an appraisal. It denotes an attitude *to be* taken, that of striving to perpetuate and to make secure.

It is worth notice that besides the instances given, there are many other recognitions in ordinary speech of the distinction. The endings "able," "worthy" and "ful" are cases in point. Noted and notable, noteworthy; remarked and remarkable; advised and advisable; wondered at and wonderful; pleasing and beautiful; loved and lovable; blamed and blameable, blameworthy; objected to and objectionable; esteemed and estimable; admired and admirable; shamed and shameful; honored and honorable; approved and approvable, worthy of approbation, etc. The multiplication of words adds nothing to the force of the distinction. But it aids in conveying a sense of the fundamental character of the distinction; of the difference between mere report of an already existent fact and judgment as to the importance and need of bringing a fact into existence; or, if it is already there, of sustaining it in existence. The latter is a genuine practical judgment, and marks the only type of judgment that has to do with the direction of action. Whether or no we reserve the term "value" for the latter (as seems to me proper) is a minor matter; that the distinction be acknowledged as the key to understanding the relation of values to the direction of conduct is the important thing.

This element of direction by an idea of value applies to science as well as anywhere else. For in every scientific undertaking, there is passed a constant succession of estimates; such as "it is worth treating these facts as data or evidence; it is advisable to try this experiment; to make that observation; to entertain such and such a hypothesis; to perform this calculation," etc.

The word "taste" has perhaps got too completely associated with arbitrary liking to express the nature of judgments of value. But if the word be used in the sense of an appreciation at once cultivated and active, one may say that the formation of taste is the chief matter wherever values enter in, whether intellectual, esthetic or moral. Relatively immediate judgments, which we call tact or to which we give the name of intuition, do not precede reflective inquiry, but are the funded products of much thoughtful experience. Expertness of taste is at once the result and the reward of constant exercise of thinking. Instead of there being no disputing about tastes, they are the one thing worth disputing about, if by "dispute" is signified discussion involving reflective inquiry. Taste, if we use the word in its best sense, is the outcome of experience brought cumulatively to bear on the intelligent appreciation of the real worth of likings and enjoyments. There is nothing in which a person so completely reveals himself as in the things which he judges enjoyable and desirable. Such judgments are the sole alternative to the domination of belief by impulse, chance, blind habit and self-interest. The formation of a cultivated and effectively operative good judgment or taste with respect to what is esthetically admirable, intellectually acceptable and morally approvable is the supreme task set to human beings by the incidents of experience.

Propositions about what is or has been liked are of instrumental value in reaching judgments of value, in as far as the conditions and consequences of the thing liked are thought about. In themselves they make no claims; they put forth no demand upon subsequent attitudes and acts; they profess no authority to direct. If one likes a thing he likes it; that *is* a point about which there can be no dispute:—although it is not so easy to state just *what* is liked as is frequently assumed. A judgment about what is *to be* desired and enjoyed is, on the other hand, a claim on future action; it possesses *de jure* and not merely *de facto* quality. It is a matter of frequent experience that likings and enjoyments are of all kinds, and that many are such as reflective judgments condemn. By way of self-justification and "rationalization," an enjoyment creates a tendency to assert that the thing enjoyed is a value. This assertion of validity adds authority to the fact. It is a decision that the object has a right to exist and hence a claim upon action to further its existence.

The analogy between the status of the theory of values and the theory of ideas about natural objects before the rise of experimental inquiry may be carried further. The sensationalistic theory of the origin and test of thought evoked, by way of reaction, the transcendental theory of *a priori* ideas. For it failed utterly to account for objective connection, order and regularity in objects observed. Similarly, any doctrine that identifies the mere fact of being liked with the value of the object liked so fails to give direction to conduct when direction is needed that it automatically calls forth the assertion that there are values eternally in Being that are the standards of all judgments and the obligatory ends of all action. Without the introduction of operational thinking, we oscillate between a theory that, in order to save the objectivity of judgments of values, isolates them from experience and nature, and a theory that, in order to save their concrete and human significance, reduces them to mere statements about our own feelings.

Not even the most devoted adherents of the notion that enjoyment and value are equivalent facts would venture to assert that because we have once liked a thing we should go on liking it; they are compelled to introduce the idea that *some* tastes are to be cultivated. Logically, there is no ground for introducing the idea of cultivation; liking is liking, and one is as good as another. If enjoyments *are* values, the judgment of value cannot regulate the form which liking takes; it cannot regulate its own conditions. Desire and purpose, and hence action, are left without guidance, although the question of regulation of their formation is the supreme problem of practical life. Values (to sum up) may be connected inherently with liking, and yet not with *every* liking but only with those that judgment has approved, after examination of the relation upon which the object liked depends. A casual liking is one that happens without knowledge of how it occurs nor to what effect. The difference between it and one which is sought because of a judgment that it is worth having and is to be striven for, makes just the difference between enjoyments which are accidental and enjoyments that have value and hence a claim upon our attitude and conduct. . . .

When theories of values do not afford intellectual assistance in framing ideas and beliefs about values that are adequate to direct action, the gap must be filled by other means. If intelligent method is lacking, prejudice, the pressure of immediate circumstance, self-interest and class-interest, traditional customs, institutions of accidental historic origin, are *not* lacking, and they tend to take the place of intelligence. Thus we are led to our main proposition: *Judgments about values are judgments about the conditions and the results of experienced objects; judgments about that which should regulate the formation of our desires, affections and enjoyments.* For whatever decides their formation will determine the main course of our conduct, personal and social.

If it sounds strange to hear that we should frame our judgments as to what has value by considering the connections in existence of what we like and enjoy, the reply is not far to seek. As long as we do not engage in this inquiry enjoyments (values if we choose to apply that term) are casual; they are given by "nature," not constructed by art. Like natural objects in their qualitative existence, they at most only supply material for elaboration in rational discourse. A *feeling* of good or excellence is as far removed from goodness in fact as a feeling that objects are intellectually thus and so is removed from their being actually so. To recognize that the truth of natural objects can be reached only by the greatest care in selecting and arranging directed operations, and then to suppose that values can be truly determined by the mere fact of liking seems to leave us in an incredible position. All the serious perplexities of life come back to the genuine difficulty of forming a judgment as to the values of the situation; they come back to a conflict of goods. Only dogmatism can suppose that serious moral conflict is between something clearly bad and something known to be good, and that uncertainty lies wholly in the will of the one choosing. Most conflicts of importance are conflicts between things which are or have been satisfying, not between good and evil. And to suppose that we can make a hierarchical table of values at large once for all, a kind of catalogue in which they are arranged in an order of ascending or descending worth, is to indulge in a gloss on our inability to frame intelligent judgments in the concrete. Or else it is to dignify customary choice and prejudice by a title of honor.

The alternative to definition, classification and systematization of satisfactions just as they happen to occur is judgment of them by means of the relations under which they occur. If we know the conditions under which the act of liking, of desire and enjoyment, takes place, we are in a position to know what are the consequences of that act. The difference between the desired and the desirable, admired and the admirable, becomes effective at just this point. Consider the difference between the proposition "That thing has been eaten," and the judgment "That thing is edible." The former statement involves no knowledge of any relation except the one stated; while we are able to judge of the edibility of anything only when we have a knowledge of its interactions with other things sufficient to enable us to foresee its probable effects when it is taken into the organism and produces effects there.

To assume that anything can be known in isolation from its connections with other things is to identify knowing with merely having some object before perception or in feeling, and is thus to lose the key to the traits that distinguish an object as known. It is futile, even silly, to suppose that some quality that is directly present constitutes the whole of the thing presenting the quality. It does not do so when the quality is that of being hot or fluid or heavy, and it does not when the quality is that of giving pleasure, or being enjoyed. Such qualities are, once more, effects, ends in the sense of closing termini of processes involving causal connections. They are something to be investigated, challenges to inquiry and judgment. The more connections and interactions we ascertain, the more we *know* the object in question. Thinking is search for these connections. Heat experienced as a consequence of directed operations has a meaning quite different from the heat that is casually experienced without knowledge of how it came about. The same is true of enjoyments. Enjoyments that issue from conduct directed by insight into relations have a meaning and a validity due to the way in which they are experienced. Such enjoyments are not repented of; they generate no after-taste of bitterness. Even in the midst of direct enjoyment, there is a sense of validity, of authorization, which intensifies the enjoyment. There is solicitude for perpetuation of the *object* having value which is radically different from mere anxiety to perpetuate the *feeling* of enjoyment.

Such statements as we have been making are, therefore, far from implying that there are values apart from things actually enjoyed as good. To find a thing enjoy*able* is, so to say, a *plus* enjoyment. We saw that it was foolish to treat the scientific object as a rival to or substitute for the perceived object, since the former is intermediate between uncertain and settled situations and those experienced under conditions of greater control. In the same way, judgment of the value of an object to be experienced is instrumental to appreciation of it when it is realized. But the notion that every object that happens to satisfy has an equal claim with every other to be a value is like supposing that every object of perception has the same cognitive force as every other. There is no knowledge without perception; but objects perceived are *known* only when they are deter-

mined as consequences of connective operations. There is
no value except where there is satisfaction, but there have
to be certain conditions fulfilled to transform a satisfaction
into a value.]

CHAPTER XII

Mathematics, Logic, and Analysis:

Bertrand Russell (b. 1872)

I HAVE ALREADY INTRODUCED SOME OF THE IDEAS OF
Bertrand Russell in Chapter II, but those were ideas associated with his name at a very early period in his career.
The metaphysical and epistemological realism which united
him and Moore at the turn of the century ceased to be
their primary concern as the century wore on. In fact Russell abandoned it pretty explicitly. Both Moore and Russell
became more and more interested in *analysis* and therefore many an old realistic ally deplored the company into
which they were falling. It is this analytic interest that links
their work with that of Ludwig Wittgenstein and Rudolf
Carnap. It has resulted in an understandable tendency to
speak of "the analytic movement" when one mentions the
later Moore, the later Russell, Wittgenstein and Carnap,
but the selections in this part of the volume will show that
it is quite wrong to think of them as belonging to a philosophical party with a fixed set of dogmas or a platform.
To link them all indiscriminately is as unsafe as it would
be to link all marxists or all psychoanalysts in the twentieth
century without qualification. There are differences as well
as similarities that should be kept in mind; moreover, there
are important shifts in attitude which make it necessary to
be even more careful.

Now that the reader has been warned of the danger implicit in the whole business, I shall try to set down in a very
general way the things that distinguish the philosophical

analysts as a group from some of the other figures we have dealt with, particularly from those considered in the first part of this book. With certain important qualifications it is safe to say that the analysts are all hostile to speculative and obscurely written metaphysics of the kind one finds in the later works of Whitehead, to the kind of writing we have seen in Bergson and Husserl. They think of philosophy not as a rival of science but rather as an activity which is partly devoted to clarifying it. They are relatively unconcerned with advancing a moral philosophy and more interested in finding out what is meant by words like "good," "bad," "right," and "wrong"; and even though Russell, unlike the others, has committed himself publicly and courageously on many moral questions and social issues, he has always insisted on distinguishing the different hats under which he operates: to be a philosopher, he thinks, is one thing, to be a moral critic or an indignant citizen is another. If one were to try adding much more to this description of their common views and attitudes, one would risk a great deal of damaging falsehood, so I shall not go any further. Nevertheless, this is enough to suggest the vast differences between them as a group and the first group of philosophers we have discussed, also enough to make it clear that analysts share more with the pragmatists than they do with those in the first group. Their differences with the pragmatists on the nature of philosophy revolve mainly around the small importance that analysts attach to philosophy as a social force or as an instrument of cultural criticism; analysts avoid anything like a philosophy of life of the kind one finds in both James and Dewey. They are content to move from one detailed problem to another, relatively undisturbed by the absence of a "rounded philosophy." There are numerous other differences but these are varied and specific.

Because of their deep interest in analysis, most of the main figures in the analytic tradition have said something about it or tried to illustrate it as a philosophical method, and it is here that their differences begin to emerge. With the exception of Wittgenstein in his later phase, they may call themselves analysts or speak of philosophy as clarification, but when they begin to say what they mean by analysis or when they actually engage in it, we can see differences that are critical, indeed so critical that they sometimes loom as large as more traditional differences between philosophers of rival schools. It is advisable to restrict ourselves here to the differences between Moore and Russell.

From the very beginning the work of Moore and Russell exhibited differences which were connected, I think, with the fact that Moore's earliest, formative training was linguistic and classical while Russell's was primarily mathematical. Moore's mind is more like that of a precise philologist with an extraordinary ear for ordinary language, and Russell's is that of the mathematician he once was. Moore reports his lack of interest in mathematics and natural science, his lack of training in both of them, his boredom with the moods and figures of logic. Russell, on the other hand, was very gifted at mathematics as a boy and was regarded as a promising mathematician by Whitehead when he examined him for entrance scholarships at Cambridge. Around 1900, the year that Russell calls "the most important year in my intellectual life" because it was then that he began to think seriously of his program of logicizing mathematics, he urged Moore to take private lessons from Whitehead in mathematics, but Moore reports that he did not take this advice. He adds characteristically: "I still have no settled opinion as to whether, if I had taken it, it would have made any great difference to me."[1]

One result of Russell's training in mathematics was his willingness to construct artificial deductive systems and a considerable lack of interest in whether the terminology he used was in absolute accord with ordinary language. He did not feel great uneasiness, for example, in so defining the notion of implication that statements of the form "*S* implies *T*" are true just in case *S* is false or *T* true, so long as it covered all of the mathematical examples, while Moore exclaimed: "Why logicians should have thus chosen to use the word 'implies' as a name for a relation

[1] *Philosophy of G. E. Moore*, p. 16.

for which it never is used by anyone else, I do not know."[2] Russell was also willing to say that all one sees when one looks at a thing is part of one's own brain, and that we do not know for certain the truth of any statement about a material thing, while Moore vehemently denied both of these contentions in the name of common sense. Moore has therefore been forced to argue against his old realistic and analytic comrade Russell in a vein similar to that in which he (Moore) argued against their common enemy the idealists, using arguments against Russell which are very much like those he used against McTaggart for saying that time is unreal. Anyone who has known Moore can appreciate Keynes's description of Moore as a master of the method of greeting one's remarks with a gasp of incredulity: *"Do* you *really* think *that,* an expression of face as if to hear such a thing said reduced him to a state of wonder verging on imbecility, with his mouth wide open and wagging his head in the negative so violently that his hair shook. *Oh!* he would say, goggling at you as if either you or he must be mad; and no reply was possible." Moore so conceives analysis that it requires the most faithful translation of ordinary language and the most religious acceptance of the truths of common sense. The result has been a critical kind of analytic philosophy, one that does not go in for systems like that of Russell and Whitehead's *Principia Mathematica* but which often consists in the deflation of outrageous redefinitions of old terms and of philosophers who flatly contradict what most ordinary men believe in their sane moments.

Russell, on the other hand, has advanced bizarre theory after theory about the meanings of terms in physics and mathematics in a way that is surprisingly pragmatic in spite of Russell's long polemic against pragmatism. He has thought of philosophy as essentially reconstructive in nature, as obliged to rebuild mathematics, physics, and common sense upon a firmer foundation, or one that dispenses with questionable assumptions and obscure entities. He has illustrated this in his theory of descriptions and his espousal of Frege's theory of cardinal number—both

[2] G. E. Moore, *Philosophical Studies* (1922), p. 296.

briefly presented in the selection to follow—and, in fact, in all of his researches in the philosophy of mathematics and science. He has disregarded ordinary usage in the way that the biologist disregards ordinary usage of the word "fish" when he redefines the word "whale," and he tries to justify this disregard very much as the biologist does: by appealing to the clarity, the economy, the scientific simplicity of the alternative definition. For this reason Russell's conception of analysis makes philosophy an integral part of science itself.

Instead of thinking of mathematics, physics, and common sense as axiomatically untouchable, instead of conceiving philosophy as essentially spectatorial or passive *vis à vis* these more solid parts of knowledge, Russell insists that the philosopher should enter science and participate in the reconstruction of its foundations. The most striking example of his success is the way in which he has contributed to the derivation of mathematics from a purified logic. As a result of his work, in the tradition of Frege and many other mathematicians and logicians, it is extremely difficult to say where logic ends and mathematics begins. They are now indissolubly linked in systems that prevent any clear demarcation of the line between them. Russell has also attempted a reconstruction of the foundations of physics but with less approval of all concerned. This willingness to regard philosophy not only as analytic of science and common sense but also as critical of them, links Russell more closely to his old friend Whitehead than to his old friend Moore. Whitehead and Russell came to differ in many ways, but not really in their attitude toward redefining old terms or in their view of philosophy's capacity to discover new truth that contradicts common sense. This trait is partly explained by their both being mathematicians and it is one they shared with the mathematician-philosopher Peirce. It makes Russell the most metaphysical of all the analytic philosophers, and Peirce the most architectonic of all the pragmatists.

Because the selection that follows presents Russell's views in outline, I need not say anything more about his philosophy in the narrow, technical sense, but it is desir-

194   THE AGE OF ANALYSIS

able to add something about him as an intellectual figure
in the twentieth century. Unlike most other philosophers
in the analytic tradition he has expressed himself vividly
on education, politics, history, manners, morals, war, and
peace. Like Croce he has lived most of his life outside of
the university and he has been one of the most prolific and
distinguished writers of English prose in this century. He
was born into a political family—the grandson of the Lord
John Russell who introduced the Reform Bill of 1832—
and he has used his immense talent in the cause of rational
and humane liberalism for over a half century. John Stuart
Mill was his godfather "so far as is possible in a non-reli-
gious sense" and it was Mill's philosophy which he read
most sympathetically between the ages of fifteen and eighteen before he was momentarily seduced by hegelianism as
a young man. His unconventional life and his hatred of
political and social tyranny is reminiscent of Mill; so is his
honesty and his desire to get to the (preferably clear) bottom of things. It is true that most of Russell's technical
philosophy runs counter to Mill's (again, I think, because
he was a mathematician and Mill was not), and it is also
true that his playfulness, his irony, and his cleverness prevent him from writing as solemn and grave a prose as
Mill's. But he is the only English philosopher since Mill to
combine so much intellectual power, so much cultivation,
and so much passion for liberty. No philosopher has had
a more salutary influence on the intellectual life of the
twentieth century.

The following selection is Chapter XXXI of Russell's
A History of Western Philosophy (1945). The title of the
chapter is "The Philosophy of Logical Analysis."[3]

[In philosophy ever since the time of Pythagoras there
has been an opposition between the men whose thought
was mainly inspired by mathematics and those who were
more influenced by the empirical sciences. Plato, Thomas
Aquinas, Spinoza, and Kant belong to what may be called

[3] This selection from *A History of Western Philosophy* by
Bertrand Russell, copyright, 1945, by Bertrand Russell, is reprinted
with the permission of Simon and Schuster, New York, and George
Allen & Unwin, Ltd., London.

the mathematical party; Democritus, Aristotle, and the modern empiricists from Locke onwards, belong to the opposite party. In our day a school of philosophy has arisen which sets to work to eliminate Pythagoreanism from the principles of mathematics, and to combine empiricism with an interest in the deductive parts of human knowledge. The aims of this school are less spectacular than those of most philosophers in the past, but some of its achievements are as solid as those of the men of science.

The origin of this philosophy is in the achievements of mathematicians who set to work to purge their subject of fallacies and slipshod reasoning. The great mathematicians of the seventeenth century were optimistic and anxious for quick results; consequently they left the foundations of analytical geometry and the infinitesimal calculus insecure. Leibniz believed in actual infinitesimals, but although this belief suited his metaphysics it had no sound basis in mathematics. Weierstrass, soon after the middle of the nineteenth century, showed how to establish the calculus without infinitesimals, and thus at last made it logically secure. Next came Georg Cantor, who developed the theory of continuity and infinite number. "Continuity" had been, until he defined it, a vague word, convenient for philosophers like Hegel, who wished to introduce metaphysical muddles into mathematics. Cantor gave a precise significance to the word, and showed that continuity, as he defined it, was the concept needed by mathematicians and physicists. By this means a great deal of mysticism, such as that of Bergson, was rendered antiquated.

Cantor also overcame the long-standing logical puzzles about infinite number. Take the series of whole numbers from 1 onwards; how many of them are there? Clearly the number is not finite. Up to a thousand, there are a thousand numbers; up to a million, a million. Whatever finite number you mention, there are evidently more numbers than that, because from 1 up to the number in question there are just that number of numbers, and then there are others that are greater. The number of finite whole numbers must, therefore, be an infinite number. But now comes a curious fact: The number of even numbers must be the same as the number of all whole numbers. Consider the two rows:

$$1, \ 2, \ 3, \ 4, \quad 5, \quad 6, \ \ldots .$$
$$2, \ 4, \ 6, \ 8, \ 10, \ 12, \ \ldots .$$

There is one entry in the lower row for every one in the top row; therefore the number of terms in the two rows must be the same, although the lower row consists of only half the terms in the top row. Leibniz, who noticed this, thought it a contradiction, and concluded that, though there are infinite collections, there are no infinite numbers. Georg Cantor, on the contrary, boldly denied that it is a contradiction. He was right; it is only an oddity.

Georg Cantor defined an "infinite" collection as one which has parts containing as many terms as the whole collection contains. On this basis he was able to build up a most interesting mathematical theory of infinite numbers, thereby taking into the realm of exact logic a whole region formerly given over to mysticism and confusion.

The next man of importance was Frege, who published his first work in 1879, and his definition of "number" in 1884; but, in spite of the epoch-making nature of his discoveries, he remained wholly without recognition until I drew attention to him in 1903. It is remarkable that, before Frege, every definition of number that had been suggested contained elementary logical blunders. It was customary to identify "number" with "plurality." But an instance of "number" is a particular number, say 3, and an instance of 3 is a particular triad. The triad is a plurality, but the class of all triads—which Frege identified with the number 3—is a plurality of pluralities, and number in general, of which 3 is an instance, is a plurality of pluralities of pluralities. The elementary grammatical mistake of confounding this with the simple plurality of a given triad made the whole philosophy of number, before Frege, a tissue of nonsense in the strictest sense of the term "nonsense."

From Frege's work it followed that arithmetic, and pure mathematics generally, is nothing but a prolongation of deductive logic. This disproved Kant's theory that arithmetical propositions are "synthetic" and involve a reference to time. The development of pure mathematics from logic was set forth in detail in *Principia Mathematica,* by Whitehead and myself.

It gradually became clear that a great part of philosophy can be reduced to something that may be called "syntax," though the word has to be used in a somewhat wider sense than has hitherto been customary. Some men, notably Carnap, have advanced the theory that all philosophical problems are really syntactical, and that, when errors in syntax are avoided, a philosophical problem is thereby either solved or shown to be insoluble. I think this is an overstatement, but there can be no doubt that the utility of philosophical syntax in relation to traditional problems is very great.

I will illustrate its utility by a brief explanation of what is called the theory of descriptions. By a "description" I mean a phrase such as "The present President of the United States," in which a person or thing is designated, not by name, but by some property which is supposed or known to be peculiar to him or it. Such phrases had given a lot of trouble. Suppose I say "The golden mountain does not exist," and suppose you ask "What is it that does not exist?" It would seem that, if I say "It is the golden mountain," I am attributing some sort of existence to it. Obviously I am not making the same statement as if I said, "The round square does not exist." This seemed to imply that the golden mountain is one thing and the round square is another, although neither exists. The theory of descriptions was designed to meet this and other difficulties.

According to this theory, when a statement containing a phrase of the form "the so-and-so" is rightly analysed, the phrase "the so-and-so" disappears. For example, take the statement "Scott was the author of *Waverley.*" The theory interprets this statement as saying:

"One and only one man wrote *Waverley,* and that man was Scott." Or, more fully:

"There is an entity c such that the statement 'x wrote *Waverley*' is true if x is c and false otherwise; moreover c is Scott."

The first part of this, before the word "moreover," is

defined as meaning: "The author of *Waverley* exists (or existed or will exist)." Thus "The golden mountain does not exist" means:

"There is no entity *c* such that '*x* is golden and mountainous' is true when *x* is *c*, but not otherwise."

With this definition the puzzle as to what is meant when we say "The golden mountain does not exist" disappears.

"Existence," according to this theory, can only be asserted of descriptions. We can say "The author of *Waverley* exists," but to say "Scott exists" is bad grammar, or rather bad syntax. This clears up two millennia of muddle-headedness about "existence," beginning with Plato's *Theaetetus*.

One result of the work we have been considering is to dethrone mathematics from the lofty place that it has occupied since Pythagoras and Plato, and to destroy the presumption against empiricism which has been derived from it. Mathematical knowledge, it is true, is not obtained by induction from experience; our reason for believing that 2 and 2 are 4 is not that we have so often found, by observation, that one couple and another couple together make a quartet. In this sense, mathematical knowledge is still not empirical. But it is also not *a priori* knowledge about the world. It is, in fact, merely verbal knowledge. "3" means "2 + 1," and "4" means "3 + 1." Hence it follows (though the proof is long) that "4" means the same as "2 + 2." Thus mathematical knowledge ceases to be mysterious. It is all of the same nature as the "great truth" that there are three feet in a yard.

Physics, as well as pure mathematics, has supplied material for the philosophy of logical analysis. This has occurred especially through the theory of relativity and quantum mechanics.

What is important to the philosopher in the theory of relativity is the substitution of space-time for space and time. Common sense thinks of the physical world as composed of "things" which persist through a certain period of time and move in space. Philosophy and physics developed the notion of "thing" into that of "material substance," and thought of material substance as consisting of particles, each very small, and each persisting throughout all time. Einstein substituted events for particles; each event had to each other a relation called "interval," which could be analysed in various ways into a time-element and a space-element. The choice between these various ways was arbitrary, and no one of them was theoretically preferable to any other. Given two events A and B, in different regions, it might happen that according to one convention they were simultaneous, according to another A was earlier than B, and according to yet another B was earlier than A. No physical facts correspond to these different conventions.

From all this it seems to follow that events, not particles, must be the "stuff" of physics. What has been thought of as a particle will have to be thought of as a series of events. The series of events that replaces a particle has certain important physical properties, and therefore demands our attention; but it has no more substantiality than any other series of events that we might arbitrarily single out. Thus "matter" is not part of the ultimate material of the world, but merely a convenient way of collecting events into bundles.

Quantum theory reinforces this conclusion, but its chief philosophical importance is that it regards physical phenomena as possibly discontinuous. It suggests that, in an atom (interpreted as above), a certain state of affairs persists for a certain time, and then suddenly is replaced by a finitely different state of affairs. Continuity of motion, which had always been assumed, appears to have been a mere prejudice. The philosophy appropriate to quantum theory, however, has not yet been adequately developed. I suspect that it will demand even more radical departures from the traditional doctrine of space and time than those demanded by the theory of relativity.

While physics has been making matter less material, psychology has been making mind less mental. We had occasion in a former chapter to compare the association of ideas with the conditioned reflex. The latter, which has replaced the former, is obviously much more physiological. (This is only one illustration; I do not wish to exaggerate the scope of the conditioned reflex.) Thus from both ends physics and psychology have been approaching each other, and making more possible the doctrine of "neutral monism" suggested by William James's criticism of "consciousness." The distinction of mind and matter came into philosophy from religion, although, for a long time, it seemed to have valid grounds. I think that both mind and matter are merely convenient ways of grouping events. Some single events, I should admit, belong only to material groups, but others belong to both kinds of groups, and are therefore at once mental and material. This doctrine effects a great simplification in our picture of the structure of the world.

Modern physics and physiology throw a new light upon the ancient problem of perception. If there is to be anything that can be called "perception," it must be in some degree an effect of the object perceived, and it must more or less resemble the object if it is to be a source of knowledge of the object. The first requisite can only be fulfilled if there are causal chains which are, to a greater or less extent, independent of the rest of the world. According to physics, this is the case. Light-waves travel from the sun to the earth, and in doing so obey their own laws. This is only roughly true. Einstein has shown that light-rays are affected by gravitation. When they reach our atmosphere, they suffer refraction, and some are more scattered than others. When they reach a human eye, all sorts of things happen which would not happen elsewhere, ending up with what we call "seeing the sun." But although the sun of our visual experience is very different from the sun of the astronomer, it is still a source of knowledge as to the latter, because "seeing the sun" differs from "seeing the moon" in ways that are causally connected with the difference between the astronomer's sun and the astronomer's moon. What we can know of physical objects in this way, however, is only certain abstract properties of structure. We can know that the sun is round in a sense, though not quite the sense in which what we see is round; but we have no reason to suppose that it is bright or warm, because physics can account for its seeming so without supposing that it is so. Our knowledge of the physical world, therefore, is only abstract and mathematical.

Modern analytical empiricism, of which I have been giving an outline, differs from that of Locke, Berkeley, and Hume by its incorporation of mathematics and its development of a powerful logical technique. It is thus able, in regard to certain problems, to achieve definite answers, which have the quality of science rather than of philosophy. It has the advantage, as compared with the philosophies of the system-builders, of being able to tackle its problems one at a time, instead of having to invent at one stroke a block theory of the whole universe. Its methods, in this respect, resemble those of science. I have no doubt that, in so far as philosophical knowledge is possible, it is by such methods that it must be sought; I have also no doubt that, by these methods, many ancient problems are completely soluble.

There remains, however, a vast field, traditionally included in philosophy, where scientific methods are inadequate. This field includes ultimate questions of value; science alone, for example, cannot prove that it is bad to enjoy the infliction of cruelty. Whatever can be known, can be known by means of science; but things which are legitimately matters of feeling lie outside its province.

Philosophy, throughout its history, has consisted of two parts inharmoniously blended: on the one hand a theory as to the nature of the world, on the other an ethical or political doctrine as to the best way of living. The failure to separate these two with sufficient clarity has been a source of much confused thinking. Philosophers, from Plato to William James, have allowed their opinions as to the constitution of the universe to be influenced by the desire for edification: knowing, as they supposed, what beliefs would make men virtuous, they have invented arguments, often very sophistical, to prove that these beliefs are true. For my part I reprobate this kind of bias, both on moral and on intellectual grounds. Morally, a philosopher who uses his professional competence for anything except a disinterested search for truth is guilty of a kind of treachery. And when he assumes, in advance of inquiry, that certain beliefs, whether true or false, are such as to promote good behaviour, he is so limiting the scope of philosophical speculation as to make philosophy trivial; the true philosopher is prepared to examine *all* preconceptions. When any limits are placed, consciously or unconsciously, upon the pursuit of truth, philosophy becomes paralyzed by fear, and the ground is prepared for a government censorship punishing those who utter "dangerous thoughts"— in fact, the philosopher has already placed such a censorship over his own investigations.

Intellectually, the effect of mistaken moral considerations upon philosophy has been to impede progress to an extraordinary extent. I do not myself believe that philosophy can either prove or disprove the truth of religious dogmas, but ever since Plato most philosophers have considered it part of their business to produce "proofs" of immortality and the existence of God. They have found fault with the proofs of their predecessors—Saint Thomas rejected Saint Anselm's proofs, and Kant rejected Descartes'—but they have supplied new ones of their own. In order to make their proofs seem valid, they have had to falsify logic, to make mathematics mystical, and to pretend that deep-seated prejudices were heaven-sent intuitions.

All this is rejected by the philosophers who make logical analysis the main business of philosophy. They confess frankly that the human intellect is unable to find conclusive answers to many questions of profound importance to mankind, but they refuse to believe that there is some "higher" way of knowing, by which we can discover truths hidden from science and the intellect. For this renunciation they have been rewarded by the discovery that many questions, formerly obscured by the fog of metaphysics, can be answered with precision, and by objective methods which introduce nothing of the philosopher's temperament except the desire to understand. Take such questions as: What is number? What are space and time? What is mind, and what is matter? I do not say that we can here and now give definite answers to all these ancient questions, but I do say that a method has been discovered by which, as in science, we can make successive approximations to the truth, in which each new stage results from an improvement, not a rejection, of what has gone before.

In the welter of conflicting fanaticisms, one of the few unifying forces is scientific truthfulness, by which I mean the habit of basing our beliefs upon observations and inferences as impersonal, and as much divested of local and temperamental bias, as is possible for human beings. To have insisted upon the introduction of this virtue into philosophy, and to have invented a powerful method by which it can be rendered fruitful, are the chief merits of the philosophical school of which I am a member. The habit of careful veracity acquired in the practice of this philosophical method can be extended to the whole sphere of human activity, producing, wherever it exists, a lessening of fanaticism with an increasing capacity of sympathy and mutual understanding. In abandoning a part of its dogmatic pretensions, philosophy does not cease to suggest and inspire a way of life.]

CHAPTER XIII

Logical Positivism:

Rudolf Carnap (b. 1891)

RUDOLF CARNAP IS ONE OF THE MOST DISTINGUISHED AND most productive representatives of a philosophical movement which is sometimes called logical postivism, sometimes logical empiricism. It is closely related to what Russell calls analytic empiricism in the previous selection, but there Russell is rather liberal in defining that view in order to depict a comparatively broad tendency in twentieth-century thought. Unlike Russell and Moore, Carnap has done a great deal of his philosophizing in a formally co-operative atmosphere, in groups that lay down platforms and manifestoes to which philosophers might sign their names. Like any small, self-conscious movement, logical positivism has often sought the protection of co-operation and even clubby solidarity; its official origin in 1923 is usually identified with a group called "The Vienna Circle" which grew out of a seminar conducted by Moritz Schlick, who had become professor of philosophy at Vienna in 1922. Its original members were mainly ex-scientists who had become philosophers and practicing scientists with an interest in philosophy, and in this respect the Circle was the culmination of a movement which had started on the continent in the latter part of the nineteenth century and which continued into the twentieth. Distinguished natural scientists like Ludwig Boltzmann, Pierre Duhem, Helmholtz, Ernst Mach, and Einstein had begun to throw off the shackles of philosophical dictators who pontificated on the nature of science with little first-hand knowledge of it. The influence of this group of scientists was primarily in the direction of empiricism, but the Vienna Circle also worshipped other gods: among them mathematical logicians like Peirce, Giuseppe Peano, Ernst Schroeder, Whitehead, the great Frege, and pre-eminently Bertrand Russell, whose work in logic was then quite recent. This marriage of the empirical and logical traditions was first solemnized by the name "Logical Positivism" in order to indicate the two families united, but this was later changed to "Logical Empiricism" when it was realized how bad the odor of the word "positivism" was for those who associated it with the narrowness of Auguste Comte.

Carnap, a German by birth, came to the University of Vienna in 1927 and participated actively in the discussions of the Vienna Circle, but Wittgenstein, whose *Tractatus Logico-Philosophicus* had appeared in 1921, was far more elusive and far less co-operative, though his book had a profound influence on the group. Very soon the doctrines of logical positivism spread throughout the world, chiefly to England and America. Schlick visited the United States in 1929; Wittgenstein settled in Cambridge, England, in the same year. When Hitler came to power, its scientific temper and its obvious incompatibility with racial and philosophical fanaticism made logical positivism too dangerous for Central Europe and vice versa. Carnap came to the United States in 1936 as professor at the University of Chicago, and Wittgenstein succeeded Moore in his chair at Cambridge in 1939. At first positivism met with the kind of reception it might have expected from philosophers who resented its desecration of the temples of metaphysics and ethics (it only called them meaningless). But soon it was treated more civilly by English philosophers who, after all, had also read Russell, and by Americans who had developed a respect for science and logic under the influence of Peirce, Royce, James, Dewey, and the younger logicians C. I. Lewis and H. M. Sheffer.

There are two sides to logical positivism: a negative, militant, critical, almost contemptuous attitude toward the previous history of philosophy, which expresses itself in hostility toward the traditional disciplines of metaphysics and ethics, and a positive, admiring attitude toward logic and the sciences. Together they led to the view that philosophy is nothing but the logic *of* science. The attack on metaphysics and ethics flowed from a very vigorous use of what is called "the empiricist criterion of meaning" and a refusal to recognize anything but mathematical and empirical statements as meaningful. The view that philosophy is the logic of science was related to the conviction that logic (including mathematics) is the only respectable cognitive activity besides empirical science, and the belief that philosophy should press forward in the tradition of *Principia Mathematica*. Philosophy was to do for other concepts and disciplines what that system had accomplished for logic and mathematics. Carnap has been a gifted and active leader in both campaigns. He was trained in physics, he is an accomplished logician, and an indefatigable worker.

The empiricist criterion of meaning was spiritually close to the pragmatic criterion of Peirce, and its development in Europe was stimulated by methodological conclusions drawn from modern physics, particularly from Einstein's conclusions about Newtonian absolutism. The distinction between mathematical and empirical truths goes back at least as far as Leibniz and Hume, both of whom had made a similar distinction only to be contradicted by Kant and therefore disregarded for most of the nineteenth century. According to many positivists, however, Kant's doctrine had been demolished by a combination of *Principia Mathematica* and Wittgenstein's *Tractatus,* so the way was presumably clear for a revival of earlier wisdom on this all-important issue. Hume is therefore one of the few figures in the history of philosophy whom positivists treat with respect. I shall devote the rest of my space in this chapter to a brief summary of the main positivistic views, particularly those of Carnap.

1. *The Empiricist Criterion of Meaning*

The point of this device was to save philosophers and scientists the trouble of disputing idly over meaningless questions. It was to disallow as nonsense any putatively scientific statement which could not possibly be confirmed or disconfirmed by appealing to sensory experience, and to admit as meaningful those that could be. Stated in this way, however, it was far too loose, almost traditionally philosophical in its vagueness. A movement dedicated to logical exactness felt obliged to specify more rigorously the connection between meaningful statements, whether true or false, and so-called observation statements like "This is red" and "That is hot." The question was: how are observation-statements logically connected with the more abstract and complicated statements of physics, for example? The formulae of physics, it was recognized, could not be translated into simple combinations of observation-statements. For one thing, because physical laws are more than summaries of sensory findings; they apply to the unobserved events of the future—that is the whole point of prediction in science. Some positivists adopted the heroic alternative of calling statements of physical laws meaningless, but Carnap and his closest friends were reluctant to take this course. Their statement of the relation between experience and meaningful theory had to be more subtle, nevertheless stringent enough to eliminate the hated metaphysical statements and sufficiently loose to admit the eminently respectable and meaningful statements of physics no matter how far removed from the direct reports of observation. The history of positivism has been hectic on this point and some positivists have come to despair of achieving any really airtight criterion by studying the relation between sensory reports and abstract theories as these occur in the actual practice of science. They have decided that a positivist should simply list a set of acceptable, observable predicates, and then propose that scientists never use sentences which cannot be put into an appropriate relation with this basic vocabulary. But even this *relation* between elected scientific terms and these charter-members, so to speak, has caused logical difficulties that are too technical to enter here. In any case, the search for logical exactitude has left a number of positivists less than optimistic about the possibility of getting airtight criteria of meaningfulness, and for them Wittgenstein's tendency to be less formalistic about such matters has been vindicated. Indeed, some philosophers—usually Englishmen—are content to "smell out" nonsense rather than try to establish rigid criteria for it, but nothing could be further from the original positivistic disdain for such "intuitions," such unscientific "private insights." Others, like Carnap, continue to think of the criterion as useful and extremely important in philosophy and deserving of further study.

2. *Empirical Truths vs. Mathematico-Logical Truths*

No matter how we formulate the nature of empirical truths, positivists say, we must recognize a fundamental distinction between them and the truths of mathematics. The truths of mathematics are *a priori,* true independently of experience. According to positivists, Leibniz and Hume —especially Hume—had correctly insisted that there are only two kinds of true statements: (a) those which are *a posteriori,* known by experience, and also *synthetic* like "All bachelors are eccentric" because the meaning of the predicate "eccentric" is not part of the meaning of the subject "bachelor"; (b) those which are *a priori,* known prior to experience, and *analytic* like "All bachelors are males" because the meaning of "bachelor" *does* contain the meaning of "male" as a part. Hume held that the statements of arithmetic fell into category (b) and, more generally, that all and only analytic statements are *a priori.*

Kant denied this and invented a hybrid category which he called the *synthetic a priori* and into which he said arithmetical truths fell. "7+5=12," he claimed, is *a priori* but we cannot discover its truth merely by observing the connections between the meanings of its terms. Most positivistic energy was directed against Kant on this point, chiefly on the basis of what Russell and Whitehead had shown in *Principia Mathematica* plus certain efforts of Wittgenstein in his *Tractatus*. Because they are so technical, they can only be stated superficially here. It was maintained that because the *Principia* had reduced all of mathematics to logic and because all of logic was what Wittgenstein called *tautologous*, it followed that all mathematical truths are analytic in this Wittgensteinian sense and therefore that the spirit of Hume's philosophy on this point had been vindicated. And even after it was shown that Wittgenstein's notion of tautology was too narrow for characterizing *all* of logic, Carnap leapt into the breach with a notion of analyticity that he thought would do the trick. This is a highly controversial field, however, and Carnap's conclusions are not accepted by all logicians.

3. *The Logical Analysis of Scientific Language*

Because he is quite convinced of the adequacy of the empiricist criterion of meaning and the distinction between analytic and synthetic, Carnap regards much of traditional metaphysics and ethical discourse as meaningless. What doesn't pass muster before the criterion of meaning (as all of empirical science must), and is not analytic (as mathematics and logic are), must be either self-contradictory or meaningless, and Carnap thinks that much of metaphysics like Heidegger's "The nothing naughts," and many so-called moral laws, fall into this category. They may have poetic or "emotive" meaning but they are cognitively meaningless. A school of ethical analysis flourishes in the light of this conclusion. It rejects the ethical naturalism of Dewey as well as Moore's view that moral goodness is a "non-natural" quality which is not detectable by scientific observation or experiment.

Under the circumstances Carnap concludes that philosophy is neither more nor less than the logical analysis of science. At one time he limited this to what he called the logical *syntax* of scientific language, which was restricted to studying the relations between signs conceived purely as syntactical shapes, but under the influence of the logician Alfred Tarski he has widened his view to include *semantics* or the study of the relation between signs and the objects they denote or connote. Both in turn are to be distinguished from *pragmatics,* which studies the relations between signs and their human senders and receivers, so to speak, for this is a more psychological question. Carnap has applied his methods to many important philosophical topics like necessity, existence, and probability and he has influenced a great many younger logicians and philosophers. Some who once followed him slavishly have come to disagree with him in recent years but even they do not question the intellectual honesty and vigor with which he has pursued his investigations for more than a generation.

The following passage consists of all but one paragraph of Chapter I, "The Rejection of Metaphysics," of Carnap's *Philosophy and Logical Syntax* (1935).[1]

{1. *Verifiability*

The problems of philosophy as usually dealt with are of very different kinds. From the point of view which I am here taking we may distinguish mainly three kinds of problems and doctrines in traditional philosophy. For the sake of simplicity we shall call these parts *Metaphysics-Psychology,* and *Logic.* Or, rather, there are not three distinct regions, but three sorts of components which in most theses and questions are combined: a metaphysical, a psychological, and a logical component.

The considerations that follow belong to the third region: we are here carrying out *Logical Analysis.* The function of logical analysis is to analyse all knowledge, all assertions of science and of everyday life, in order to

[1] Grateful acknowledgment is made to the Orthological Institute of London and to Mr. C. K. Ogden for permission to reprint the passage from *Philosophy and Logical Syntax* by Rudolf Carnap.

make clear the sense of each such assertion and the connections between them. One of the principal tasks of the
logical analysis of a given proposition is to find out the
method of verification for that proposition. The question
is: What reasons can there be to assert this proposition; or:
How can we become certain as to its truth or falsehood?
This question is called by the philosophers the epistemological question; epistemology or the philosophical theory
of knowledge is nothing other than a special part of logical
analysis, usually combined with some psychological questions concerning the process of knowing.

What, then, is the method of verification of a proposition? Here we have to distinguish between two kinds of
verification: direct and indirect. If the question is about
a proposition which asserts something about a present
perception, *e.g.* "Now I see a red square on a blue ground,"
then the proposition can be tested directly by my present
perception. If at present I do see a red square on a blue
ground, the proposition is directly verified by this seeing;
if I do not see that, it is disproved. To be sure, there are
still some serious problems in connection with direct verification. We will however not touch on them here, but give
our attention to the question of *indirect* verification, which
is more important for our purposes. A proposition P which
is not directly verifiable can only be verified by direct verification of propositions deduced from P together with other
already verified propositions.

Let us take the proposition P_1: "This key is made of
iron." There are many ways of verifying this proposition;
e.g.: I place the key near a magnet; then I perceive that
the key is attracted. Here the deduction is made in this way:
Premises: P_1: "This key is made of iron;" the proposi-
            tion to be examined.

$\qquad\qquad$ P_2: "If an iron thing is placed near a magnet,
            it is attracted;" this is a physical law, al-
            ready verified.

$\qquad\qquad$ P_3: "This object—a bar—is a magnet;" propro-
            sition already verified.

$\qquad\qquad$ P_4: "The key is placed near the bar;" this is now
            directly verified by our observation.

From these four premises we can deduce the conclusion:

P_5: "The key will now be attracted by the bar."

This proposition is a prediction which can be examined by observation. If we look, we either observe the attraction or we do not. In the first case we have found a positive instance, an instance of verification of the proposition P_1 under consideration; in the second case we have a negative instance, an instance of disproof of P_1.

In the first case the examination of the proposition P_1 is not finished. We may repeat the examination by means of a magnet, *i.e.* we may deduce other propositions similar to P_5 by the help of the same or similar premises as before. After that, or instead of that, we may make an examination by electrical tests, or by mechanical, chemical, or optical tests, etc. If in these further investigations all instances turn out to be positive, the certainty of the proposition P_1 gradually grows. We may soon come to a degree of certainty sufficient for all practical purposes, but *absolute* certainty we can never attain. The number of instances deducible from P_1 by the help of other propositions already verified or directly verifiable is *infinite*. Therefore there is always a possibility of finding in the future a negative instance, however small its probability may be. Thus the proposition P_1 *can never be completely verified*. For this reason it is called an *hypothesis*.

So far we have considered an individual proposition concerning one single thing. If we take a general proposition concerning all things or events at whatever time and place, a so-called natural *law*, it is still clearer that the number of examinable instances is infinite and so the proposition is an hypothesis.

Every assertion P in the wide field of science has this character, that it either asserts something about present perceptions or other experiences, and therefore is verifiable by them, or that propositions about future perceptions are deducible from P together with some other already verified propositions. If a scientist should venture to make an assertion from which no perceptive propositions could be deduced, what should we say to that? Suppose, *e.g.*, he asserts that there is not only a gravitational field having an effect on bodies according to the known laws of gravitation, but also a *levitational field,* and on being asked what sort of effect this levitational field has, according to his theory, he answers that there is no observable effect; in other words, he confesses his inability to give rules according to which we could deduce perceptive propositions from his assertion. In that case our reply is: your assertion is no assertion at all; it does not speak about anything; it is nothing but a series of empty words; it is simply without sense.

It is true that he may have images and even feelings connected with his words. This fact may be of psychological importance; logically, it is irrelevant. What gives theoretical meaning to a proposition is not the attendant images and thoughts, but the possibility of deducing from it perceptive propositions, in other words, the possibility of verification. To give sense to a proposition the presence of images is not sufficient; it is not even necessary. We have no actual image of the electro-magnetic field, nor even, I should say, of the gravitational field. Nevertheless the propositions which physicists assert about these fields have a perfect sense, because perceptive propositions are deducible from them. I by no means object to the proposition just mentioned about a levitational field that we do not know how to imagine or conceive such a field. My only objection to that proposition is that we are not told how to verify it.

2. *Metaphysics*

What we have been doing so far is *logical analysis.* Now we are going to apply these considerations not to propositions of physics as before, but to propositions of *metaphysics.* Thus our investigation belongs to *logic,* to the third of the three parts of philosophy spoken about before, but the *objects* of this investigation belong to the first part.

I will call *metaphysical* all those propositions which claim to represent knowledge about something which is over or beyond all experience, *e.g.* about the real Essence of things, about Things in themselves, the Absolute, and such like. I do not include in metaphysics those theories—sometimes called metaphysical—whose object is to arrange the most general propositions of the various regions of scientific knowledge in a well-ordered system; such theories belong actually to the field of empirical science, not of philosophy, however daring they may be. The sort of propositions I wish to denote as metaphysical may most easily be made clear by some examples: "The Essence and Principle of the world is Water," said Thales; "Fire," said Heraclitus; "the Infinite," said Anaximander; "Number," said Pythagoras. "All things are nothing but shadows of eternal ideas which themselves are in a spaceless and timeless sphere," is a doctrine of Plato. From the Monists we learn: "There is only one principle on which all that is, is founded"; but the Dualists tell us: "There are two principles." The Materialists say: "All that is, is in its essence material," but the Spiritualists say: "All that is, is spiritual." To metaphysics (in our sense of the word) belong the principal doctrines of Spinoza, Schelling, Hegel, and—to give at least one name of the present time—Bergson.

Now let us examine this kind of proposition from the point of view of *verifiability*. It is easy to realise that such propositions are not verifiable. From the proposition: "The Principle of the world is Water" we are not able to deduce any proposition asserting any perceptions or feelings or experiences whatever which may be expected for the future. Therefore the proposition, "The Principle of the world is Water," asserts nothing at all. It is perfectly analogous to the proposition in the fictive example above about the levitational field and therefore it has no more sense than that proposition. The Water-Metaphysician—as we may call him—has no doubt many images connected with his doctrine; but they cannot give sense to the proposition, any more than they could in the case of the levitational field. Metaphysicians cannot avoid making their propositions non-verifiable, because if they made them verifiable, the decision about the truth or falsehood of their doctrines would depend upon experience and therefore belong to the region of empirical science. This consequence they

wish to avoid, because they pretend to teach knowledge
which is of a higher level than that of empirical science.
Thus they are compelled to cut all connection between their
propositions and experience; and precisely by this procedure they deprive them of any sense.

3. Problems of Reality

So far I have considered only examples of such propositions as are usually called metaphysical. The judgment
I have passed on these propositions, namely, that they have
no empirical sense, may perhaps appear not very astonishing, and even trivial. But it is to be feared that the reader
will experience somewhat more difficulty in agreement
when I now proceed to apply that judgment also to philosophical doctrines of the type which is usually called epistemological. I prefer to call them also metaphysical because of their similarity, in the point under consideration,
to the propositions usually so called. What I have in mind
are the doctrines of Realism, Idealism, Solipsism, Positivism and the like, taken in their traditional form as asserting or denying the Reality of something. The Realist asserts
the Reality of the external world; the Idealist denies it. The
Realist—usually at least—asserts also the Reality of other
minds; the Solipsist—an especially radical Idealist—denies
it, and asserts that only his own mind or consciousness is
real. Have these assertions sense?

Perhaps it may be said that assertions about the reality
or unreality of something occur also in empirical science,
where they are examined in an empirical way, and that
therefore they have sense. This is quite true. But we have
to distinguish between two concepts of reality, one occurring in empirical propositions and the other occurring in
the philosophical propositions just mentioned. When a
zoologist asserts the reality of kangaroos, his assertion
means that there are things of a certain sort which can be
found and perceived at certain times and places; in other
words that there are objects of a certain sort which are
elements of the space-time system of the physical world.
This assertion is of course verifiable; by empirical investiga-

tion every zoologist arrives at a positive verification, independent of whether he is a Realist or an Idealist. Between
the Realist and the Idealist there is full agreement as to the
question of the reality of things of such and such sort, *i.e.*
of the possibility of locating elements of such and such sort
in the system of the physical world. The disagreement begins only when the question about the Reality of the physical world as a whole is raised. But this question has no
sense, because the reality of anything is nothing else than
the possibility of its being placed in a certain system, in
this case, in the space-time system of the physical world,
and such a question has sense only if it concerns elements
or parts, not if it concerns the system itself.

The same result is obtained by applying the criterion
explained before: the possibility of deducing perceptive
propositions. While from the assertion of the reality or the
existence of kangaroos we *can* deduce perceptive propositions, from the assertion of the Reality of the physical
world this is not possible; neither is it possible from the
opposite assertion of the Unreality of the physical world.
Therefore both assertions have no empirical content—no
sense at all. It is to be emphasized that this criticism of
having no sense applies equally to the assertion of Unreality. Sometimes the views of the *Vienna Circle* have been
mistaken for a denial of the Reality of the physical world,
but we make no such denial. It is true that we reject the
thesis of the Reality of the physical world; but we do not
reject it as false, but as having no sense, and its Idealistic
anti-thesis is subject to exactly the same rejection. We
neither assert nor deny these theses, we reject the whole
question.

All the considerations which apply to the question of
the Reality of the physical world apply also to the other
philosophical questions of Reality, *e.g.* the Reality of other
minds, the Reality of the given, the Reality of universals,
the Reality of qualities, the Reality of relations, the Reality
of numbers, etc. If any philosophical thesis answering any
of these questions positively or negatively is added to the
system of scientific hypotheses, this system will not in the
least become more effective; we shall not be able to make

any further prediction as to future experiences. Thus all these philosophical theses are deprived of empirical content, of theoretical sense; they are pseudo-theses.

If I am right in this assertion, the philosophical problems of Reality—as distinguished from the empirical problems of Reality—have the same logical character as the problems (or rather, pseudo-problems) of transcendental metaphysics earlier referred to. For this reason I call those problems of Reality not epistemological problems—as they usually are called—but metaphysical.

Among the metaphysical doctrines that have no theoretical sense I have also mentioned *Positivism,* although the *Vienna Circle* is sometimes designated as Positivistic. It is doubtful whether this designation is quite suitable for us. In any case we do not assert the thesis that only the Given is Real, which is one of the principal theses of traditional Positivism. The name Logical Positivism seems more suitable, but this also can be misunderstood. At any rate it is important to realize that our doctrine is a logical one and has nothing to do with metaphysical theses of the Reality or Unreality of anything whatever. What the character of a *logical* thesis is, will be made clear in the following chapters.

4. *Ethics*

One division of philosophy, which by some philosophers is considered the most important, has not been mentioned at all so far, namely, the philosophy of values, with its main branch, moral philosophy or *Ethics.* The word "Ethics" is used in two different senses. Sometimes a certain empirical investigation is called "Ethics," *viz.* psychological and sociological investigations about the actions of human beings, especially regarding the origin of these actions from feelings and volitions and their effects upon other people. Ethics in this sense is an empirical, scientific investigation; it belongs to empirical science rather than to philosophy. Fundamentally different from this is ethics in the second sense, as the philosophy of moral values or moral norms, which one can designate normative ethics. This is not an investigation of facts, but a pretended investigation of what is good and what is evil, what it is right to do and what it is wrong to do. Thus the purpose of this philosophical, or normative, ethics is to state norms for human action or judgments about moral values.

It is easy to see that it is merely a difference of formulation, whether we state a norm or a value judgment. A norm or rule has an imperative form, for instance: "Do not kill!" The corresponding value judgment would be: "Killing is evil." This difference of formulation has become practically very important, especially for the development of philosophical thinking. The rule, "Do not kill," has grammatically the imperative form and will therefore not be regarded as an assertion. But the value statement, "Killing is evil," although, like the rule, it is merely an expression of a certain wish, has the grammatical form of an assertive proposition. Most philosophers have been deceived by this form into thinking that a value statement is really an assertive proposition, and must be either true or false. Therefore they give reasons for their own value statements and try to disprove those of their opponents. But actually a value statement is nothing else than a command in a misleading grammatical form. It may have effects upon the actions of men, and these effects may either be in accordance with our wishes or not; but it is neither true nor false. It does not assert anything and can neither be proved nor disproved.

This is revealed as soon as we apply to such statements our method of logical analysis. From the statement "Killing is evil" we cannot deduce any proposition about future experiences. Thus this statement is not verifiable and has no theoretical sense, and the same thing is true of all other value statements.

Perhaps somebody will contend in opposition that the following proposition is deducible: "If a person kills anybody he will have feelings of remorse." But this proposition is in no way deducible from the proposition "Killing is evil." It is deducible only from psychological propositions about the character and the emotional reactions of the person. These propositions are indeed verifiable and not without sense. They belong to psychology, not to philosophy; to psychological ethics (if one wishes to use this word), not to philosophical or normative ethics. The propositions of normative ethics, whether they have the form of rules or the form of value statements, have no theoretical sense, are not scientific propositions (taking the word scientific to mean any assertive proposition).

To avoid misunderstanding it must be said that we do not at all deny the possibility and importance of a scientific investigation of value statements as well as of acts of valuation. Both of these are acts of individuals and are, like all other kinds of acts, possible objects of empirical investigation. Historians, psychologists, and sociologists may give analyses and causal explanations of them, and such historical and psychological propositions about acts of valuation and about value statements are indeed meaningful scientific propositions which belong to ethics in the first sense of this word. But the value statements themselves are here only objects of investigation; they are not propositions in these theories, and have, here as elsewhere, no theoretical sense. Therefore we assign them to the realm of metaphysics.

5. *Metaphysics as Expression*

Now we have analysed the propositions of metaphysics in a wide sense of this word, including not only transcendental metaphysics, but also the problems of philosophical Reality and lastly normative ethics. Perhaps many will agree that the propositions of all these kinds of metaphysics are not verifiable, *i.e.* that their truth cannot be examined by experience. And perhaps many will even grant that for this reason they have not the character of scientific propositions. But when I say that they are without sense, assent will probably seem more difficult. Someone may object: these propositions in the metaphysical books obviously have an effect upon the reader, and sometimes a very strong effect; therefore they certainly *express* something. That is quite true, they *do* express something, but nevertheless they have no sense, no theoretical content.

We have here to distinguish two functions of language, which we may call the expressive function and the representative function. Almost all the conscious and unconscious movements of a person, including his linguistic utterances, express something of his feelings, his present mood, his temporary or permanent dispositions to reaction, and the like. Therefore we may take almost all his movements and words as symptoms from which we can infer something about his feelings or his character. That is the expressive function of movements and words. But besides that, a certain portion of linguistic utterances (*e.g.* "this book is black"), as distinguished from other linguistic utterances and movements, has a second function: these utterances represent a certain state of affairs; they tell us that something is so and so; they assert something, they predicate something, they judge something.

In special cases, this asserted state may be the same as that which is inferred from a certain expressive utterance; but even in such cases we must sharply distinguish between the assertion and the expression. If, for instance, somebody is laughing, we may take this as a symptom of his merry mood; if on the other hand he tells us without laughing: "Now I am merry," we can learn from his words the same thing which we inferred in the first case from his laughing. Nevertheless, there is a fundamental difference between the laughter and the words: "I am merry now." This linguistic utterance *asserts* the merry mood, and therefore it is either true or false. The laughter does not assert the merry mood but *expresses* it. It is neither true nor false, because it does not assert anything, although it may be either genuine or deceptive.

Now many linguistic utterances are analogous to laughing in that they have only an expressive function, no representative function. Examples of this are cries like "Oh, Oh" or, on a higher level, lyrical verses. The aim of a lyrical poem in which occur the words "sunshine" and "clouds," is not to inform us of certain meteorological facts, but to express certain feelings of the poet and to excite similar feelings in us. A lyrical poem has no assertional sense, no theoretical sense, it does not contain knowledge.

The meaning of our anti-metaphysical thesis may now be more clearly explained. This thesis asserts that metaphysical propositions—like lyrical verses—have only an expressive function, but no representative function. Metaphysical propositions are neither true nor false, because they assert nothing, they contain neither knowledge nor error, they lie completely outside the field of knowledge, of theory, outside the discussion of truth or falsehood. But they are, like laughing, lyrics, and music, expressive. They express not so much temporary feelings as permanent emotional or volitional dispositions. Thus, for instance, a Metaphysical system of Monism may be an expression of an even and harmonious mode of life, a Dualistic system may be an expression of the emotional state of someone who takes life as an eternal struggle; an ethical system of Rigorism may be expressive of a strong sense of duty or perhaps of a desire to rule severely. Realism is often a symptom of the type of constitution called by psychologists extroverted, which is characterized by easily forming connections with men and things; Idealism, of an opposite constitution, the so-called introverted type, which has a tendency to withdraw from the unfriendly world and to live within its own thoughts and fancies.

Thus we find a great similarity between metaphysics and lyrics. But there is one decisive difference between them. Both have no representative function, no theoretical content. A metaphysical proposition, however—as distinguished from a lyrical verse—*seems* to have some, and by this not only is the reader deceived, but the metaphysician himself. He believes that in his metaphysical treatise he has asserted something, and is led by this into argument and polemics against the propositions of some other metaphysician. A poet, however, does not assert that the verses of another are wrong or erroneous; he usually contents himself with calling them bad.

The non-theoretical character of metaphysics would not be in itself a defect; all arts have this non-theoretical character without thereby losing their high value for personal as well as for social life. The danger lies in the *deceptive* character of metaphysics; it gives the illusion of knowledge without actually giving any knowledge. This is the reason why we reject it.

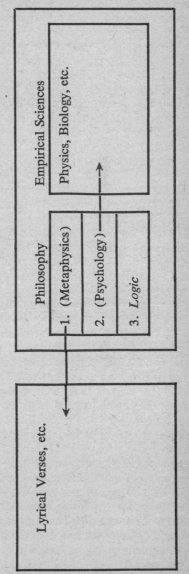

6. *Psychology*

When we have eliminated metaphysical problems and
doctrines from the region of knowledge or theory, there
remain still two kinds of philosophical questions: psychological and logical. Now we shall eliminate the psychological questions also, not from the region of knowledge, but
from philosophy. Then, finally, philosophy will be reduced to logic alone (in a wide sense of this word).

Psychological questions and propositions are certainly
not without sense. From such propositions we can deduce
other propositions about future experiences and by their
help we can verify the psychological propositions. But the
propositions of psychology belong to the region of empirical science in just the same way as do the propositions of
chemistry, biology, history and the like. The character of
psychology is by no means more philosophical than that
of the other sciences mentioned. When we look at the
historical development of the sciences we see that philosophy has been the mother of them all. One science after
another has been detached from philosophy and has become an independent science. Only in our time has the
umbilical cord between psychology and philosophy been
cut. Many philosophers have not yet realized quite clearly
that psychology is no longer an embryo, but an independent
organism, and that psychological questions have to be left
to empirical research.

Of course we have no objection to connecting psychological and logical investigations, any more than to connecting investigations of any scientific kind. We reject only
the confusion of the two kinds of questions. We demand
that they should be clearly distinguished even where in
practice they are combined. The confusion sometimes
consists in dealing with a logical question as if it were a
psychological one. This mistake—called Psychologism—
leads to the opinion that logic is a science concerning thinking, that is, either concerning the actual operation of thinking or the rules according to which thinking should proceed.
But as a matter of fact the investigation of operations of

thinking as they really occur is a task for psychology and has nothing to do with logic. And learning how to think *aright* is what we do in every other science as well as in logic. In astronomy we learn how to think aright about stars; in logic we learn how to think aright about the special objects of logic. What these special objects of logic are, will be seen in the next chapter. In any case thinking is not an object of logic, but of psychology.

Psychological questions concern all kinds of so-called psychic or mental events, all kinds of sensations, feelings, thoughts, images, etc., whether they are conscious or unconscious. These questions of psychology can be answered only by experience, not by philosophising.

7. *Logical Analysis*

The only proper task of *Philosophy* is *Logical Analysis*. And now the principal question to be answered here will be: *"What is logical analysis?"* In our considerations so far we have already practised logical analysis: we have tried to determine the character of physical hypotheses, of metaphysical propositions (or rather, pseudo-propositions), of psychological propositions. And now we have to apply logical analysis to logical analysis itself; we have to determine the character of the propositions of logic, of those propositions which are the results of logical analysis.

The opinion that metaphysical propositions have no sense because they do not concern any facts, has already been expressed by *Hume*. He writes in the last chapter of his *Enquiry Concerning Human Understanding* (published in the year 1748) as follows: "It seems to me, that the only objects of the abstract sciences or of demonstration, are quantity and number. . . . All other enquiries of men regard only matter of fact and existence; and these are evidently incapable of demonstration. . . . When we run over libraries, persuaded of these principles, what havoc must we make? If we take in our hand any volume, of divinity or school metaphysics, for instance; let us ask, Does it contain any abstract reasoning concerning quantity or number? No. Does it contain any experimental reasoning concerning matter of fact and existence? No. Commit it then to the flames: for it can contain nothing but sophistry and illusion." We agree with this view of Hume, which says—translated into our terminology—that only the propositions of mathematics and empirical science have sense, and that all other propositions are without sense.

. But now it may perhaps be objected: "How about your own propositions? In consequence of your view your own writings, including this book, would be without sense, for they are neither mathematical nor empirical, that is, verifiable by experience." What answer can be given to this objection? What is the character of my propositions and in general of the propositions of logical analysis? This question is decisive for the consistency of the view which has been explained here.

An answer to the objection is given by Wittgenstein in his book *Tractatus Logico-Philosophicus*. This author has developed most radically the view that the propositions of metaphysics are shown by logical analysis to be without sense. How does he reply to the criticism that in that case his own propositions are also without sense? He replies by agreeing with it. He writes: "The result of philosophy is not a number of 'philosophical propositions,' but to make propositions clear" (p. 77). "My propositions are elucidatory in this way: he who understands me finally recognizes them as senseless, when he has climbed out through them, on them, over them. (He must so to speak throw away the ladder, after he has climbed up on it.) He must surmount these propositions; then he sees the world rightly. Whereof one cannot speak, thereof one must be silent" (p. 189).

I, as well as my friends in the Vienna Circle, owe much to Wittgenstein, especially as to the analysis of metaphysics. But on the point just mentioned I cannot agree with him. In the first place he seems to me to be inconsistent in what he does. He tells us that one cannot state philosophical propositions and that whereof one cannot speak, thereof one must be Silent; and then instead of keeping silent, he writes a whole philosophical book. Secondly, I do not agree with his statement that all his propositions are quite as much without sense as metaphysical propositions are. My opinion is that a great number of his propositions (unfortunately not all of them) have in fact sense; and that the same is true for all propositions of logical analysis.]

CHAPTER XIV

The Uses of Language:

Ludwig Wittgenstein (1889–1951)

THE PHILOSOPHY OF LUDWIG WITTGENSTEIN IS MORE difficult to abstract and summarize than that of any other philosopher in this volume, and they all present difficulties. It's not that he uses obscure words or doubtful modes of inference or unilluminating metaphors, for he doesn't. Explaining his meaning is less like expounding a straightforward philosophical text and more like explaining just why or how a conversation with an understanding wife, lover, friend, or psychiatrist relieves anxiety. And Wittgenstein saw this, as the passage just quoted by Carnap suggests. Even in his posthumous *Philosophical Investigations,* written when Wittgenstein had renounced a good deal of his *Tractatus,* he reveals the same desire to produce philosophical insight by a kind of rearrangement of his reader's mental patterns, by a kind of intellectual shock treatment. It is not surprising, therefore, that some of his disciples have tried to relate his philosophizing to the art of psychoanalysis, or that others have compared it to the conversational dialectic of Socrates. Nor is it difficult to see why Wittgenstein's methods as a teacher have been compared to the whacks on the back delivered by Zen Buddhist masters, and his effect with the liberating experience of *Satori* of which Zen Buddhists speak. There are similarities, but, as Wittgenstein himself might have insisted, there are differences too.

Wittgenstein's first book, the *Tractatus,* bristles with logical symbols and shows the great influence of Russell, with whom he studied, and of Frege, whose work he greatly admired. In it he advanced a theory of the nature of logical truth, as we have seen in the last chapter, and a view of metaphysics and ethics which was quite congenial in outline to positivists. But even then his intellectual waywardness and his dark, aphoristic paragraphs were less than congenial to earnest logicians eager to transmit a coded but clear philosophical message to scientists. The gap between Wittgenstein's methods and those of more orthodox logical positivists grew even wider after he came to Cambridge, England. There his philosophizing was done mainly in lectures and conversations: after the *Tractatus* the only publication to appear in his lifetime was an article in a philosophical periodical. But against his wishes, his lecture notes were clandestinely typed and clandestinely circulated throughout the philosophical world. Those who did not know him sought to penetrate the mystery while those who did often encouraged a mystique and began to make faces like Wittgenstein in argument. Even the clear-headed Moore, who would terrorize some people by asking "What *exactly* do you mean?", had enormous regard for Wittgenstein in spite of not understanding a great deal of what he said. Moore attended Wittgenstein's lectures (some notes of which he published after Wittgenstein's death), spoke of Wittgenstein as more clever and more profound than himself, and said "He has made me think that what is required for the solution of philosophical problems which baffle me, is a method quite different from any which I have ever used—a method which he himself uses quite successfully, but which I have never been able to understand clearly enough to use it myself."[1] Russell, on the other hand, who knew him extremely well in his earlier and more logical period when he regarded him as a man of genius, lost touch with his views after 1919 and seems to think of them as excessively mystical in their tendency.

There are great differences between the philosophizing of Moore and Wittgenstein but they are far smaller than

---

[1] *Philosophy of G. E. Moore,* p. 33.

those between Russell and Wittgenstein. More and more,
Wittgenstein came to concentrate on the details of ordinary
language as Moore had before him; less and less did he
concern himself with building systems of logic like Russell,
and he was never interested in anything like the semantical
systems of Carnap. Instead of trying to reconstruct ordinary
language as Carnap did, and instead of asking "What
exactly do you mean?" and expecting a one-sentence answer like Moore's "To be a brother is to be a male sibling,"
Wittgenstein turned his attention to a different kind of
question. He was rather concerned with the origin and
therapy of metaphysical puzzlement and perplexity. This
was, of course, linked to his earlier and baldly stated view
that philosophical statements are meaningless, but later he
took a greater interest in the things that drove philosophers
into queer views or maddening puzzles and even greater
interest in how to help them out. He believed, as I understand him, that philosophical puzzlement can be eliminated
by a careful, scrupulous description of language as we actually use it. It is only when we study it in this way and
see how it works that we can disengage ourselves from the
traps of traditional philosophies like platonism and cartesianism. (These are not Wittgenstein's terms.) By platonism I mean the view that there are abstract entities called
meanings which exist above and over the words that express
them and the people who utter them; by cartesianism I
mean what Gilbert Ryle has called the doctrine of the
ghost in the machine, a purely spiritual soul joined mysteriously with a purely material body. Wittgenstein also objected to the view that there are special, momentary or
relatively short, inner *acts* of understanding in which cartesian souls grasp platonic meanings. He held, rather, that
to understand a word is to be able to use it in accord with
customary social practice and that philosophical puzzlement arises from our pressing unwarranted analogies between some linguistic habits and others that are related to
them by what he called "family resemblance."

In all of this, historically minded philosophers are likely
to see connections with other thinkers. Wittgenstein's distrust of queer entities reminds one of Russell's attack on

Meinong's golden-mountain argument and of his belief that philosophers should try to eliminate queer entities by the use of Occam's Razor. Wittgenstein's passionate interest in describing the use of language without metaphysical presuppositions is reminiscent of Husserl. His interest in describing the role, job, and function of words is like the pragmatists'. His hostility to cartesian dualism and his preoccupation with shared, social linguistic activity sound more like John Dewey than Dewey or Wittgenstein would have dreamed. The notion that _ch word is embedded in a large, linguistic contex* _.at swells into a "form of life" is certainly not utterly removed from idealism. And yet all of these attitudes and views are expressed by Wittgenstein in an original and very compelling way which cannot be explained by historical root-tracing or by textbook summary. Moreover, there are details that cannot be classified under any of the attitudes I have mentioned. "The meaning is the use" was Wittgenstein's most famous slogan and it applies tenfold to his own words. To understand him one must read him and see the use of it.

Today his philosophy is at the height of its influence in academic circles, chiefly as a result of the appearance of his *Philosophical Investigations*. When he was alive and teaching at Cambridge that university was the center of his English influence, particularly since he did not publish. Since then it has spread to Oxford too where it is a source of a great deal of new activity. There are a number of ironies in this, chief among them the fact that Oxford has long been the home of the kind of metaphysics for which Wittgenstein sought the diagnosis and cure. But it is also less scientifically oriented than Cambridge and therefore initially well-disposed to a philosophy that requires no more than attention to ordinary language as a prerequisite. So far the main concern of philosophy under the influence of Wittgenstein has been with the language of very ordinary men, but it shows signs of seriously spreading to the language of law, history, politics, literature, and esthetics. When it does, at least one circle of twentieth-century thought will have been completed, for an offshoot of the analytic tradition will have come closer to the study of human problems and matters of common concern. Whether for good or ill remains to be seen, but at any rate such an outcome would effectively silence those who hold that *only* philosophers like Bergson, Croce, Sartre, Whitehead, and Santayana are even remotely interested in the problems of human life.

The passage below gives a glimpse of the contrast between the later Wittgenstein and all three of the other "analytic" philosophers represented in this volume: Carnap, Moore, and Russell. In fact the contrast is great enough to warrant our not calling the later Wittgenstein an analytic philosopher at all. He abandoned Moore's effort to produce clear and logically complex synonyms for obscure philosophical words. He had grave doubts about the philosophical value of constructing artificial systems in the manner of the early Russell and Carnap. Instead he became interested in seeing what he calls the "family resemblances" and differences among different uses, jobs, or functions of the same word. In large measure, therefore, Wittgenstein's philosophizing consisted in distinguishing the various fibers of usage connected with words that give rise to philosophical puzzles, stressing the fact that we cannot always find one fiber that runs through the length of the thread. When we insist that there is, we propel ourselves into philosophical perplexity that can be escaped only by distinguishing and connecting the various strands. That is why, to use another metaphor of Wittgenstein's, his last work is a philosophical album rather than a monumental picture of the whole of things.

The passage reproduced below (sections 65-77) comes from a part of his *Philosophical Investigations* which Wittgenstein had completed in 1945.[1] The editors of the volume explain that certain passages which they print beneath a line at the foot of some pages were written on slips which Wittgenstein had cut from other writings and inserted at

[1] I wish to thank Basil Blackwell of Oxford for permission to reprint these sections from *Philosophical Investigations* by Ludwig Wittgenstein, translated by G. E. M. Anscombe (1953). The original German text of this passage is printed in an appendix on page 244 in response to a request of the publishers. They have followed Wittgenstein's wish that his German text always be available to the reader of his work.

these pages, without any further indication of where they were to come in. The one such passage here (between No. 70 and No. 71) is preceded and followed by a line.

[65. Here we come up against the great question that lies behind all these considerations.—For someone might object against me: "You take the easy way out! You talk about all sorts of language-games, but have nowhere said what the essence of a language-game, and hence of language, is: what is common to all these activities, and what makes them into language or parts of language. So you let yourself off the very part of the investigation that once gave you yourself most headache, the part about the *general form of propositions* and of language."

And this is true.—Instead of producing something common to all that we call language, I am saying that these phenomena have no one thing in common which makes us use the same word for all,—but that they are *related* to one another in many different ways. And it is because of this relationship, or these relationships, that we call them all "language." I will try to explain this.

66. Consider for example the proceedings that we call "games." I mean board-games, card-games, ball-games, Olympic games, and so on. What is common to them all?—Don't say: "There *must* be something common, or they would not be called 'games' "—but *look and see* whether there is anything common to all.—For if you look at them you will not see something that is common to *all,* but similarities, relationships, and a whole series of them at that. To repeat: don't think, but look!—Look for example at board-games, with their multifarious relationships. Now pass to card-games; here you find many correspondences with the first group, but many common features drop out, and others appear. When we pass next to ball-games, much that is common is retained, but much is lost.—Are they all 'amusing'? Compare chess with noughts and crosses. Or is there always winning and losing, or competition between players? Think of patience. In ball-games there is winning and losing; but when a child throws his ball at the wall and catches it again, this feature has disappeared.

Look at the parts played by skill and luck; and at the difference between skill in chess and skill in tennis. Think now of games like ring-a-ring-a-roses; here is the element of amusement, but how many other characteristic features have disappeared! And we can go through the many, many other groups of games in the same way; can see how similarities crop up and disappear.

And the result of this examination is: we see a complicated network of similarities overlapping and criss-crossing: sometimes overall similarities, sometimes similarities of detail.

67. I can think of no better expression to characterize these similarities than "family resemblances"; for the various resemblances between members of a family: build, features, colour of eyes, gait, temperament, etc. etc. overlap and criss-cross in the same way.—And I shall say: 'games' form a family.

And for instance the kinds of number form a family in the same way. Why do we call something a "number"? Well, perhaps because it has a—direct—relationship with several things that have hitherto been called number; and this can be said to give it an indirect relationship to other things we call the same name. And we extend our concept of number as in spinning a thread we twist fibre on fibre. And the strength of the thread does not reside in the fact that some one fibre runs through its whole length, but in the overlapping of many fibres.

But if someone wished to say: "There is something common to all these constructions—namely the disjunction of all their common properties"—I should reply: Now you are only playing with words. One might as well say: "Something runs through the whole thread—namely the continuous overlapping of those fibres."

68. "All right: the concept of number is defined for you as the logical sum of these individual interrelated concepts: cardinal numbers, rational numbers, real numbers, etc.; and in the same way the concept of a game as the logical sum of a corresponding set of sub-concepts."——It need not be so. For I *can* give the concept 'number' rigid limits in this way, that is, use the word "number" for

a rigidly limited concept, but I can also use it so that the extension of the concept is *not* closed by a frontier. And this is how we do use the word "game." For how is the concept of a game bounded? What still counts as a game and what no longer does? Can you give the boundary? No. You can *draw* one; for none has so far been drawn. (But that never troubled you before when you used the word "game.")

"But then the use of the word is unregulated, the 'game' we play with it is unregulated."—It is not everywhere circumscribed by rules; but no more are there any rules for how high one throws the ball in tennis, or how hard; yet tennis is a game for all that and has rules too.

69. How should we explain to someone what a game is? I imagine that we should describe *games* to him, and we might add: "This *and similar things* are called 'games.'" And do we know any more about it ourselves? Is it only other people whom we cannot tell exactly what a game is? —But this is not ignorance. We do not know the boundaries because none have been drawn. To repeat, we can draw a boundary—for a special purpose. Does it take that to make the concept usable? Not at all! (Except for that special purpose.) No more than it took the definition: 1 pace = 75 cm. to make the measure of length 'one pace' usable. And if you want to say "But still, before that it wasn't an exact measure," then I reply: very well, it was an inexact one.—Though you still owe me a definition of exactness.

70. "But if the concept 'game' is uncircumscribed like that, you don't really know what you mean by a 'game.'" —When I give the description: "The ground was quite covered with plants"—do you want to say I don't know what I am talking about until I can give a definition of a plant?

My meaning would be explained by, say, a drawing and the words "The ground looked roughly like this." Perhaps I even say "it looked *exactly* like this."—Then were just *this* grass and *these* leaves there, arranged just like this? No, that is not what it means. And I should not accept any picture as exact in *this* sense.

Someone says to me: "Show the children a game." I
teach them gaming with dice, and the other says "I didn't
mean that sort of game." Must the exclusion of the game
with dice have come before his mind when he gave me the
order?

---

71. One might say that the concept 'game' is a concept
with blurred edges.—"But is a blurred concept a concept
at all?"—Is an indistinct photograph a picture of a person
at all? Is it even always an advantage to replace an indistinct picture by a sharp one? Isn't the indistinct one often
exactly what we need?

Frege compares a concept to an area and says that an
area with vague boundaries cannot be called an area at all.
This presumably means that we cannot do anything with it.
—But is it senseless to say: "Stand roughly there"? Suppose that I were standing with someone in a city square
and said that. As I say it I do not draw any kind of
boundary, but perhaps point with my hand—as if I were
indicating a particular *spot*. And this is just how one might
explain to someone what a game is. One gives examples
and intends them to be taken in a particular way.—I do
not, however, mean by this that he is supposed to see in
those examples that common thing which I—for some
reason—was unable to express; but that he is now to *employ* those examples in a particular way. Here giving examples is not an *indirect* means of explaining—in default of
a better. For any general definition can be misunderstood
too. The point is that *this* is how we play the game. (I mean
the language-game with the word "game.")

72. *Seeing what is common.* Suppose I show someone
various multi-coloured pictures, and say: "The colour you
see in all these is called 'yellow ochre.' "—This is a definition, and the other will get to understand it by looking for
and seeing what is common to the pictures. Then he can
look *at,* can point *to,* the common thing.

Compare with this a case in which I show him figures of
different shapes all painted the same colour, and say:
"What these have in common is called 'yellow ochre.' "

And compare this case: I show him samples of different shades of blue and say: "The colour that is common to all these is what I call 'blue'."

73. When someone defines the names of colours for me by pointing to samples and saying "This colour is called 'blue,' this 'green' . . ." this case can be compared in many respects to putting a table in my hands, with the words written under the colour-samples.—Though this comparison may mislead in many ways.—One is now inclined to extend the comparison: to have understood the definition means to have in one's mind an idea of the thing defined, and that is a sample or picture. So if I am shown various different leaves and told "This is called a 'leaf,' " I get an idea of the shape of a leaf, a picture of it in my mind.—But what does the picture of a leaf look like when it does not show us any particular shape, but "what is common to all shapes of leaf?" Which shade is the "sample in my mind" of the colour green—the sample of what is common to all shades of green?

"But might there not be such 'general' samples? Say a schematic leaf, or a sample of *pure* green?"—Certainly there might. But for such a schema to be understood as a *schema,* and not as the shape of a particular leaf, and for a slip of pure green to be understood as a sample of all that is greenish and not as a sample of pure green—this in turn resides in the way the samples are used.

Ask yourself: what *shape* must the sample of the colour green be? Should it be rectangular? Or would it then be the sample of a green rectangle?—So should it be "irregular" in shape? And what is to prevent us then from regarding it—that is, from using it—only as a sample of irregularity of shape?

74. Here also belongs the idea that if you see this leaf as a sample of "leaf shape in general" you *see* it differently from someone who regards it as, say, a sample of this particular shape. Now this might well be so—though it is not so—for it would only be to say that, as a matter of experience, if you *see* the leaf in a particular way, you use it in such-and-such a way or according to such-and-such rules. Of course, there is such a thing as seeing in *this* way

or *that*; and there are also cases where whoever sees a sample like *this* will in general use it in *this* way, and whoever sees it otherwise in another way. For example, if you see the schematic drawing of a cube as a plane figure consisting of a square and two rhombi you will, perhaps, carry out the order "Bring me something like this" differently from someone who sees the picture three-dimensionally.

75. What does it mean to know what a game is? What does it mean, to know it and not be able to say it? Is this knowledge somehow equivalent to an unformulated definition? So that if it were formulated I should be able to recognize it as the expression of my knowledge? Isn't my knowledge, my concept of a game, completely expressed in the explanations that I could give? That is, in my describing examples of various kinds of game; showing how all sorts of other games can be constructed on the analogy of these; saying that I should scarcely include this or this among games; and so on.

76. If someone were to draw a sharp boundary I could not acknowledge it as the one that I too always wanted to draw, or had drawn in my mind. For I did not want to draw one at all. His concept can then be said to be not the same as mine, but akin to it. The kinship is that of two pictures, one of which consists of colour patches with vague contours, and the other of patches similarly shaped and distributed, but with clear contours. The kinship is just as undeniable as the difference.

77. And if we carry this comparison still further it is clear that the degree to which the sharp picture *can* resemble the blurred one depends on the latter's degree of vagueness. For imagine having to sketch a sharply defined picture "corresponding" to a blurred one. In the latter there is a blurred red rectangle: for it you put down a sharply defined one. Of course—several such sharply defined rectangles can be drawn to correspond to the indefinite one.— But if the colours in the original merge without a hint of any outline won't it become a hopeless task to draw a sharp picture corresponding to the blurred one? Won't you then have to say: "Here I might just as well draw a circle or heart as a rectangle, for all the colours merge." Anything—

and nothing—is right.—And this is the position you are in if you look for definitions corresponding to our concepts in aesthetics or ethics.

In such a difficulty always ask yourself: How did we *learn* the meaning of this word ("good" for instance)? From what sort of examples? in what language-games? Then it will be easier for you to see that the word must have a family of meanings.]

CHAPTER XV

Philosophy and Man:

An Exhortation

THE READER WHO HAS HAD THE INTEREST AND THE courage to come this far may well be bewildered by the variety of philosophical thought he has encountered. He has read about a dozen doctrines, as many methods, and a variety of concepts from essence to existence, life to language, logic to love, and practice to perfection. But within this welter several contrasts stand out: first of all the fundamental one between philosophers who strive to know big things and those who are less ambitious; and secondly, the peculiarly geographical character of this division. It does seem as though the continent of Europe is the land of the hedgehog while the English-speaking world is the home of the philosophical fox. No matter how one resists the idea of geographical determinism in intellectual matters, it is true that Bergson and Sartre span an enormous amount of French thinking in the twentieth century; that Croce was the spiritual leader of Italy for more than a generation; that philosophers like Husserl, Wilhelm Dilthey, and Max Weber encouraged the tradition of philosophical vastness in Germany for years, and that they were succeeded by Jaspers and Heidegger. Moreover, the continental philosophers' interest in subjects outside of philosophy, particularly in biology, history, literature, and the social sciences, is naturally accompanied by an influence that extends well beyond professional philosophical circles, and in this respect they emulate Hegel without being hegelians. It is also true that English thinkers like Russell and Moore are engaged in a more deflationary effort, in whittling philosophy down to manageable size, while the main American philosophers like Dewey and James try to blunt the point and the edge of scientific and analytic methods, to soften the blow at traditional philosophical sensibility. This is undoubtedly why so many English and American observers of the present philosophical scene in Europe deplore the persistence of obscurity and pretentiously displayed learning that seem so irrelevant to the real problems of philosophy. It is also why so many continental philosophers—whether they are existentialists, marxists, or phenomenologists—regard English and American analysts and positivists as heartless philistines.

Writing in the magazine *Horizon* in 1949 a distinguished Oxford professor, H. H. Price, said of the British philosophers' concern with perception: "I have been told that Continental philosophers find this national pastime of ours very puzzling; and I have heard one of them suggest that it is connected in some way with the Wordsworthian attitude to Nature, and with our national taste for landscape painting. Perhaps there is some connection (if there is, it is nothing to be ashamed of). But for my part I find it puzzling that so many Continental philosophers are *not* interested in perception at all, and prefer to spend their lives talking about dreary subjects like *Kulturphilosophie*." And it is reported that when Henry Sidgwick, the last great utilitarian, was asked by a German philosopher how the English got along without an equivalent for the word "Gelehrte," Sidgwick (a stutterer) replied: "We call them p-p-prigs." But a match for both of these is the reply of the French existentialist who was asked for his comment on a particularly careful criticism of his views by a logical positivist: "He is a cow!"

One wonders about the likelihood of effective communication between cows and prigs, or between hedgehogs and foxes, especially when they are of different nationalities. Nevertheless it is a mistake to think of this geographical division of the Western philosophers as more than a rough generalization having deep historical roots and understandable social and political concomitants. One should not conclude that it is psychologically impossible for courageous souls to penetrate the thick fog that has dropped between some philosophers of the continent and some English-speaking philosophers. For after all, much of contemporary Anglo-American interest in logical analysis, science, and language originates in the work of the Austrians Wittgenstein and Schlick, and the Germans Carnap and Reichenbach who had learned a great deal from Russell, who in turn had learned from Frege in a more internationally minded period. Moreover, Dewey, Santayana, and Whitehead—three of the great English-speaking philosophers of the twentieth century—have been philosophers in the grand manner, and even the language of the existentialists, which seems so difficult to our ears, has its English translators and, I think, its affinities with developments in England and America.

If there is any gulf between the style, the terminology, and the interests of philosophers all over the world it cannot be laid up merely to difference of tongue, or location, or historical background, for we know that there are political forces which foster and indeed demand the continuation of such a gulf. The philosophers behind the iron curtain are forbidden to espouse any philosophy other than dialectical materialism, and there are religious institutions in the world which impose rigid limits upon the philosophical beliefs of their adherents. An honest man, therefore, can hardly point to philosophy itself and accuse it of an incapacity to come to universal agreement when such agreement is blocked by terror and orthodoxy.

But let us perform an experiment in imagination—unfortunately only in imagination. Let us suppose that the various social and political curtains and bans have been lifted and ask whether philosophers of different lands and tongues might, even in this state of nature, *understand* each other—to say nothing about agreeing with each other. What then? Would we come to anything like the kind of co-operation that we find in the sciences? One must answer no, I think, but this time we are in paradise, so we cannot explain our failures by terror and orthodoxy. This time philosophers must look into themselves and there they will find divisions which are at least as effective as terror and orthodoxy in blocking philosophical communication. They will find the doctrine that there are methods of arriving at *knowledge* which transcend reason and experience; they will find a sharp and untenable dualism between reason and experience themselves enshrined in the distinction between analytic and synthetic statements; they will meet a similar contrast between the so-called normative statements of ethics and the descriptive statements of science. And all of this is the result of a desperate effort to maintain that there are fundamentally different methods of arriving at knowledge which correspond to the supposedly different subject matters of metaphysics, ethics, and science—to say nothing of theology. The hedgehogs do not merely think they know one big thing; they think they know it in a special way; the self-appointed custodians of our morals think they know what *they* claim to know in a special way; the logicians persuade themselves that they need only look at meanings or words when justifying their formulae.

But let it be supposed for a moment that these dichotomies are surrendered and see how much of the fog can be lifted. Let it be recognized that a philosopher has as much responsibility to defend what he says by appealing to experience as a scientist or an historian, and that he has no special insights that set him above the crowd; let it be supposed that every statement is, as Wittgenstein says, part of a "form of life" and therefore that the decision to accept it or reject it involves reverberations beyond itself; let it be supposed that something analogous is true of the decision to accept or reject a moral judgment; let it be supposed, in short, that all of our knowledge, whether moral, metaphysical, logical, or scientific, is bound into one system, a way of life from which no statement escapes or enters without affecting, however remotely, the status of another. Then what? I suggest that the effort to draw sharp lines between the analytic and the synthetic, the metaphysical and the logical, the descriptive and the normative, will appear silly and futile. There will be judgments to which we attach more weight than others, of course, but they will come from many different fields, so that our stock of fundamental beliefs at a given moment will be pluralistically composed. It won't be possible to isolate all of them as truths of logic, or truths of mathematics, or truths of metaphysics, or truths of science. Disciplinary labeling will not be a mark of certainty, and indeed, the search for a sharp *criterion* of certainty or necessity will emerge as equally futile.

Traditional preoccupation with finding a criterion of certainty and identifying it with a given discipline, whether it be mathematics or the empirical sciences, has gone hand in hand with the notion that such a solid criterion could provide a philosopher's stone. In the medieval age of belief, and the seventeenth century's age of reason we see classic examples of this effort to single out one faculty or one science as key to the universe or the intellectual globe. One kind of knowing is set up as a model whose method the others are asked to follow whether it be theology or mathematics. In the eighteenth century the triumph of Newton's physics made mechanics king; in the nineteenth Hegel's history and Darwin's biology took on a similar importance, and toward the close of that century psychology made a strong bid to dominate philosophical studies. In place of this disciplinary imperialism the twentieth century tends to be more democratic and pluralistic. Not only does it avoid setting up one kind of *knowledge* as central, but it even denies the centrality of knowing as a form of human activity. This is evident not only in the extreme vitalism of Bergson, but also in Wittgenstein's effort to show that language has many different uses, which are all of interest to a philosopher. It is reflected in the pluralistic metaphysics of James and even in Dewey's denial of what he calls the ubiquity of the knowing experience. It is illustrated by the later tendency of logical positivists to avoid what has been called the reductive fallacy. Once it becomes clear that there are no sharp lines of demarcation between the disciplines and that no one of them can claim a fundamental position in the scheme of knowing, and once it becomes clear that there are forms of human experience which are just as important as knowing, the way is open to a philosophical study of man in the broadest sense.

If such a dream were realized, which means if the point of view outlined were to be generally accepted, can there be any question but that *some* of the conflicts and misunderstandings of contemporary philosophy would be resolved? If it were accepted, the grand philosophers would surrender the notion that they can know one big thing without knowing or feeling lots of little things, and the minute philosophers would make an effort to know big things. The analysts would have recognized the absurdity of doing analysis without knowing a great deal more of science than they usually know; they would realize that the task of analyzing moral notions cannot be separated sharply from that of making moral judgments or describing or feeling the emotions associated with them. The tradition of philosophy which has been preoccupied with the methods of physics and mathematics would have recognized the need and the importance of treating human behavior in a rational way. Science would no longer be the bugbear or the underling of philosophy but a less than constant companion. The philosopher would profit through knowledge of other disciplines, to say nothing of profiting through absorbing other experiences. Differences of all kinds might be drawn, but they would not be made in the sledge-hammer fashion of the philosopher who announces that all ethical statements are like this and all scientific statements are like that in a manner that is more like simple Thales and the rest of the pre-Socratics than moderns prefer to admit. Each statement would be studied in its own right, but always in a context that transcends the single isolated statement itself.

It should be realized, of course, that I am not calling for

a revival of absolute idealism. But I am prepared to recognize an affinity between that wrongheaded doctrine and the one I advance. Idealism's insight into the interconnectedness of all things should be transported to a linguistic level. Instead of saying that everything is mysteriously connected with everything else, it is better to say that all statements which express knowledge are logically connected with each other inasmuch as we can always reject some other statement than the one ostensibly under fire by feeling or experience. The significance of this point of view is obvious. If he takes it seriously, the philosopher is obliged to familiarize himself with more than *one part* of philosophy as traditionally conceived, indeed with more than *philosophy* as traditionally conceived. The hedgehog may lie down with the fox, and the result need not be grotesque. So long as we think of philosophy as a tightly compartmentalized subject in which there are Sartres who move us, and Carnaps who prove for us, we are bound to see the philosophical world torn by something far more depressing than disagreement, and that is the complete incapacity of philosophers to *understand* each other.

Throughout this volume I have tried my hardest, with an excusable amount of irony in some cases, to present the views of some philosophers whose views are very far from my own. I trust that in my efforts at objectivity I have not succeeded in hiding the fact that my own philosophical sympathies are closest to the pragmatic and analytic traditions, but I must also add that I sympathize with the *concerns* of some of the philosophers in the first part of the volume. I believe, therefore, that nothing could be more important than reuniting these two contrasting elements in twentieth-century philosophy—the analytic, pragmatic, linguistic concern of the recent Anglo-American tradition supplemented by some of the insights and the more humane, cultivated concerns of the predominantly continental tradition. As long as they are kept separate, as long as the custodians of philosophical technique develop axes with which to sharpen other axes, they risk developing a sense of weariness and emptiness in themselves and in those who read them. As long as the more literate and more cultivated devotees of philosophy persist in ignoring the great achievements of Russell, Moore, Carnap, and Wittgenstein, in forgetting that the giants of the old days to whom they look back nostalgically—Plato, Aristotle, Descartes, Locke, Hume, and Kant, for example—were tough, technical thinkers as well as men of feeling and vision, they will impede the revival of philosophy's strength. What Hegel saw in a Gothic dream and conveyed in a myth was a little close to the truth. For while a philosopher is not obliged to make himself an expert in all fields, and to produce dull or bogus summaries of all knowledge in the manner of Herbert Spencer or Hegel himself, he should be trained to discover the important similarities and the important differences between the chief activities of man. Knowing, as Bergson insisted, is not everything, and there are interesting general facts about feeling and doing which a philosopher might well relate to knowing—his main traditional concern. Should he heed the call to examine them without becoming a charlatan he will have done a great deal to bolster the strength of philosophy. We live in dreadful times, when a world in conflict seeks and despises that combination of technique and vision for which the great philosophers are justly famous; their successors should not shirk the responsibility to carry on with equal respect for logic and life.

Appendix

Original German Text of Sections 65-77 of Wittgenstein's *Philosophical Investigations*

65. Hier stossen wir auf die grosse Frage, die hinter allen diesen Betrachtungen steht.—Denn man könnte mir nun einwenden: "Du machst dir's leicht! Du redest von allen möglichen Sprachspielen, hast aber nirgends gesagt, was denn das Wesentliche des Sprachspiels, und also der Sprache, ist. Was allen diesen Vorgängen gemeinsam ist und sie zur Sprache, oder zu Teilen der Sprache macht. Du schenkst dir also gerade den Teil der Untersuchung, der dir selbst seinerzeit das meiste Kopfzerbrechen gemacht hat, nämlich den, die *allgemeine Form des Satzes* und der Sprache betreffend."

Und das ist wahr.—Statt etwas anzugeben, was allem, was wir Sprache nennen, gemeinsam ist, sage ich, es ist diesen Erscheinungen garnicht Eines gemeinsam, weswegen wir für alle das gleiche Wort verwenden,—sondern sie sind mit einander in vielen verschiedenen Weisen *verwandt*. Und dieser Verwandtschaft, oder dieser Verwandtschaften wegen nennen wir sie alle "Sprachen". Ich will versuchen, dies zu erklären.

66. Betrachte z. B. einmal die Vorgänge, die wir "Spiele" nennen. Ich meine Brettspiele, Kartenspiele, Ballspiele, Kampfspiele, u.s.w.. Was ist allen diesen gemeinsam?—Sag nicht: "Es *muss* ihnen etwas gemeinsam sein, sonst hiessen sie nicht 'Spiele'"—sondern *schau*, ob ihnen allen etwas gemeinsam ist.—Denn, wenn du sie anschaust, wirst du zwar nicht etwas sehen, was *allen* gemeinsam wäre, aber du wirst Aehnlichkeiten, Verwandtschaften, sehen, und zwar eine ganze Reihe. Wie gesagt: denk nicht, sondern schau!—Schau z.B. die Brettspiele an, mit ihren mannigfachen Verwandtschaften. Nun geh zu den Kartenspielen über: hier findest du viele Entsprechungen mit jener ersten Klasse, aber viele gemeinsame Züge verschwinden, andere treten auf. Wenn wir nun zu den Ballspielen übergehen, so bleibt manches Gemeinsame erhalten, aber vieles geht verloren.— Sind sie alle *'unterhaltend'*? Vergleiche Schach mit dem Mühlfahren. Oder gibt es überall ein Gewinnen und Verlieren, oder eine Konkurrenz der Spielenden? Denk an die Patiencen. In den Ballspielen gibt es Gewinnen und Verlieren; aber wenn ein Kind den Ball an die Wand wirft und wieder auffängt, so ist dieser Zug verschwunden. Schau,

welche Rolle Geschick und Glück spielen. Und wie verschieden ist Geschick im Schachspiel und Geschick im Tennisspiel. Denk nun an die Reigenspiele: Hier ist das Element der Unterhaltung, aber wie viele der anderen Charakterzüge sind verschwunden! Und so können wir durch die vielen, vielen anderen Gruppen von Spielen gehen. Aehnlichkeiten auftauchen und verschwinden sehen.

Und das Ergebnis dieser Betrachtung lautet nun: Wir sehen ein kompliziertes Netz von Aehnlichkeiten, die einander übergreifen und kreuzen. Aehnlichkeiten im Grossen und Kleinen.

67. Ich kann diese Aehnlichkeiten nicht besser charakterisieren, als durch das Wort "Familienähnlichkeiten"; denn so übergreifen und kreuzen sich die verschiedenen Aehnlichkeiten, die zwischen den Gliedern einer Familie bestehen: Wuchs, Gesichtszüge, Augenfarbe, Gang, Temperament, etc. etc..—Und ich werde sagen: die 'Spiele' bilden eine Familie.

Und ebenso bilden z. B. die Zahlenarten eine Familie. Warum nennen wir etwas "Zahl"? Nun etwa, weil es eine —direkte—Verwandtschaft mit manchem hat, was man bisher Zahl genannt hat; und dadurch, kann man sagen, erhält es eine indirekte Verwandtschaft zu anderem, was wir auch *so* nennen. Und wir dehnen unseren Begriff der Zahl aus, wie wir beim Spinnen eines Fadens Faser an Faser drehen. Und die Stärke des Fadens liegt nicht darin, dass irgend eine Faser durch seine ganze Länge läuft, sondern darin, dass viele Fasern einander übergreifen.

Wenn aber Einer sagen wollte: "Also ist allen diesen Gebilden etwas gemeinsam,—nämlich die Disjunktion aller dieser Gemeinsamkeiten"—so würde ich antworten: hier spielst du nur mit einem Wort. Ebenso könnte man sagen: es läuft ein Etwas durch den ganzen Faden,—nämlich das lückenlose Uebergreifen dieser Fasern.

68. "Gut; so ist also der Begriff der Zahl für dich erklärt als die logische Summe jener einzelnen mit einander verwandten Begriffe: Kardinalzahl, Rationalzahl, reelle Zahl, etc., und gleicherweise der Begriff des Spiels als logische Summe entsprechender Teilbegriffe."—Dies muss nicht sein. Denn ich *kann* so dem Begriff 'Zahl' feste Grenzen geben, d.h. das Wort "Zahl" zur Bezeichnung eines fest begrenzten Begriffs gebrauchen, aber ich kann es auch so gebrauchen, dass der Umfang des Begriffs *nicht* durch eine Grenze abgeschlossen ist. Und so verwenden wir ja das Wort "Spiel". Wie ist denn der Begriff des Spiels abgeschlossen? Was ist noch ein Spiel und was ist keines mehr? Kannst du die Grenzen angeben? Nein. Du kannst welche *ziehen*: denn es sind noch keine gezogen. (Aber das

hat dich noch nie gestört, wenn du das Wort "Spiel" angewendet hast.)

"Aber dann ist ja die Anwendung des Wortes nicht geregelt; das 'Spiel', welches wir mit ihm spielen, ist nicht geregelt."—Es ist nicht überall von Regeln begrenzt; aber es gibt ja auch keine Regel dafür z.B., wie hoch man im Tennis den Ball werfen darf, oder wie stark, aber Tennis ist doch ein Spiel und es hat auch Regeln.

69. Wie würden wir denn jemandem erklären, was ein Spiel ist? Ich glaube, wir werden ihm *Spiele* beschreiben, und wir könnten der Beschreibung hinzufügen: "das, *und Aehnliches*, nennt man 'Spiele'". Und wissen wir selbst denn mehr? Können wir etwa nur dem Andern nicht genau sagen, was ein Spiel ist?—Aber das ist nicht Unwissenheit. Wir kennen die Grenzen nicht, weil keine gezogen sind. Wie gesagt, wir können — für einen besondern Zweck — eine Grenze ziehen. Machen wir dadurch den Begriff erst brauchbar? Durchaus nicht! Es sei denn, für diesen besondern Zweck. So wenig, wie der das Längenmass '1 Schritt' brauchbar machte, der die Definition gab: 1 Schritt = 75cm. Und wenn du sagen willst "Aber vorher war es doch kein exaktes Längenmass", so antworte ich: gut, dann war es ein unexaktes.—Obgleich du mir noch die Definition der Exaktheit schuldig bist.

70. "Aber wenn der Begriff 'Spiel' auf diese Weise unbegrenzt ist, so weisst du ja eigentlich nicht, was du mit 'Spiel' meinst."—Wenn ich die Beschreibung gebe: "Der Boden war ganz mit Pflanzen bedeckt",—willst du sagen, ich weiss nicht, wovon ich rede, ehe ich nicht eine Definition der Pflanze geben kann?

Eine Erklärung dessen, was ich meine, wäre etwa eine Zeichnung und die Worte "So ungefähr hat der Boden ausgesehen". Ich sage vielleicht auch: "*genau* so hat er ausgesehen".—Also waren genau *diese* Gräser und Blätter, in diesen Lagen, dort? Nein, das heisst es nicht. Und kein Bild würde ich, in *diesem* Sinne, als das genaue anerkennen.

Jemand sagt mir: "Zeige den Kindern ein Spiel!" Ich lehre sie, um Geld würfeln, und der Andere sagt mir "Ich habe nicht so ein Spiel gemeint". Musste ihm da, als er mir den Befehl gab, der Ausschluss des Würfelspiels vorschweben?

---

71. Man kann sagen, der Begriff 'Spiel' ist ein Begriff mit verschwommenen Rändern.—"Aber ist ein verschwommener Begriff überhaupt ein *Begriff?*"—Ist eine unscharfe Photographie überhaupt ein Bild eines Menschen? Ja, kann

man ein unscharfes Bild immer mit Vorteil durch ein scharfes ersetzen? Ist das unscharfe nicht oft gerade das, was wir brauchen?

Frege vergleicht den Begriff mit einem Bezirk und sagt: einen unklar begrenzten Bezirk könne man überhaupt keinen Bezirk nennen. Das heisst wohl, wir können mit ihm nichts anfangen.—Aber ist es sinnlos zu sagen: "Halte dich ungefähr hier auf!"? Denk dir, ich stünde mit einem Andern auf einem Platz und sagte dies. Dabei werde ich nicht einmal irgend eine Grenze ziehen, sondern etwa mit der Hand eine zeigende Bewegung machen—als zeigte ich ihm einen bestimmten *Punkt*. Und gerade so erklärt man etwa, was ein Spiel ist. Man gibt Beispiele und will, dass sie in einem gewissen Sinne verstanden werden.—Aber mit diesem Ausdruck meine ich nicht: er solle nun in diesen Beispielen das Gemeinsame sehen, welches ich—aus irgend einem Grunde—nicht aussprechen konnte. Sondern: er solle diese Beispiele nun in bestimmter Weise *verwenden*. Das Exemplifizieren ist hier nicht ein *indirektes* Mittel der Erklärung, —in Ermanglung eines Bessern. Denn, missverstanden kann auch jede allgemeine Erklärung werden. *So* spielen wir eben das Spiel. (Ich meine das Sprachspiel mit dem Worte "Spiel".)

72. *Das Gemeinsam sehen.* Nimm an, ich zeige jemand verschiedene bunte Bilder, und sage: "Die Farbe, die du in allen siehst, heisst 'Ocker'."—Das ist eine Erklärung, die verstanden wird, indem der Andere aufsucht und sieht, was jenen Bildern gemeinsam ist. Er kann dann auf das Gemeinsame blicken, darauf zeigen.

Vergleiche damit: Ich zeige ihm Figuren verschiedener Form, alle in der gleichen Farbe gemalt und sage: "Was diese mit einander gemein haben, heisst 'Ocker'".

Und vergleiche damit: Ich zeige ihm Muster verschiedener Schattierungen von Blau und sage: "Die Farbe, die allen gemeinsam ist, nenne ich 'Blau'".

73. Wenn Einer mir die Namen der Farben erklärt, indem er auf Muster zeigt und sagt "Diese Farbe heisst 'Blau', diese 'Grün',....", so kann dieser Fall in vieler Hinsicht dem verglichen werden, dass er mir eine Tabelle an die Hand gibt, in der unter den Mustern von Farben die Wörter stehen.—Wenn auch dieser Vergleich in mancher Weise irreführen kann.—Man ist nun geneigt, den Vergleich auszudehnen: Die Erklärung verstanden haben, heisst, einen Begriff des Erklärten im Geiste besitzen, und d.i. ein Muster, oder Bild. Zeigt man mir nun verschiedene Blätter und sagt "Das nennt man 'Blatt'", so erhalte ich einen Begriff der Blattform, ein Bild von ihr im Geiste.—Aber wie schaut denn das Bild eines Blattes aus, das keine

bestimmte Form zeigt, sondern 'das, was allen Blattformen
gemeinsam ist'? Welchen Farbton hat das 'Muster in mei-
nem Geiste' der Farbe Grün—dessen, was allen Tönen von
Grün gemeinsam ist?

"Aber könnte es nicht solche 'allgemeine' Muster geben?
Etwa ein Blattschema, oder ein Muster von *reinem* Grün?"
—Gewiss! Aber, dass dieses Schema als *Schema* verstanden
wird, und nicht als die Form eines bestimmten Blattes, und
dass ein Täfelchen von reinem Grün als Muster alles dessen
verstanden wird, was grünlich ist, und nicht als Muster
für reines Grün—das liegt wieder in der Art der Anwendung
dieser Muster.

Frage dich: Welche *Gestalt* muss das Muster der Farbe
Grün haben? Soll es viereckig sein? oder würde es dann das
Muster für grüne Vierecke sein?—Soll es also 'unregel-
mässig' geformt sein? Und was verhindert uns, es dann
nur als Muster der unregelmässigen Form anzusehen—d.h.
zu verwenden?

74.   Hierher gehört auch der Gedanke, dass der, welcher
dieses Blatt als Muster 'der Blattform im allgemeinen' an-
sieht, es anders *sieht*, als der, welcher es etwa als Muster
für diese bestimmte Form betrachtet. Nun, das könnte ja
so sein—obwohl es nicht so ist—, denn es würde nur
besagen, dass erfahrungsgemäss der, welcher das Blatt in
bestimmter Weise *sieht*, es dann so und so, oder den und
den Regeln gemäss, verwendet. Es gibt natürlich ein *so* und
anders Sehen; und es gibt auch Fälle, in denen der, der
ein Muster *so* sieht, es im allgemeinen in *dieser* Weise verwenden wird, und wer es anders sieht, in anderer Weise.
Wer z.B., die schematische Zeichnung eines Würfels als
ebene Figur sieht, bestehend aus einem Quadrat und zwei
Rhomben, der wird den Befehl "Bringe mir so etwas!" vielleicht anders ausführen, als der, welcher das Bild räumlich
sieht.

75.   Was heisst es: wissen, was ein Spiel ist? Was heisst
es, es wissen und es nicht sagen können? Ist dieses Wissen
irgendein Aequivalent einer nicht ausgesprochenen Definition? So dass, wenn sie ausgesprochen würde, ich sie als
den Ausdruck meines Wissens anerkennen könnte? Ist nicht
mein Wissen, mein Begriff vom Spiel, ganz in den Erklä-
rungen ausgedrückt, die ich geben könnte? Nämlich darin,
dass ich Beispiele von Spielen verschiedener Art beschreibe;
zeige, wie man nach Analogie dieser auf alle möglichen
Arten andere Spiele konstruieren kann; sage, dass ich das
und das wohl kaum mehr ein Spiel nennen würde; und der-
gleichen mehr.

76.   Wenn Einer eine scharfe Grenze zöge, so könnte ich
sie nicht als die anerkennen, die ich auch schon immer

ziehen wollte, oder im Geist gezogen habe. Denn ich wollte
gar keine ziehen. Man kann dann sagen: sein Begriff ist
nicht der gleiche wie der meine, aber ihm verwandt. Und
die Verwandtschaft ist die zweier Bilder, deren eines aus
unscharf begrenzten Farbflecken, das andere aus ähnlich
geformten und verteilten, aber scharf begrenzten, besteht.
Die Verwandtschaft ist dann ebenso unleugbar, wie die
Verschiedenheit.

77. Und wenn wir diesen Vergleich noch etwas weiter
führen, so ist es klar, dass der Grad, bis zu welchem das
scharfe Bild dem verschwommenen ähnlich sein *kann*, vom
Grade der Unschärfe des zweiten abhängt. Denn denk dir,
du solltest zu einem verschwommenen Bild ein ihm 'entsprechendes' scharfes entwerfen. In jenem ist ein unscharfes
rotes Rechteck; du setzt dafür ein scharfes. Freilich—es
liessen sich ja mehrere solche scharfe Rechtecke ziehen, die
dem unscharfen entsprächen.—Wenn aber im Original die
Farben ohne die Spur einer Grenze ineinanderfliessen,—
wird es dann nicht eine hoffnungslose Aufgabe werden, ein
dem verschwommenen entsprechendes scharfes Bild zu
zeichnen? Wirst du dann nicht sagen müssen: "Hier könnte
ich ebensogut einen Kreis, wie ein Rechteck, oder eine Herz-
form zeichnen; es fliessen ja alle Farben durcheinander.
Es stimmt alles; und nichts."—Und in dieser Lage befindet
sich z.B. der, der in der Aesthetik, oder Ethik nach Defini-
tionen sucht, die unseren Begriffen entsprechen.

Frage dich in dieser Schwierigkeit immer: Wie haben wir
denn die Bedeutung dieses Wortes ("gut" z.B.) *gelernt?*
An was für Beispielen; in welchen Sprachspielen? Du wirst
dann leichter sehen, dass das Wort eine Familie von Be-
deutungen haben muss.

Some Important Works
By The Philosophers Discussed

G. E. MOORE
Principia Ethica, Cambridge, 1903; *Ethics,* New York, 1912; *Philosophical Studies,* New York, 1922.

BENEDETTO CROCE
Philosophy of the Spirit, London, 1913-1922, 4 vols.

GEORGE SANTAYANA
The Life of Reason, New York, 1905-1906, 5 vols.; *Scepticism and Animal Faith,* New York, 1923; *The Realms of Being,* New York, 1927-1940, 4 vols.

HENRI BERGSON
Creative Evolution, New York, 1911; *Matter and Memory,* New York, 1911; *Time and Free Will,* New York, 1910.

EDMUND HUSSERL
Ideas: General Introduction to Pure Phenomenology, New York, 1931.

ALFRED NORTH WHITEHEAD
(With Bertrand Russell) *Principia Mathematica,* Cambridge, 1910-1913, 3 vols.; *Science and the Modern World,* New York, 1925; *Process and Reality,* New York, 1929.

JEAN-PAUL SARTRE
Psychology of Imagination, New York, 1948.

CHARLES SANDERS PEIRCE
Collected Papers, ed. Charles Hartshorne and Paul Weiss, Cambridge, Mass., 1931-1935.

WILLIAM JAMES
The Will to Believe and Other Essays, New York, 1897; *Pragmatism,* New York, 1907; *A Pluralistic Universe,* New York, 1909; *Essays in Radical Empiricism* (posthumous), ed. R. B. Perry, New York, 1912.

JOHN DEWEY
Human Nature and Conduct, New York, 1922; *Experience and Nature,* New York, 1929; *The Quest for Certainty,* New York, 1929.

BERTRAND RUSSELL
The Problems of Philosophy, New York, 1912; *Our Knowledge of the External World,* London, 1914; *Introduction to Mathematical Philosophy,* New York, 1919; *An Inquiry into Meaning and Truth,* New York, 1940; *Human Knowledge—Its Scope and Limits,* New York, 1948.

RUDOLF CARNAP
Logical Syntax of Language, New York, 1937; *Logical Foundations of Probability,* Chicago, 1950.

LUDWIG WITTGENSTEIN
Tractatus Logico-Philosophicus, London, 1922; *Philosophical Investigations,* New York, 1953.

Index of Names

Abelard, Peter, 150

Anselm, St., 202

Aquinas, St. Thomas, 194, 202

Aristotle, 14, 54, 64, 195, 243

Bacon, Francis, 49

Bergson, Henri, 18, 20, 45, 65-81, 82, 83, 84, 101, 104, 116, 135, 154, 160, 190, 195, 228, 236, 240, 243

Berkeley, George, 16, 36-37, 138, 173, 201

Boltzmann, Ludwig, 204

Bradley, F. H., 16, 23, 84, 137, 138, 142

Brentano, Franz, 24, 101, 102

Caird, Edward, 137

Caird, John, 137

Cantor, Georg, 195-96

Carnap, Rudolf, 17, 20, 82, 102, 189, 197, 203-25, 227, 228, 238, 242, 243

Clifford, W. K., 138

Coleridge, Samuel Taylor, 137

Comte, Auguste, 47, 66, 120-21, 204

Croce, Benedetto, 17, 18, 20, 43-53, 54, 65, 66, 81, 82, 84, 101, 122, 135, 154, 194, 228, 236

Darwin, Charles, 65, 137, 240

Democritus, 195

Descartes, René, 20, 66, 97, 102, 111, 113, 122, 133, 142, 150, 202, 243

Dewey, John, 13, 16, 19, 55, 65, 101, 137, 138, 154, 155, 164-65, 173-89, 190, 205, 208, 228, 237, 238, 241

Diderot, Denis, 123

Dilthey, Wilhelm, 236

Dostoevski, Fedor, 66, 117, 128

Duhem, Pierre, 204

Eddington, A. S., 84

Edwards, Jonathan, 136

Einstein, Albert, 142, 199, 204, 205

Eliot, T. S., 56

Emerson, Ralph Waldo, 137, 138

Erigena, John Scotus, 149

Euclid, 164

Fichte, Johann, 73-74

Fizeau, Armand, 151

Foucault, Jean, 151

Franklin, Benjamin, 137

Frege, Gottlob, 24, 193, 196, 204, 226, 238

Gibbs, Willard, 140

THE AGE OF BELIEF

The Medieval Philosophers

By ANNE FREMANTLE

Here, in one volume, is the wisdom of the most spiritually harmonious age that Western man has known. In this age of belief, the period from the fifth to the fifteenth centuries A.D., when religion and social institutions were closely related, philosophers discussed the nature of God, of Being, and of Man, with an intensity not known before or since.

In this remarkable book, Anne Fremantle, religious scholar and author, presents selections from the basic writings of such dominant philosophers of the medieval period as Augustine, Thomas Aquinas, Boethius, Erigena, Anselm, Abelard, Bonaventura, and Averroës, with an interpretation of their work woven throughout the texts.

ANNE FREMANTLE, *an associate editor of* Commonweal, *an editor of the Catholic Book Club, an associate professor at Fordham University, an editor-on-loan to the United Nations during the General Assembly, is also the author of numerous books, reviews, and articles.*

THE AGE OF ADVENTURE
The Renaissance Philosophers
By GIORGIO DE SANTILLANA

The Renaissance was a time when men turned from abstractions, from thoughts of other-worldly perfection, to explore new seas, new continents, new notions, new images of man, and they brought forth such bold creations in art, psychology, politics, and manners as were never known in the ancient world.

Giorgio de Santillana presents in this volume the basic writings of Bruno, Galileo, Machiavelli, Montaigne, Michelangelo, Leonardo da Vinci, More, and Kepler—and contributes an introduction and connecting commentary which illustrates the love of life that characterized this age of adventure.

GIORGIO DE SANTILLANA *has taught at Harvard and is currently Professor of History and Philosophy of Science at Massachusetts Institute of Technology.*

THE AGE OF REASON
The 17th Century Philosophers
By STUART HAMPSHIRE

The great modern philosopher, Alfred North Whitehead, has described the 17th century as the "century of genius." In this challenging volume, Stuart Hampshire has selected from Galileo, Bacon, Descartes, Hobbes, Pascal, Spinoza and Leibniz and linked their work with his interpretive commentary. The conflict between the new ideas of these 17th century thinkers and traditional theology and logic led to the modern discipline of philosophy.

STUART HAMPSHIRE, *Fellow of All Souls College, Oxford, and author of many articles on logical theory, has also been visiting professor of philosophy at Columbia University.*

THE AGE OF
ENLIGHTENMENT

The 18th Century Philosophers

By ISAIAH BERLIN

The philosophy of the 18th century begins with a systematic effort to apply to the study of man those methods which Newton had so triumphantly applied to nature. The editor of this volume, Isaiah Berlin, traces the development of the influence of scientific thought through the writings of the great philosophers and popularizers whose work remains the foundation of liberal humanism and rationalism in the West. Berlin's selections, and his penetrating introduction and interpretive commentary, shed light upon the philosophy of Locke, Berkeley, Hume, Voltaire, Reid and Condillac, and their German critics.

ISAIAH BERLIN, *a Fellow of All Souls College, Oxford, has lectured on philosophy and intellectual history at Harvard and other American universities.*

THE AGE OF IDEOLOGY

The 19th Century Philosophers

By HENRY D. AIKEN

One great new development of philosophy in the 19th century was the attempt to construct consistent attitudes toward the human situation. In this time of great religious, political and economic change, philosophy became a technique for adjustment to a changing environment. The major thought of the period is elucidated here through Henry D. Aiken's commentary and his selections from the great thinkers of the age—Kant, Fichte, Hegel, Schopenhauer, Comte, Mill, Spencer, Marx, Mach, Kierkegaard, and Nietzsche.

HENRY D. AIKEN, *now Professor of Philosophy at Harvard, has also been on the teaching staffs of Columbia University and the University of Washington.*